IMAGES
of Rail

SACRAMENTO SOUTHERN RAILROAD

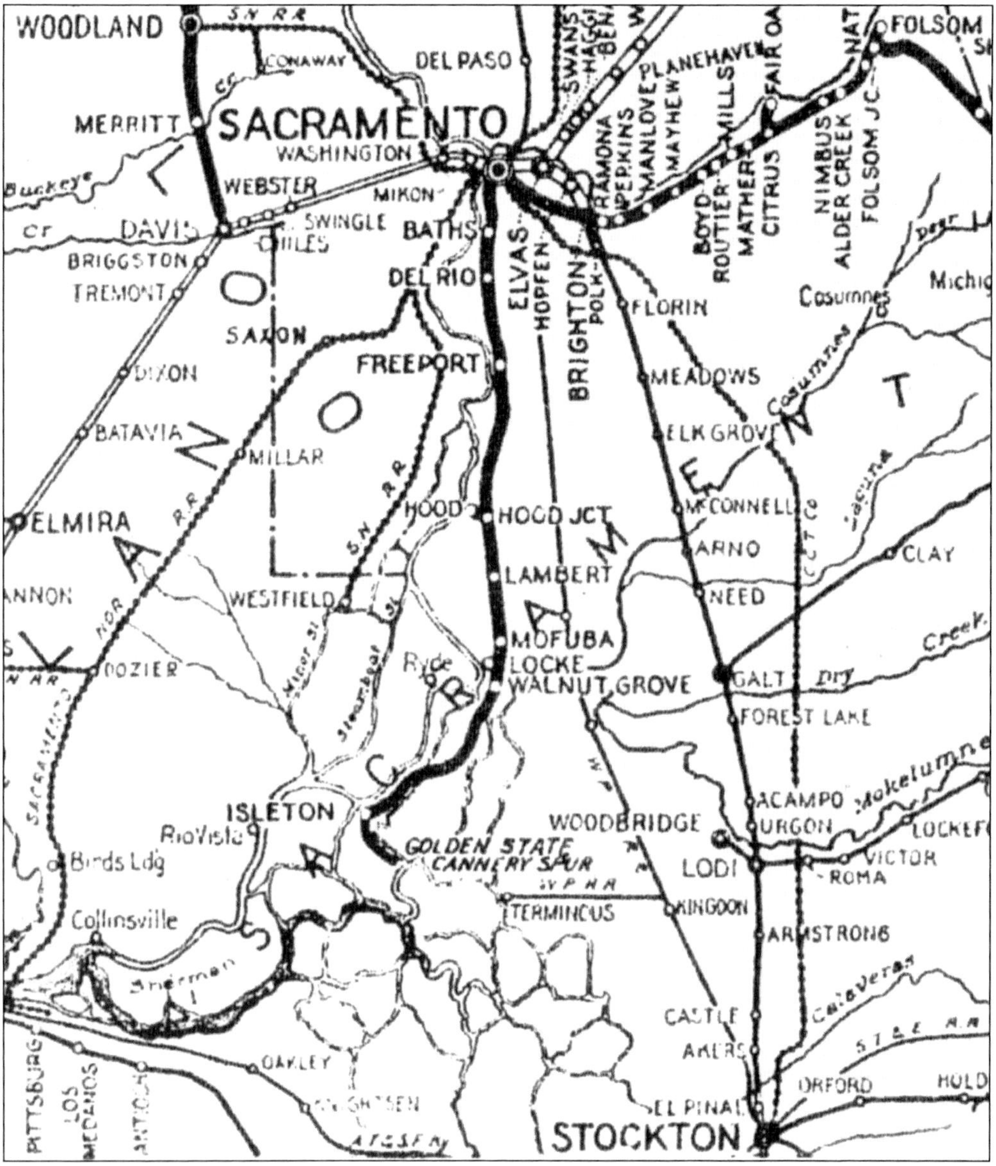

This map from a 1951 Southern Pacific Lines Sacramento Division employee timetable shows the route of the Walnut Grove Branch at its longest. The spur from Isleton to the Golden State Cannery was abandoned that year. At present, only the segment from Sacramento to Baths is operational, though tracks remain in place as far as Hood Junction. (Courtesy of the California State Railroad Museum Library.)

On the Cover: A Southern Pacific locomotive and train crew pose at Freeport around 1915. Second from the left is SP track worker Joseph Contente, whose story is told in detail on page 56. (Courtesy of the Portuguese Historical and Cultural Society, Sacramento.)

IMAGES
of Rail

SACRAMENTO SOUTHERN RAILROAD

Kevin W. Hecteman

ARCADIA
PUBLISHING

ISBN 978-0-7385-6986-4

Published by Arcadia Publishing
Charleston, South Carolina

Printed in the United States of America

Library of Congress Catalog Card Number: 2008934517

For all general information contact Arcadia Publishing at:
Telephone 843-853-2070
Fax 843-853-0044
E-mail sales@arcadiapublishing.com
For customer service and orders:
Toll-Free 1-888-313-2665

Visit us on the Internet at www.arcadiapublishing.com

This book is dedicated to my late grandfather Shirley Edwin "Smitty" Smith, who more than anyone else is responsible for inspiring my love of railroading, and to the men and women of the Sacramento Southern Railroad—past, present, and future.

Contents

ACKNOWLEDGMENTS

Just because my name is on the cover does not mean that I am solely responsible for bringing this book into being. Without the generous assistance of a multitude of people, this project would have been impossible.

I wish to start by thanking Dick Noonan, general manager of the Sacramento Southern Railroad, who lent valuable insights and assistance to this project. Marilyn Sommerdorf of the California State Railroad Museum was of invaluable assistance. Her family goes back several generations in the delta region, and her interest in the Walnut Grove Branch goes back decades. Several of the images in this book are from her personal collection.

Without the skill and dedication of the staff of the California State Railroad Museum Library, you would not be reading this. Many thanks to Ellen Halteman, Kathryn Santos, and Cara Randall for going above and beyond the call of duty in assisting with my endless stream of requests and scanning in a boxcar load of images. Thanks to Paul Hammond, director of the California State Railroad Museum in Sacramento, for his support of the project. Thanks to the staff of the Sacramento Archives and Museum Collection Center. Carson Hendricks, Pat Johnson, and Rebecca Crowther were instrumental in helping me dig up photographs and information. Hendricks also deserves thanks for scanning in a sizable photograph order. Thanks to the staff of the Sacramento Room, a historical repository housed in the Sacramento Public Library, for helping me track down photographs and information. A debt of gratitude is also owed to the California State Library; Arnold Menke; the California State Archives; Terri White and Dolores Greenslate of the Portuguese Historical and Cultural Society in Sacramento; Pam Bulaban and Charlene Andersson of the Isleton Brannan-Andrus Historical Society; John Perez, longtime Isleton resident and realtor; Esther Koopman, Bobbi Collier, and Tom Herzog of the Sacramento River Delta Historical Society in Walnut Grove; Chuck Vercelli and the staff of the Western Railway Museum Library at Rio Vista Junction; John Poultney, my editor at Arcadia; Bill Burg, for proofreading the manuscript; and my parents, Roy and Barbara, for their love and support (and in Dad's case, his business sense as well).

The author, who volunteers on the modern Sacramento Southern Railroad, will contribute his royalties to the California State Railroad Museum Foundation in order that the trains may keep on rolling for generations to come.

INTRODUCTION

KNOW ALL MEN BY THESE PRESENTS that we, the undersigned, all of whom are residents of the State of California, have this day voluntarily associated ourselves for the purpose of forming a corporation under the laws of the State of California, and we do hereby certify:

I. That the name of said corporation is SACRAMENTO SOUTHERN RAILROAD COMPANY.

—From the Articles of Incorporation of the Sacramento Southern Railroad Company, July 7, 1903

Thus was the Sacramento Southern Railroad launched.

The railroad was not an independent venture; it was controlled from the outset by the mighty Southern Pacific Company. The articles of incorporation stated that the Sacramento Southern's corporate business would be transacted in San Francisco, home of SP's headquarters, and all five initial directors—I. W. Hellman Jr., Charles Hollbrook, J. M. Israel, C. A. Harp, and John C. Kirkpatrick—were residents of the "City by the Bay."

The Sacramento Southern proposed to build south from its namesake city to Stockton, with two branch lines. One of these would split from the main line at or near the delta town of Walnut Grove and run to Antioch, in Contra Costa County, where connections would be made with either the SP; the Atchison, Topeka, and Santa Fe Railway; or with both. The other branch would run to Woodbridge, west of Lodi in San Joaquin County, and make connections with the SP's valley lines. The directors proposed to build a common-carrier, standard-gauge railroad "operated by steam, electricity or other lawful motive power" for the purpose of hauling passengers and freight. (Remember the part about that "branch" to Antioch. The apparent truth will emerge before long.)

In 1905 and 1906, the Sacramento Southern turned up frequently in the *Sacramento Union*, one of the California capital's newspapers, as the railroad worked to secure a right-of-way through town, initiating several condemnation suits against various landowners and reclamation districts.

One protracted dispute pitted the railroad against the City of Sacramento and landowner Frederick A. Miller. The Sacramento Southern looked to build its line out of town along a city-owned riverfront levee. The *Union* reported on December 18, 1905, that on the previous day, a Sunday, railroad work crews swooped in and built track atop the river levee extending 450 feet north from Y Street to W Street to connect with an SP spur coming down from what is now Old Sacramento. (At the time, Y Street was the southern edge of town; the street is now Broadway.) Miller, who was of the opinion that the city had an easement on his property only for a levee, erected a fence across the levee to try to stop the construction crews. (The final score there: steam locomotive 1, fence 0.)

Miller told the *Union* that he had been bargaining with the Western Pacific Railroad, which was also trying to gain access to the waterfront, and that this burst of construction was aimed at keeping the WP away. City officials did not know what was happening until a *Union* reporter filled them in. The SP believed it had a right to build upon the levee that dated back to 1852; the city believed otherwise.

On December 19, 1905, on orders from Sacramento mayor W. J. Hassett, superintendent of streets D. J. Mannix showed up with a work party intent on tearing up the newly laid track on the levee. The problem was several freight cars just happened to be parked on the new section of track. Mannix's men actually managed to move a couple of them before an SP freight train arrived and coupled to the cars. With the train occupying most of the trackage Mannix wanted to destroy, he and his crew settled for pulling up a few lengths of rail between the train and Y Street. Later that day, SP superintendent Thomas R. Jones and attorney W. H. Devlin met with Mayor Hassett and agreed the SP would take no further action while the legal tangle was sorted out.

Matters between Miller and the railroad were resolved on April 9, 1906, when Miller deeded to the Sacramento Southern a strip of land across his property near Front and Y Streets inside the city levee for a railroad right-of-way, and condemnation proceedings were dismissed. To get around the city's objections to using the riverfront levee north of the Y Street levee, the Sacramento Southern began acquiring a right-of-way inside the levee. Then, on March 3, 1907, the *San Francisco Chronicle* disclosed that the SP had plans for a new all-rail route linking Sacramento with San Francisco. The new route would be 147 miles long—57 miles longer than the route then in use—but would relieve the SP of two major operational headaches. One headache was the two time-consuming ferry segments required for a Sacramento–San Francisco journey—the Carquinez Strait between Benicia and Martinez, wherein the entire train was ferried, and from Oakland Pier (also known as the Oakland Mole) to the Ferry Building at the foot of San Francisco's Market Street. The other headache was the fact that the SP's Sacramento-Benicia line, built as the California Pacific in the late 1860s, was sinking into the marshes near Suisun Bay, playing havoc with SP's operations.

The Sacramento Southern figured big in SP's plans. In its report on the SP's intentions, the *Chronicle* wrote: "Officials of the company admitted yesterday that this is the real purpose of the so-called Sacramento Southern, which is being projected southward from Sacramento on the east side of the river, ostensibly for a reach of twenty miles to tap into an agricultural region. The Sacramento Southern will be a direct short cut line from Sacramento to Antioch in Contra Costa county."

At Antioch, the *Chronicle* reported, a drawbridge spanning the San Joaquin River would carry trains toward Concord, thence to Walnut Creek and San Ramon over what was at the time a lightly traveled branch line. New track would be laid from San Ramon to Pleasanton; trains would then steam through scenic Niles Canyon to the Dumbarton cutoff (then under construction) at Newark, cross San Francisco Bay to Redwood City, and ramble up the peninsula to San Francisco. This idea never came to pass. The SP ultimately resolved the marsh problem near Suisun Bay and eventually took care of the Martinez-Benicia ferry problem by way of a giant lift bridge, opened in 1930, spanning Carquinez Strait. This route is in heavy use today by Union Pacific, Capitol Corridor, and Amtrak trains.

The Sacramento Southern finally won its franchise from the City of Sacramento in October 1907 to build within the city. The line opened to Freeport, just south of Sacramento, in 1909. On March 12, 1912, the railroad arrived in Walnut Grove. That same year, the Sacramento Southern's name disappeared from Southern Pacific's annual reports, as its assets were transferred to the Central Pacific Railway Company as part of a corporate reorganization. (The Central Pacific, builder of the western half of the first transcontinental railroad, still existed on paper as a railroad leased and operated by the Southern Pacific.) Before long, the Sacramento Southern came to be known by its timetable description: the Walnut Grove Branch. Passenger service was never all that extensive. The SP, for the most part, used McKeen motorcars—essentially buses on rails—to take care of passenger traffic on the branch. This lasted until 1924, when the passenger schedules disappeared from the timetable in favor of a single mixed train, leaving Sacramento in the morning and returning in the afternoon. Regular passenger service was discontinued in 1932.

What really paid the bills was agriculture. The branch's main purpose was to haul the fruits (and vegetables) of delta farmers' labors to the SP's massive yards in Sacramento and Roseville for forwarding to points around the country. In March 1920, the *S. P. Bulletin* boasted of the year-round bounty of the delta. The Walnut Grove station, it stated, shipped celery from November to February, asparagus from February to May, fruit from May through September, and seeds from September through November. Competition existed on the rails and on the water. Riverboats, some owned by the Southern Pacific itself, plied the Sacramento River, hauling people and goods to points as far away as San Francisco. The Western Pacific and its subsidiary, the electric-powered Sacramento Northern, were also building branches to serve delta agriculture. The WP opened a branch from its own Sacramento-Stockton main line to Terminous, on Potato Slough, in October 1927. The Sacramento Northern, meanwhile, built a branch from its namesake city to the west of the Sacramento River. The Holland Branch opened in June 1929.

SP's response to the WP's activities was an extension of the Walnut Grove Branch to Isleton, on Andrus Island in the Sacramento River Delta. The extension, about 7.8 miles in length, opened in October 1929. Two years later, over the WP's objections, the Interstate Commerce Commission approved a 3-mile spur from Isleton to the Golden State Asparagus Cannery on the banks of the Mokelumne River. This proved to be the ultimate reach of the original Sacramento Southern/Walnut Grove Branch. Two things doomed the branch: 18-wheelers and Mother Nature. From the 1950s onward, more and more freight traffic, especially of the perishable variety, deserted the rails for the roads. Though the spur to Golden State was abandoned in 1951, the Walnut Grove Branch soldiered on. Then the levee burst.

A disastrous flood in June 1972, instigated by a levee failure, inundated Isleton and destroyed much of the railroad's physical plant on Andrus Island. With a sizable portion of the line knocked out—permanently, as it happened—traffic began dwindling and the SP began to think hard about getting out.

The branch was abandoned in two segments; from Hood Junction to Isleton in 1977 and from Miller Park in Sacramento to Hood Junction in 1978. One of the last remaining customers on the line—Sacramento's sewage-treatment plant near Del Rio south of town, which received shipments of chemicals via the branch—lost rail service with the final abandonment. On October 10, 1978, a pair of Southern Pacific diesel locomotives trundled down to Hood Junction, picked up a string of derelict freight cars, and rumbled into history.

As the SP exited stage left, the California State Railroad Museum entered stage right. The first phase, a reconstruction of Sacramento's old Central Pacific Railroad passenger station on Front Street between I and J Streets, had opened in 1976. The Museum of Railroad History followed in 1981. After that, the museum went to work on the next phase: steam-powered excursion trains.

Several museum staffers and volunteers began formulating plans to bring the operation into being. Chief among them were Walter Gray III, one of the early employees of the California State Railroad Museum; Terry Stefani; Mark Spellman; Cathy Taylor; and Dick Noonan.

More than 100 museum docents answered the call for volunteers for the railroad. Extensive training and preparation culminated in the operation of the first steam-powered excursion trains on June 2, 1984, between Old Sacramento and Miller Park, a round-trip of about 3 miles in length. Several years later, service was extended about a mile and a half to Baths.

Except for several miles within Sacramento owned by Regional Transit, the California State Railroad Museum owns the right-of-way from Baths to Hood, including the presently trackless spur from Hood Junction to the wharf. From Hood Junction south, the tracks have been removed.

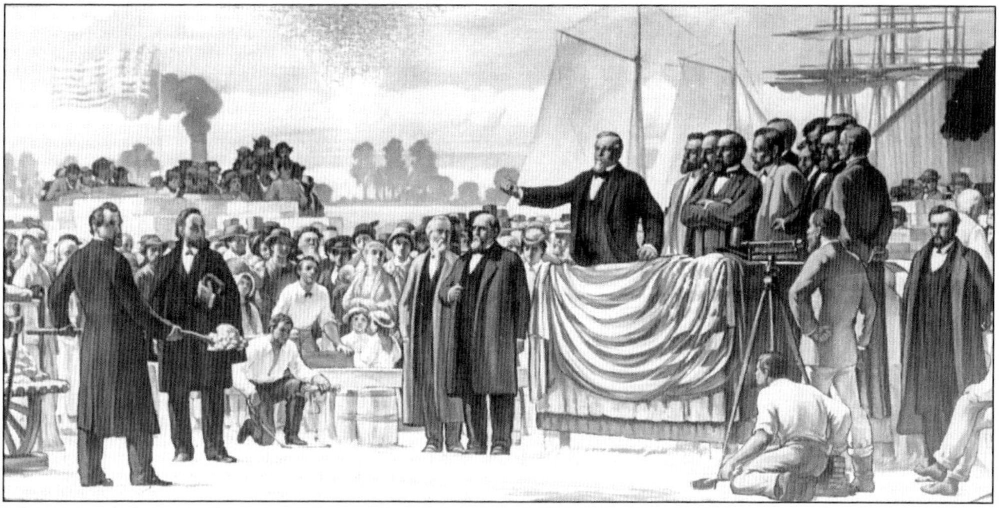

This mural depicts the Central Pacific's ground-breaking ceremony held on January 8, 1863, at Front and K Streets in Sacramento. That is Leland Stanford, president of the Central Pacific and also governor of California, speaking at center right. Sacramento Southern's excursion trains still roll through this spot on most weekends. The mural can be seen in the waiting room of Amtrak's former Southern Pacific depot in Sacramento. (Courtesy of the Sacramento Archives and Museum Collection Center.)

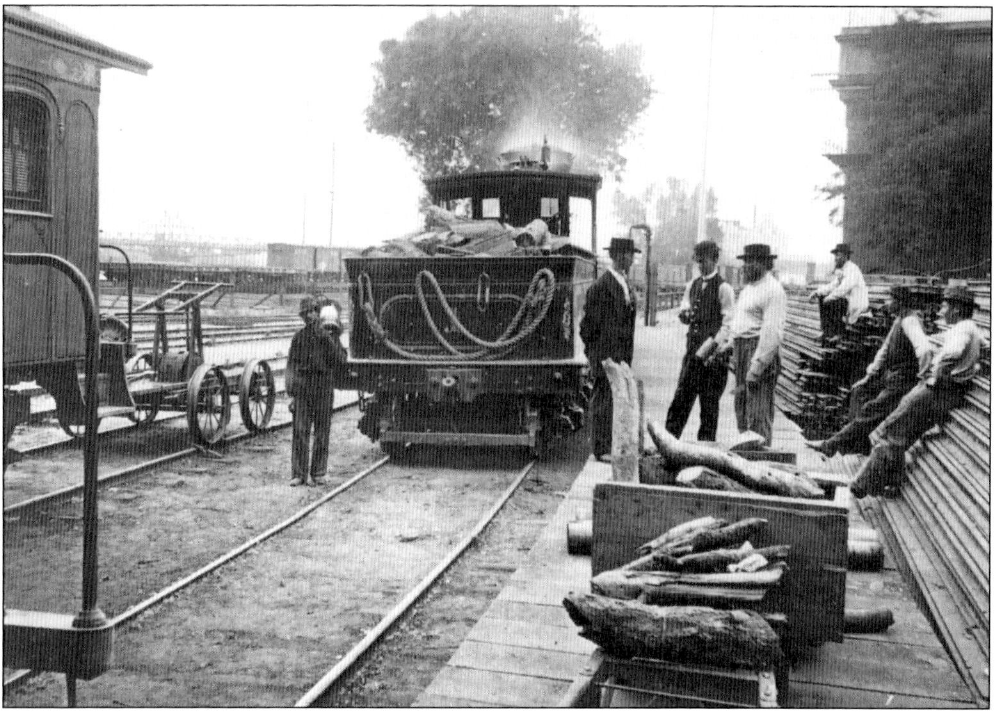

The *Gov. Stanford*, the Central Pacific's first locomotive, stands in the CP's Front Street yard around 1864. At left, visible next to the passenger car, is a bridge over the Sacramento River; the I Street Bridge occupies this spot today. At right is Sacramento's city hall/waterworks/jail. This building has been replicated in its original location and now houses the Sacramento History Museum. (Courtesy of the California History Room, California State Library.)

One

The Prehistory of the Sacramento Southern

Railroading on the Sacramento waterfront predates the Sacramento Southern Railroad by half a century. California's first common-carrier railroad, the Sacramento Valley, had opened for business in 1856, connecting the California capital with Folsom. The SVRR's passenger depot was at Third and R Streets, near the waterfront; freight trains operated north on Front Street to the steamer landing at the foot of K Street. The Central Pacific absorbed the SVRR in 1865; the SVRR's line to Folsom evolved into the SP's Placerville Branch. In 1863, the Central Pacific broke ground in Sacramento and began building east toward the Sierra Nevada and a date with history at Promontory, Utah. The CPRR's passenger depot was on Front Street between I and J Streets; the freight depot was one block south on Front Street. The 1870s iterations of these depots have been reconstructed in approximately their original locations. Trackage on Front Street and R Street allowed SVRR, CP, and later SP trains to access freight customers along the waterfront as well as interchange traffic with other railroads and with steamboats plying the Sacramento River.

The photographs in this chapter depict railroading on and around Sacramento's waterfront in the days before the Sacramento Southern's incorporation in 1903. The "new" Sacramento Southern is the only railroad operating in this territory today.

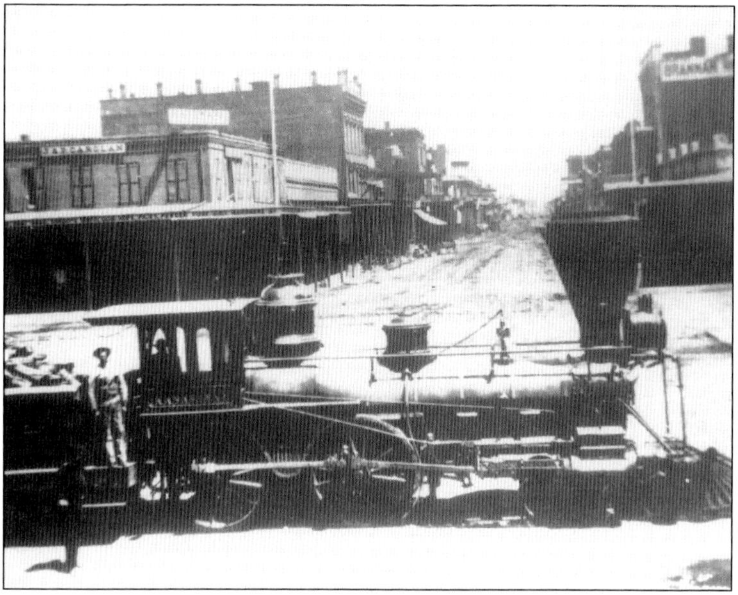

Central Pacific locomotive No. 7, the A.A. *Sargent*, stands at Front and J Streets. This scene will look familiar to visitors of today's Old Sacramento, as many of the buildings on J Street still stand, including the Brannan House. (Courtesy of the Sacramento Archives and Museum Collection Center.)

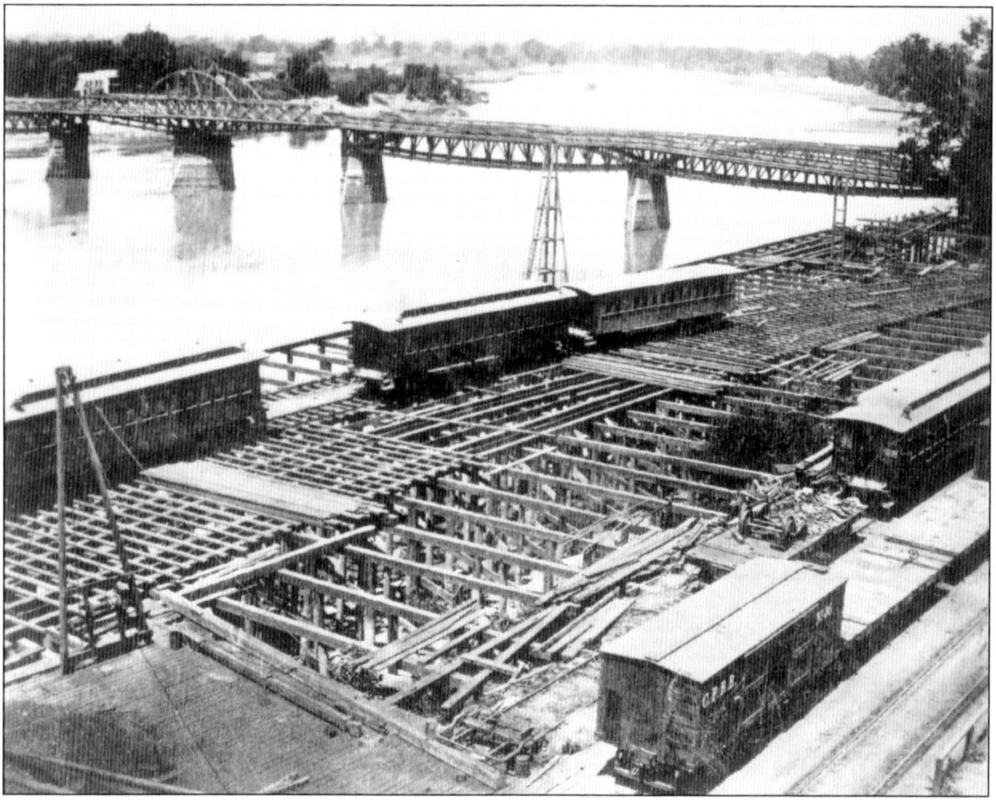

The Central Pacific was putting its new Sacramento wharf to use even as it was under construction around 1870. In the background is the bridge connecting Sacramento with the towns of Washington and Broderick (now part of West Sacramento); this is about where I Street Bridge stands today. (Courtesy of the Sacramento Archives and Museum Collection Center.)

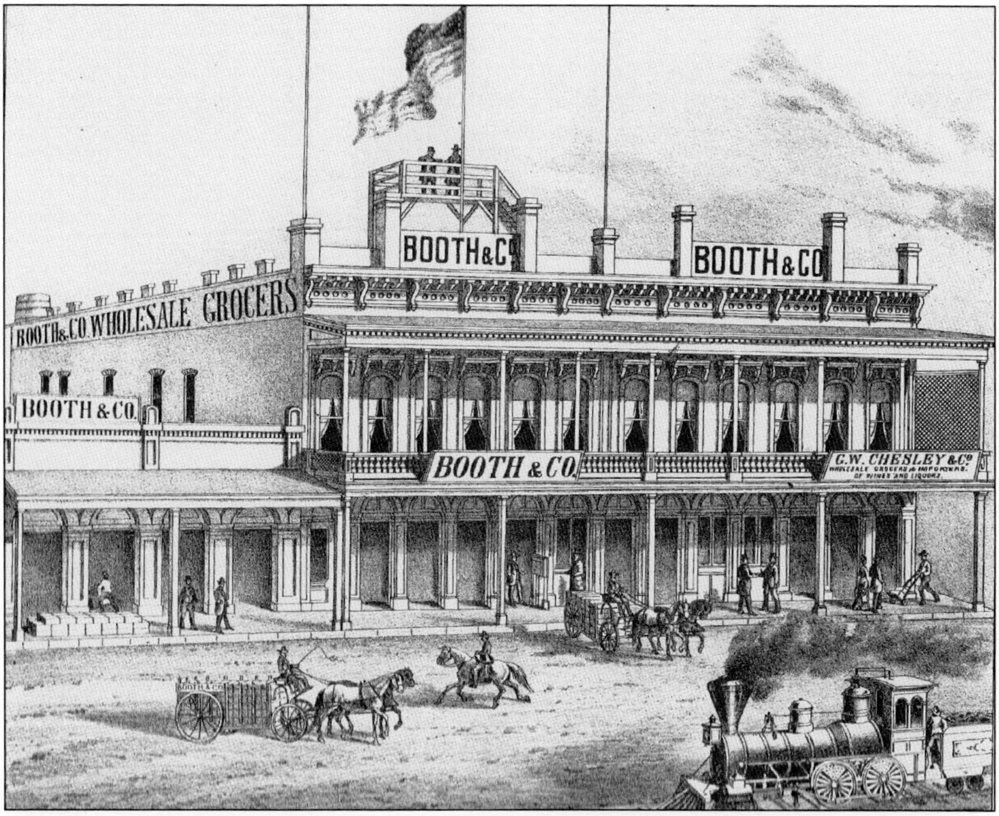

Booth and Company maintained a large warehouse on Front Street, between J and K Streets, across from the Central Pacific freight depot. The building, complete with observation platform, still stands today. (Courtesy of the Sacramento Room, Sacramento Public Library.)

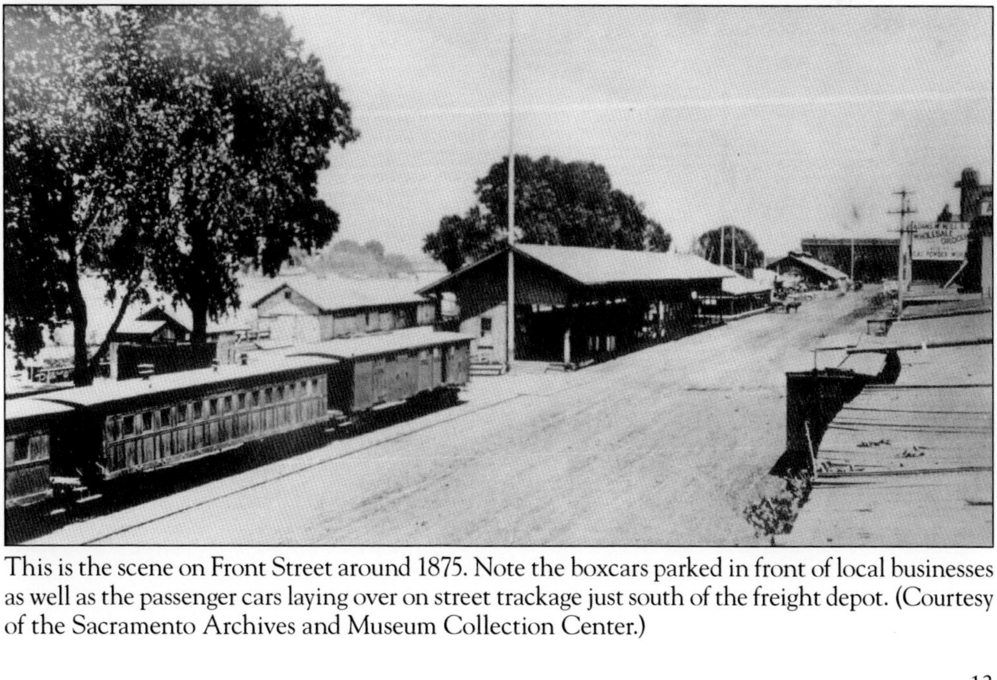
This is the scene on Front Street around 1875. Note the boxcars parked in front of local businesses as well as the passenger cars laying over on street trackage just south of the freight depot. (Courtesy of the Sacramento Archives and Museum Collection Center.)

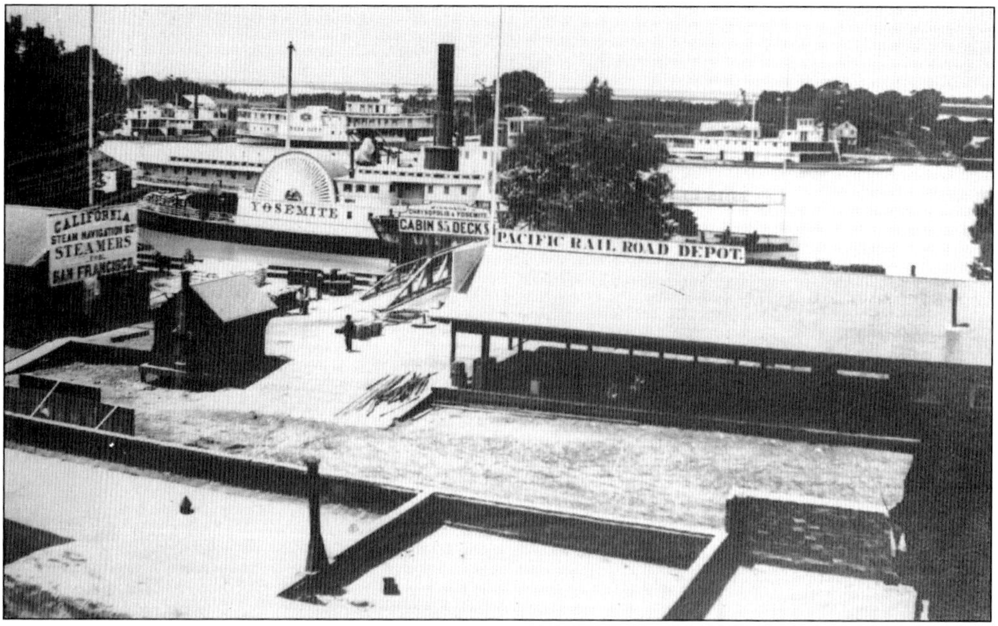

The California Steam Navigation Company steamboat *Yosemite* is docked at the foot of K Street around 1870; she and her sister boat, the *Chrysopolis*, were in the passenger trade between Sacramento and San Francisco. To the right is the Central Pacific Railroad's freight depot. The CPRR depot and the steam-navigation buildings have been reconstructed, complete with signage. (Courtesy of the Sacramento Archives and Museum Collection Center.)

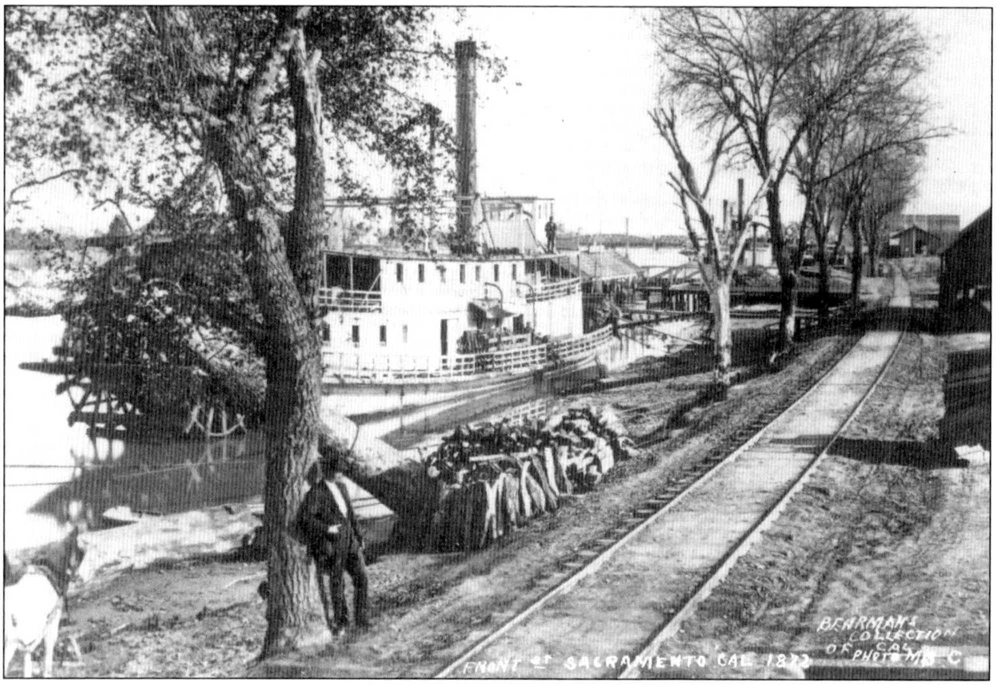

A steamboat is docked along the riverfront near the foot of K Street around 1870. The boilers of riverboats and steam locomotives at the time used wood for fuel, hence the large woodpile in the foreground. (Courtesy of the Sacramento Archives and Museum Collection Center.)

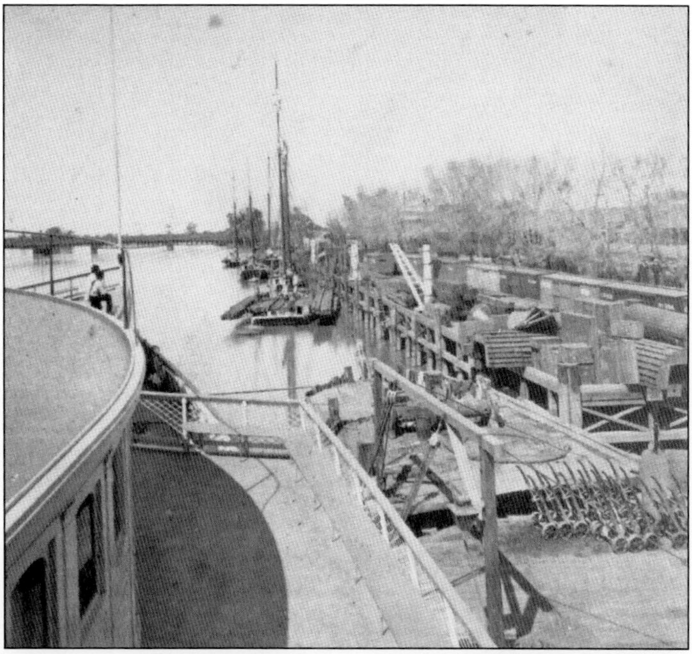

This steamboat's-eye view of activity along the Sacramento riverfront is pictured here in the 1870s. Note the rail yard full of freight cars, mainly boxcars. The CPRR's bridge over the Sacramento River is visible in the background. (Courtesy of the Sacramento Archives and Museum Collection Center.)

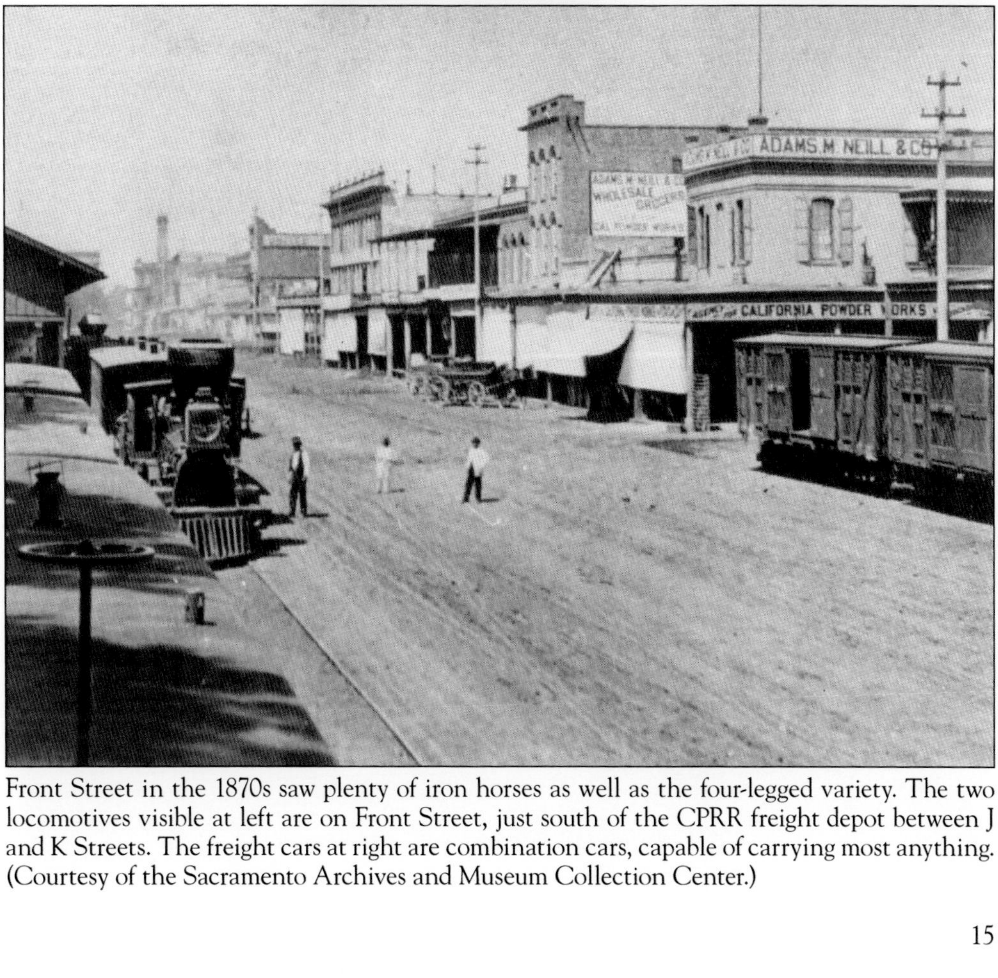

Front Street in the 1870s saw plenty of iron horses as well as the four-legged variety. The two locomotives visible at left are on Front Street, just south of the CPRR freight depot between J and K Streets. The freight cars at right are combination cars, capable of carrying most anything. (Courtesy of the Sacramento Archives and Museum Collection Center.)

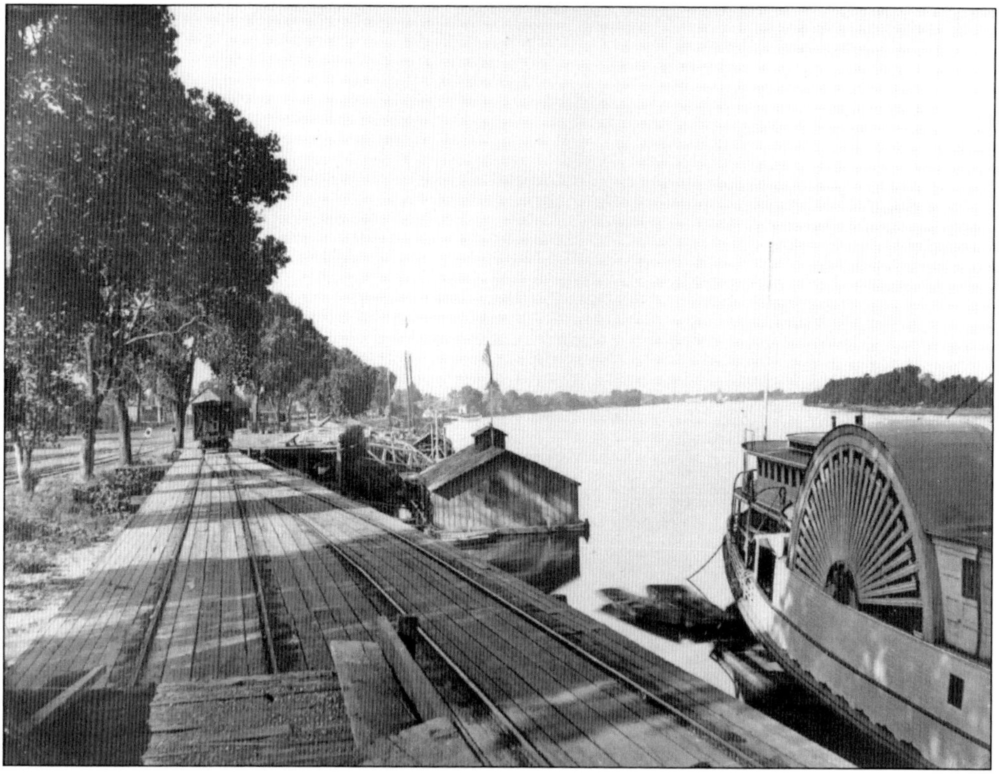

This is the Sacramento riverfront about 1875, looking south from the vicinity of M Street (now called Capitol Mall). The Sacramento Valley Railroad, California's first railroad, had used these tracks to reach the riverfront from its Third and R Streets terminus. (Courtesy of the Sacramento Archives and Museum Collection Center.)

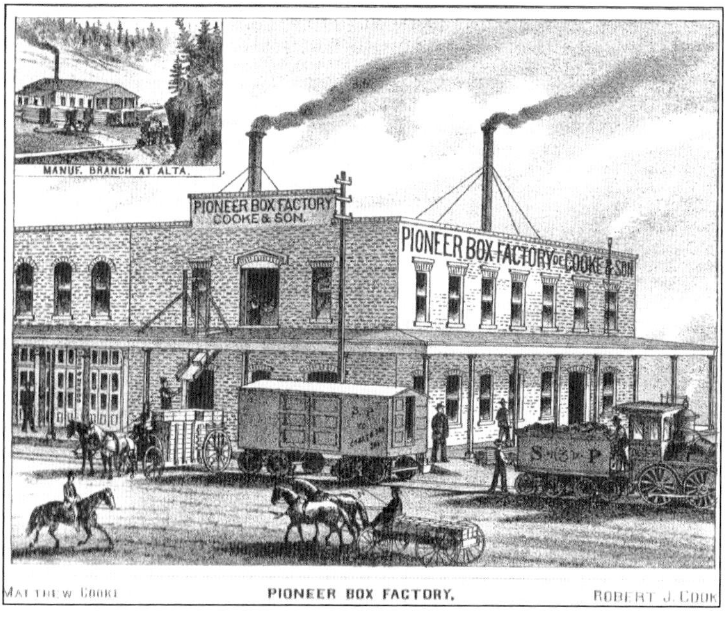

The confluence of river and rails brought many a business to Sacramento. This one, the Pioneer Box Factory, stood at the corner of Front and M Streets, about where Tower Bridge Garage is now. This and the following two illustrations come from the 1880 Thompson and West compendium of Sacramento County history, people, and enterprises. (Courtesy of the Sacramento Room, Sacramento Public Library.)

One block south, at Front and N Streets, stood the Guttenberg foundry. The Sacramento Valley Railroad freight train is traveling the same route still used today by Sacramento Southern trains. The Embassy Suites Hotel now occupies this general area. (Courtesy of the Sacramento Room, Sacramento Public Library.)

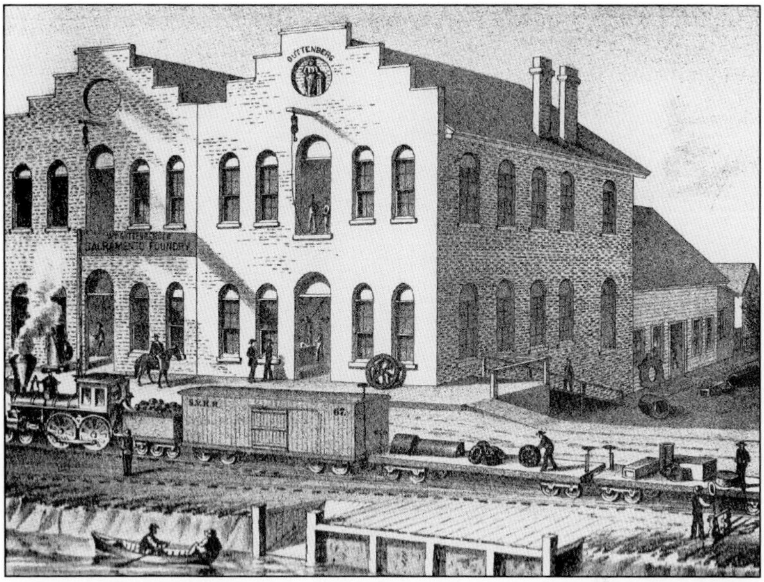

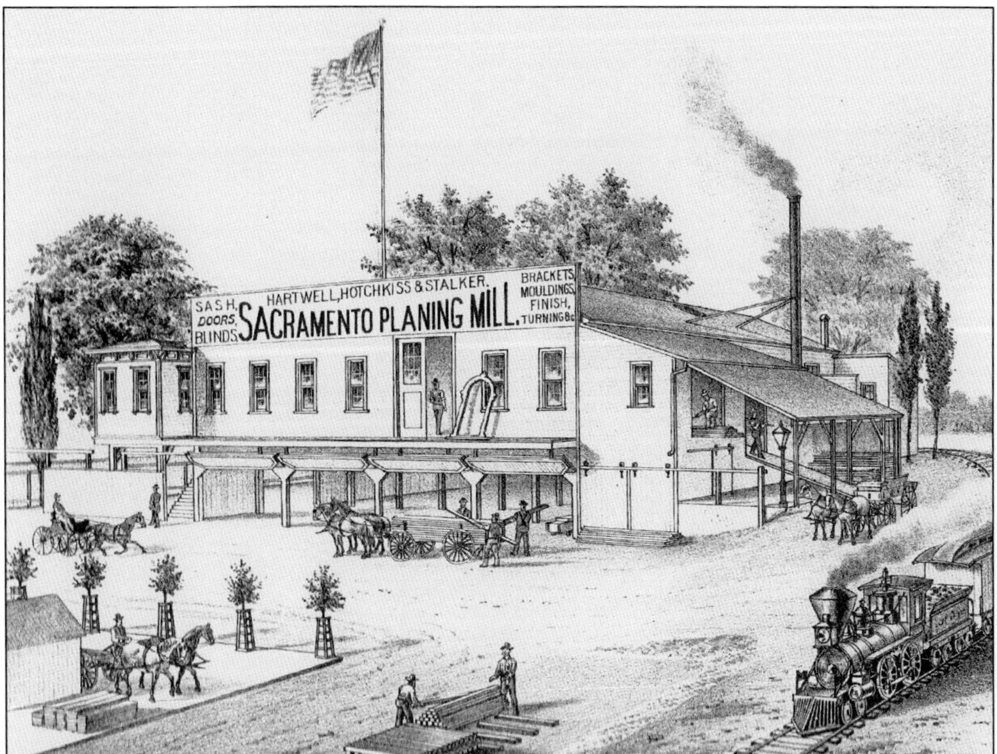

The Sacramento Planing Mill at Front and Q Streets turned out wood products for the booming construction business. The train is turning north onto Front Street from the Sacramento Valley's main line on R Street. (Courtesy of the Sacramento Room, Sacramento Public Library.)

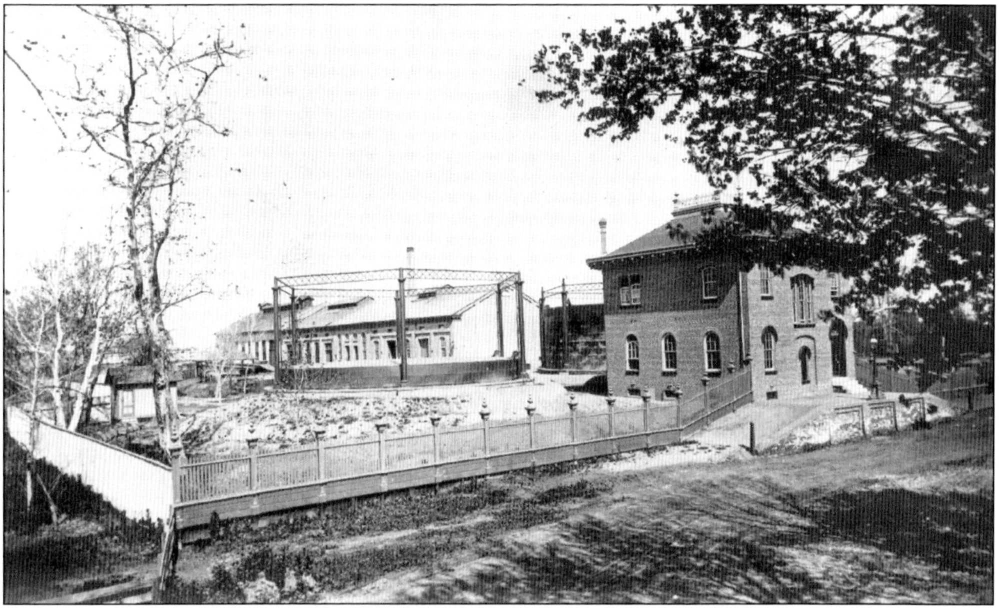

The Pacific Gas and Electric works stood at Front and T Streets. The works was served via a railroad spur. (Courtesy of the Sacramento Archives and Museum Collection Center.)

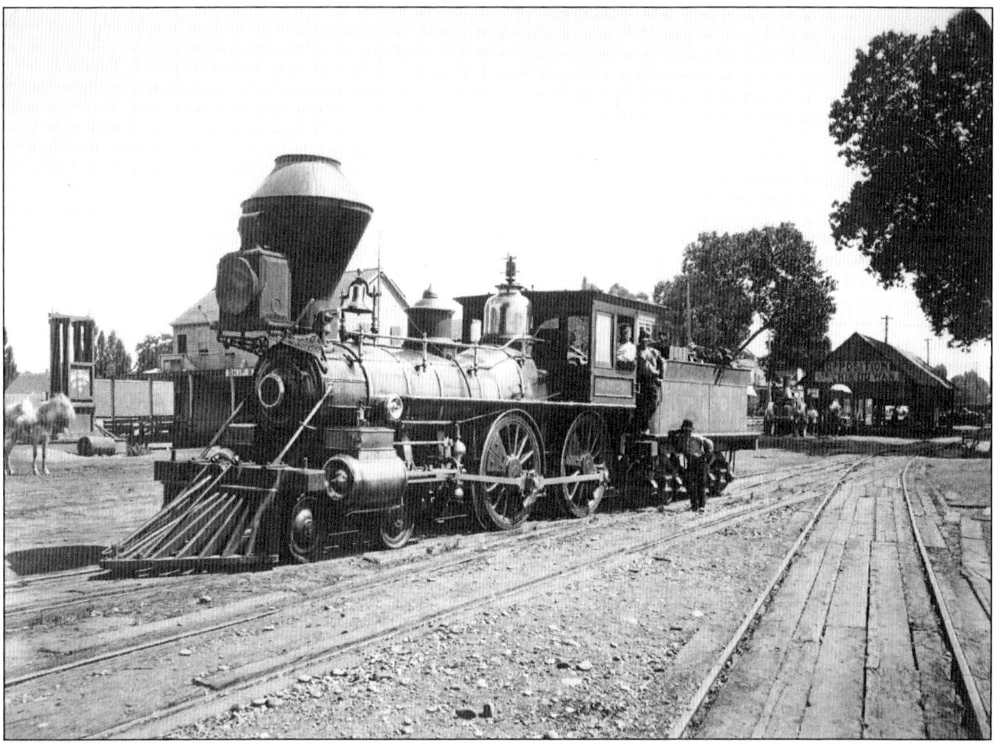

Central Pacific locomotive No. 162 and crew pose at the foot of U Street in Sacramento. The shed at right is home to the Opposition Steamship Line and its riverboat, the *Chin Du Wan*. (Courtesy of the California History Room, California State Library.)

Two

Beginnings and Purpose

Most people who came to California during the Gold Rush and struck it rich were doing something other than looking for gold. Some found their fortunes in the fields and orchards in the Sacramento River Delta, then as now noted for its rich soil. With the Sacramento River and various tributaries, known as sloughs (pronounced "slews"), access to waterborne transportation was easy. The "Big Four" of Central Pacific fame—Leland Stanford, Collis Huntington, Mark Hopkins, and Charles Crocker—certainly knew this. They were in the riverboat business as well as the railroad business. SP steamers were among the armada of riverboats patrolling the rivers and sloughs, picking up produce and other goods and bringing them to railheads for transfer to trains.

Even without the main line intentions spelled out in the introduction, the SP certainly had good reason to build a rail line into the delta. The Atchison, Topeka, and Santa Fe Railway had invaded SP's territory. It was a naval invasion of sorts—steamboats would haul produce to the Santa Fe's railhead at Antioch, near the confluence of the Sacramento and San Joaquin Rivers, where the goods were transferred to trains for shipment. The Santa Fe even bought its own boat, the *Frances*, for the produce trade. The *Topeka Journal* of May 5, 1905, reported that the *Frances* was capable of carrying 600 tons of goods.

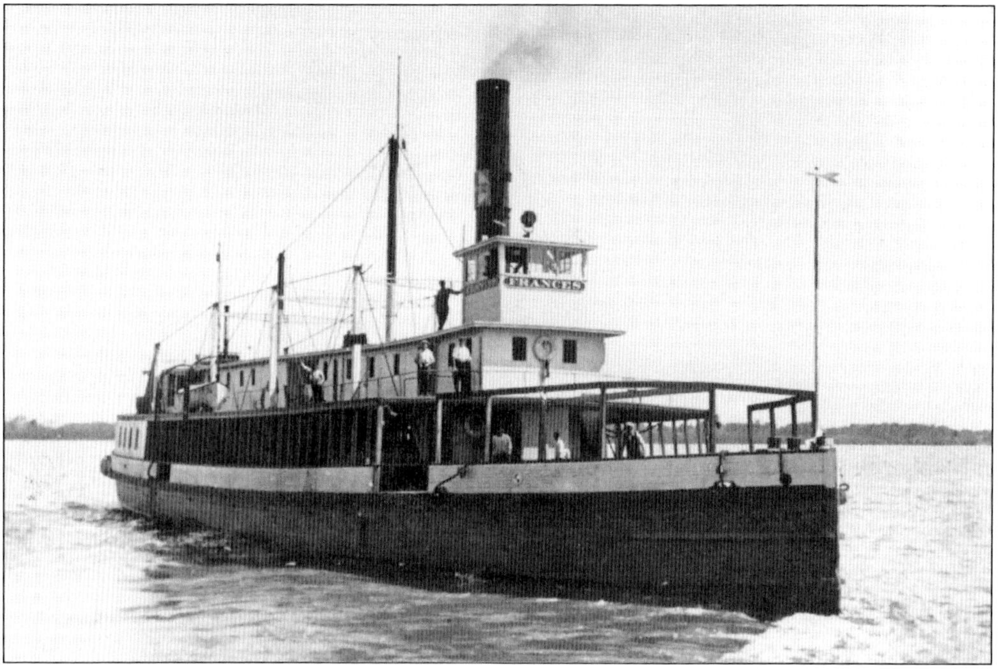

This is the steamboat that may have helped launch the Sacramento Southern Railroad. The *Frances*, owned by the Atchison, Topeka, and Santa Fe Railway, collected produce at various delta landings and brought the goods to its railhead at Antioch for shipment by rail. Note the Santa Fe herald on the stack. (Courtesy of the Sacramento Archives and Museum Collection Center.)

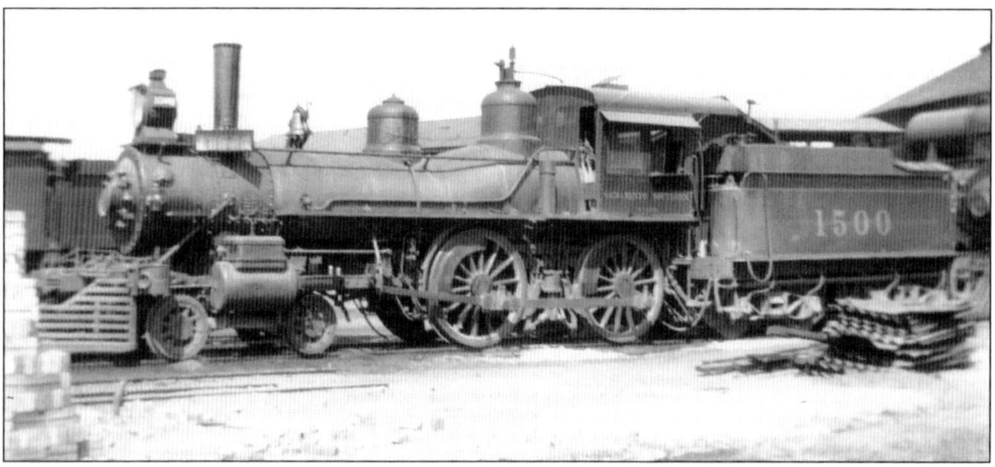

This was the only steam locomotive to wear the Sacramento Southern name. The Southern Pacific re-lettered this locomotive in 1906, when it was No. 1240. As the 1500, this 4-4-0 "American" type carried SSRR lettering until 1910. (Photograph by Robert McFarland; courtesy of the Arnold Menke collection.)

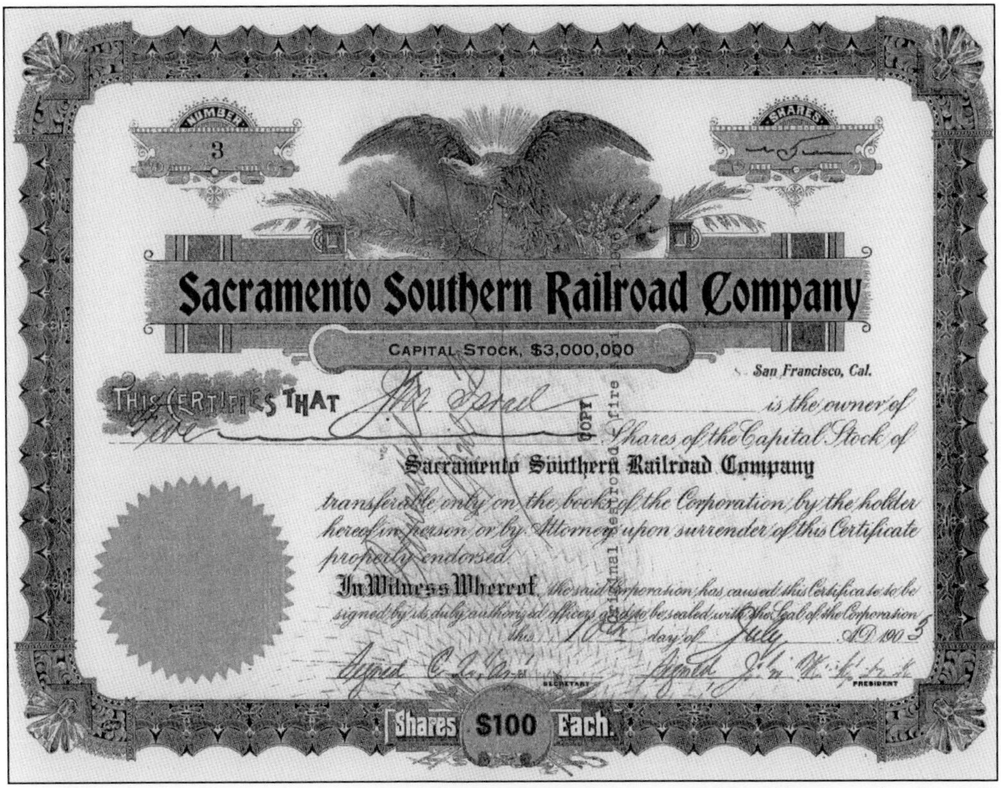

As a duly organized corporation, the Sacramento Southern issued $3 million worth of capital stock at $100 per share. A $500 investment in the new railroad is represented here. (Courtesy of the California State Railroad Museum Library.)

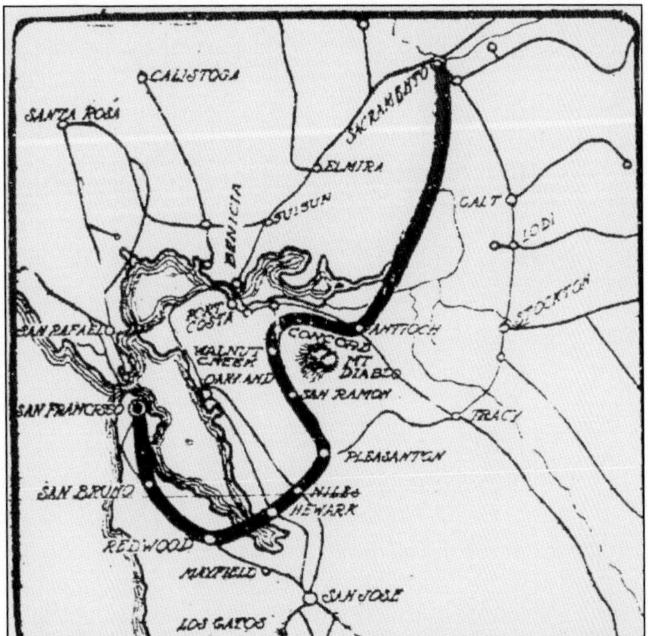

This map, published in the *San Francisco Chronicle* on March 3, 1907, illustrates the SP's proposed all-rail route from Sacramento to San Francisco. The Sacramento Southern was an integral part of the plan, comprising the Sacramento-Antioch leg of the route. This plan did not come to fruition. (Courtesy of the *San Francisco Chronicle*.)

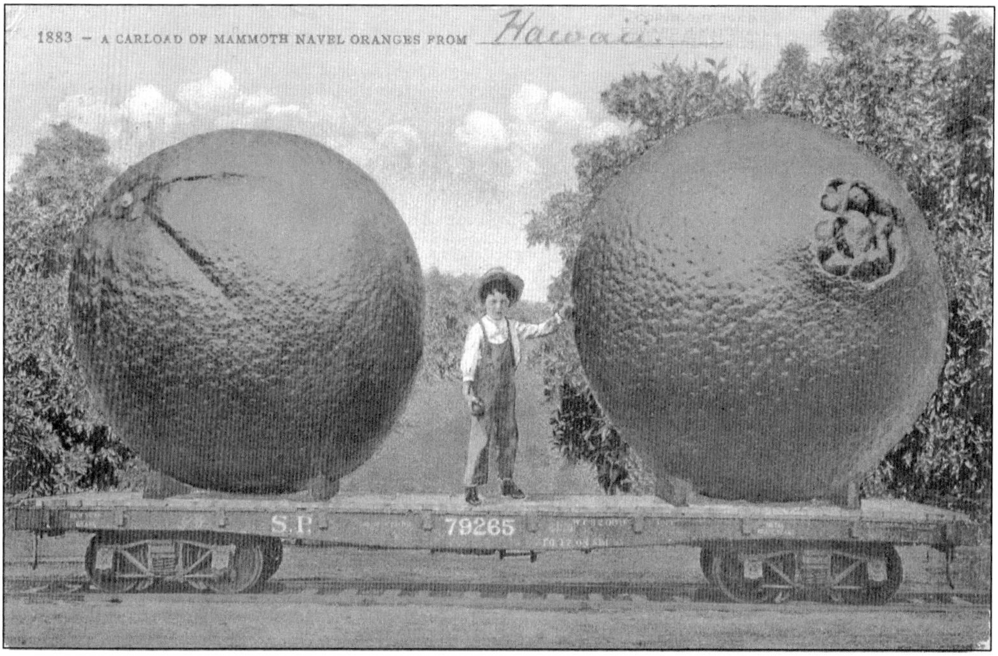

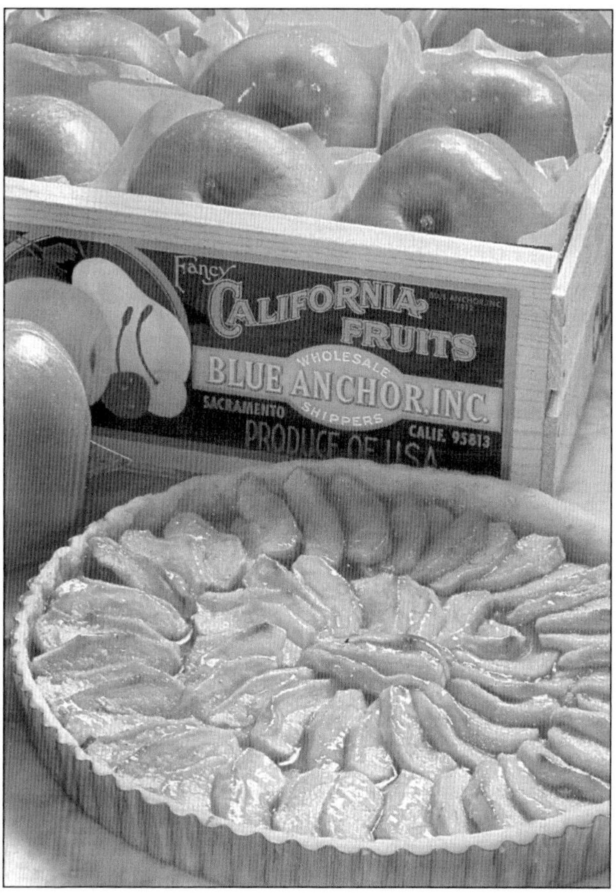

The Southern Pacific used postcards such as these to promote the agricultural richness of the Sacramento River Delta, not to mention its own transportation services. (Courtesy of the Sacramento Archives and Museum Collection Center.)

One of the Southern Pacific's largest customers on the Walnut Grove Branch was the California Fruit Exchange, which sold its fruits and vegetables under the Blue Anchor brand. The company maintained packing sheds at Hood and Walnut Grove. (Courtesy of the Sacramento Archives and Museum Collection Center.)

Reaching Walnut Grove required the Sacramento Southern to build a drawbridge over Snodgrass Slough, just north of town. The dredger *Argyle* is seen preparing the site of the bridge on February 8, 1911. (Courtesy of the California State Railroad Museum Library.)

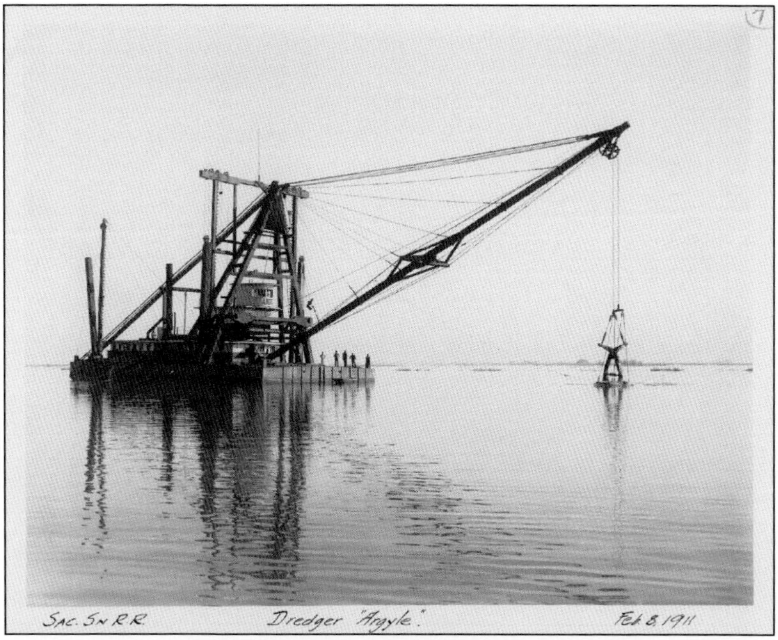

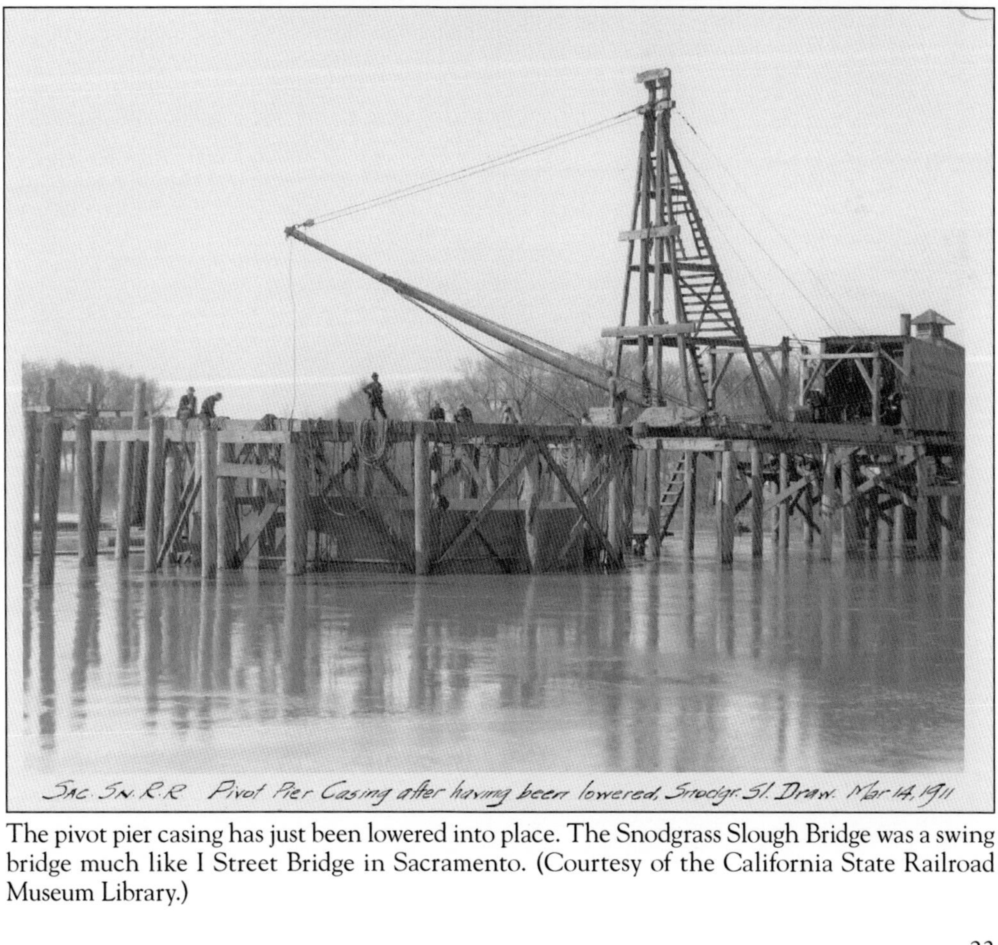

The pivot pier casing has just been lowered into place. The Snodgrass Slough Bridge was a swing bridge much like I Street Bridge in Sacramento. (Courtesy of the California State Railroad Museum Library.)

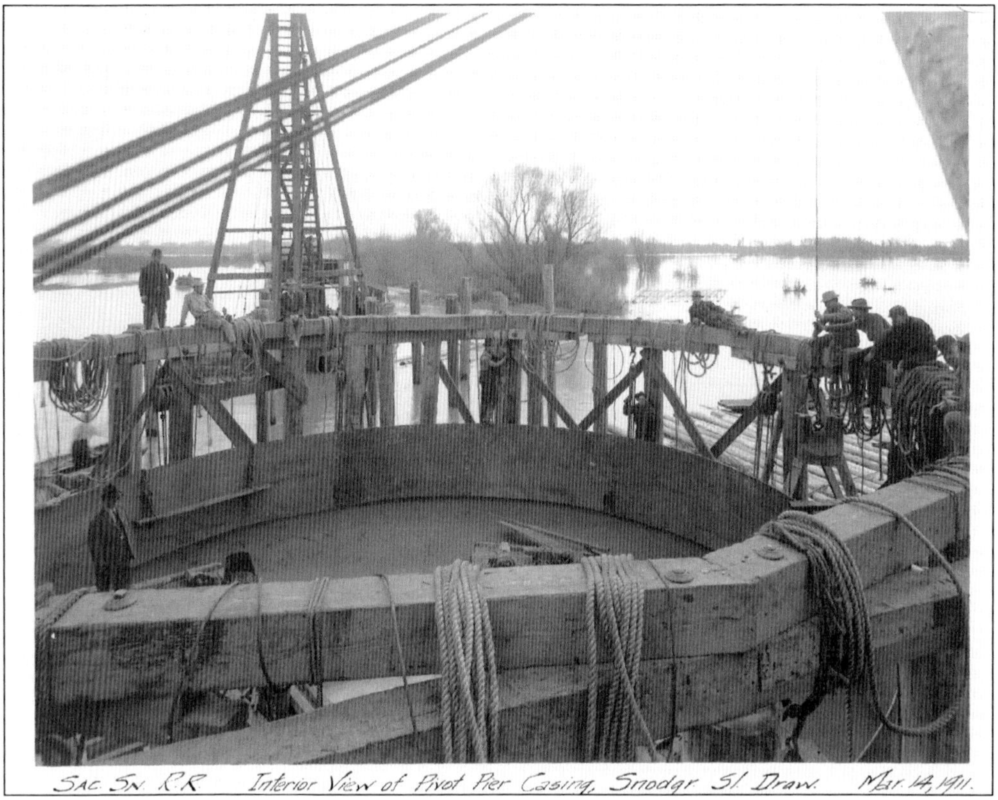

Workers inspect the pivot pier casing while others appear to be relaxing. The SP company photographer captured this scene on March 4, 1911. (Courtesy of the California State Railroad Museum Library.)

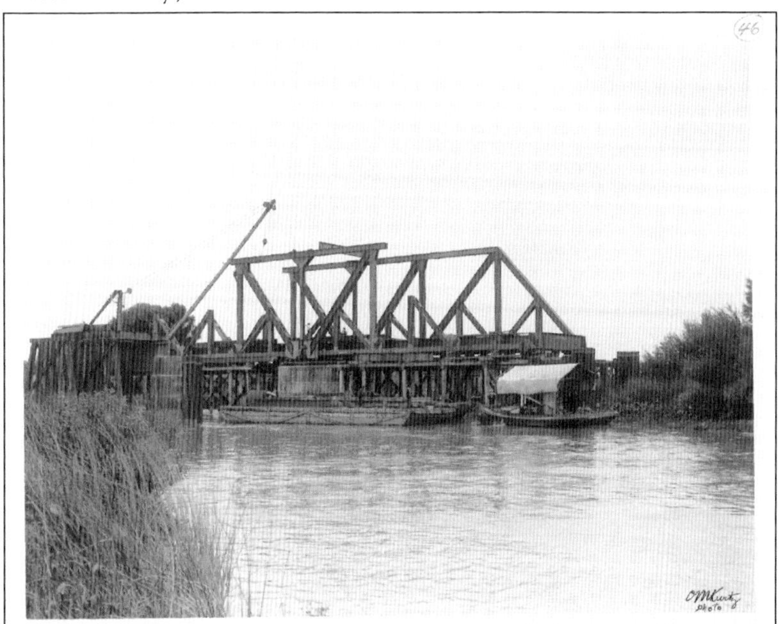

It is now September 21, 1911, and the Snodgrass Slough Bridge is taking shape. The opening of the line to Walnut Grove is still six months away. (Courtesy of the California State Railroad Museum Library.)

Later the same day, a floating crane hoists girders into place. This bridge used a cantilever structure, much like the I Street Bridge in Sacramento, which was built the same year. Unlike the I Street Bridge, however, this bridge no longer stands. (Courtesy of the California State Railroad Museum Library.)

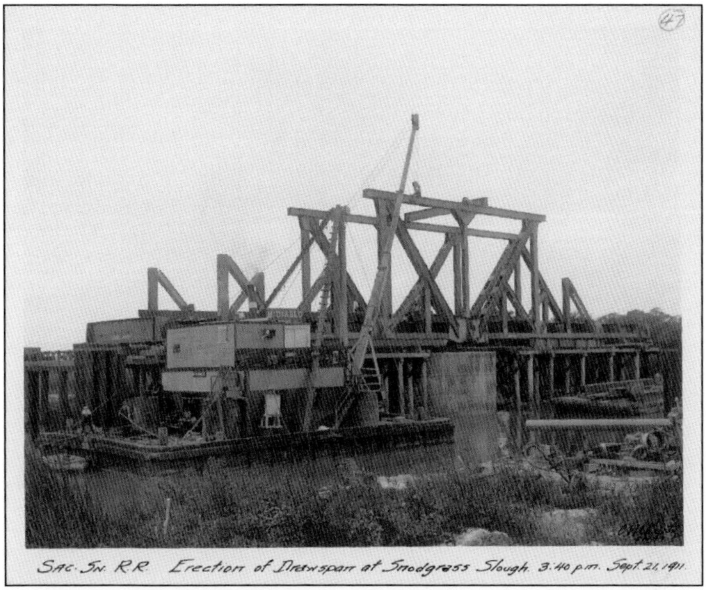

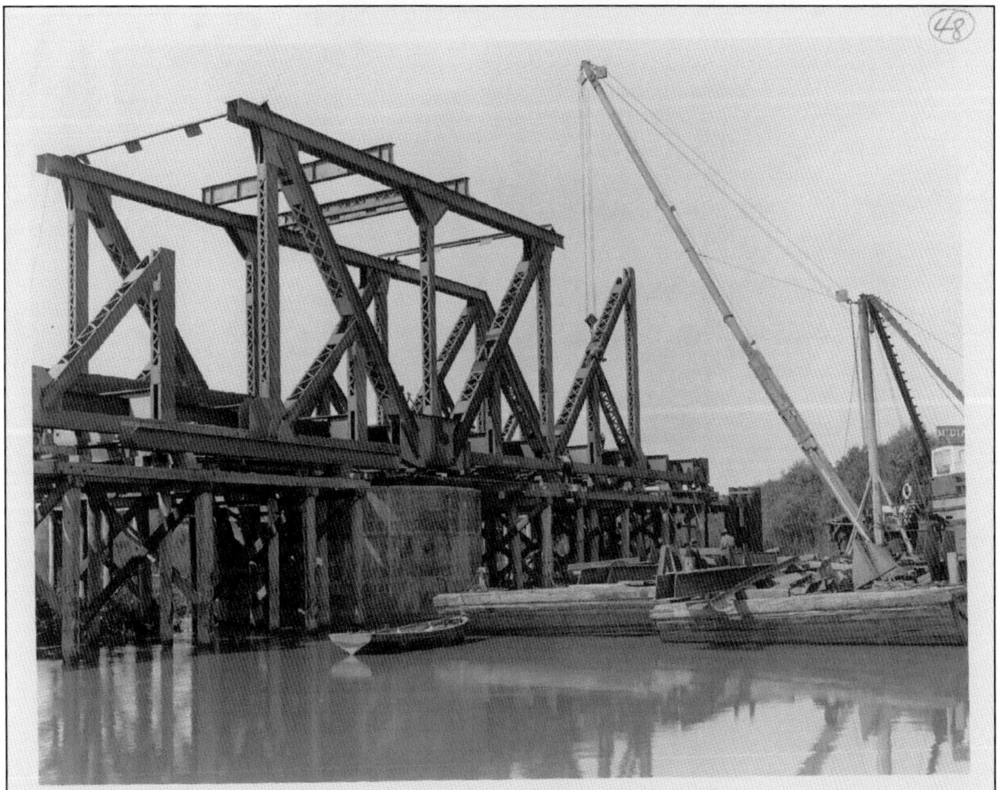

The next day, the Snodgrass Slough Drawbridge has just about achieved its final form. In keeping with the SP's original main line intentions for the Sacramento Southern, this bridge was designed to accommodate two tracks. It never carried more than one. (Courtesy of the California State Railroad Museum Library.)

FROM SAN FRANCISCO—WALNUT GROVE BRANCH—TOWARD SAN FRANCISCO

518 Walnut Grove MOTOR	604 Walnut Grove Passenger	602 Walnut Grove Mixed	Distance from San Francisco	Time Table No. 89 June 8, 1913	Distance from Walnut Grove	601 Walnut Grove Passenger	603 Walnut Grove Mixed	519 Walnut Grove MOTOR
Leave Saturday and Sunday only	Leave Daily	Leave Daily		STATIONS		Arrive Daily	Arrive Daily	Arrive Saturday and Sunday only
4.00PM	5.30PM	7.30AM	88.8	DNR **SACRAMENTO**	24.6	10.45AM	8.30PM	6.50PM
				0.5				
			89.3	Sacramento Woodland Railway Crossing	24.1			
				0.3				
4.05	5.35	7.35	89.6	JCT. SWITCH R STREET	23.8	10.40	8.25	6.45
				2.2				
f 4.12	f 5.42	f 7.40	91.8	BATHS	21.6	f 10.33	f 8.20	f 6.40
				2.4				
f 4.18	f 5.47	f 7.50	94.2	DEL RIO	19.2	f 10.28	f 8.15	f 6.35
				3.3				
s 4.27	s 5.55	s 8.00	97.5	FREEPORT	15.9	s 10.19	s 8.05	s 6.25
				7.1				
f 4.42	f **6.10**	f 8.15	104.6	HOOD JUNCTION	9.8	f 10.04	f 7.50	f **6.10**
				0.7				
s 4.50	s 6.17	s 8.35	105.3	*WHARF	9.5	s 10.00	s 7.45	s 6.05
				4.0				
f 5.02	f 6.28	f 8.50	107.9	GLANN	5.5	f 9.47	f 7.05	f 5.52
				5.5				
5.15PM	6.40PM	9.05AM	113.4	DR **WALNUT GROVE**	0.0	9.35AM	6.50PM	5.40PM
Ar. Sat. and Sunday only	Arrive Daily	Arrive Daily		(24.6)		Leave Daily	Leave Daily	Lv. Sat. and Sunday only
(1.15)	(1.10)	(1.35)		Time over District		(1 10)	(1.40)	(1.10)
19.68	21.09	15.54		Average speed per hour		21.09	14.76	21.09

On March 12, 1912, the Sacramento Southern line to Walnut Grove became operational. This scan from a Southern Pacific Sacramento Division employee timetable shows the line's scheduled trains as of June 1913. (Courtesy of the California State Railroad Museum Library.)

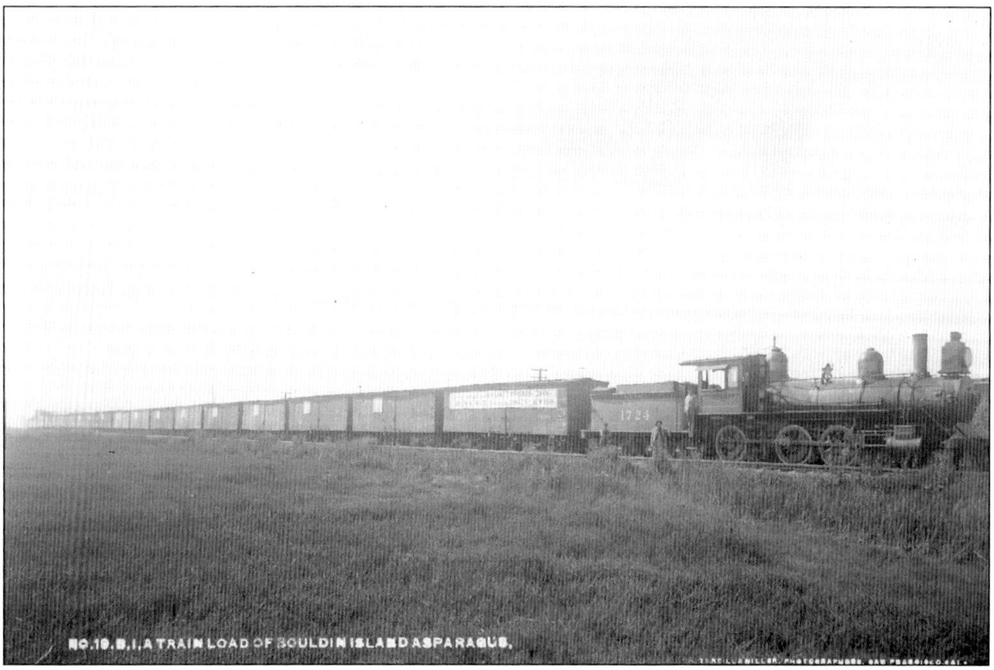

A trainload of Bouldin Island asparagus poses, likely for publicity purposes, somewhere on the Walnut Grove Branch around the 1920s. Asparagus, then as now, was a principal delta crop and was one of the main cargos hauled on the branch. (Courtesy BAERA Archives Collection/ Western Railway Museum.)

Three
SACRAMENTO

Sacramento has played many roles in California history—the jumping-off point for the hills supposedly teeming with gold, capital of California, origin of California's first railroad, busy steamboat terminal, western terminus of the transcontinental telegraph line, origin of the Central Pacific Railroad, and home of a major shops complex for the Central Pacific and Southern Pacific that for decades was Sacramento's largest employer.

Sacramento was the headquarters and namesake of the SP's Sacramento Division. This division was responsible for the famous Donner Pass route through the Sierra Nevada as well as Sacramento Valley lines north to Redding and Dunsmuir. The Walnut Grove Branch was one of several coming under the division's jurisdiction. A train arriving in town from the Sacramento Southern/Walnut Grove Branch came upon a Sacramento waterfront teeming with activity on the rails and on the water. Besides the Sacramento Southern, there was also the Western Pacific, with a wharf on the riverfront and a line extending east along R Street toward the WP main line; the Northern Electric Railway, later part of the Sacramento Northern, with electric-powered freight and passenger trains; and the Central California Traction, also an electric road, which interchanged traffic with the Sacramento Southern-SP at X Street south of downtown. And that does not even take into account SP's own extensive operations in what is now Old Sacramento. Two large SP freight depots stood along Front Street near the riverfront, each two blocks long, stretching from I Street (near where the California State Railroad Museum is now) to M Street (now Capitol Mall). The SP, one of several companies operating riverboats to and from Sacramento, also maintained a steamer terminal stretching for two blocks north of M Street, opposite one of the SP's freight houses.

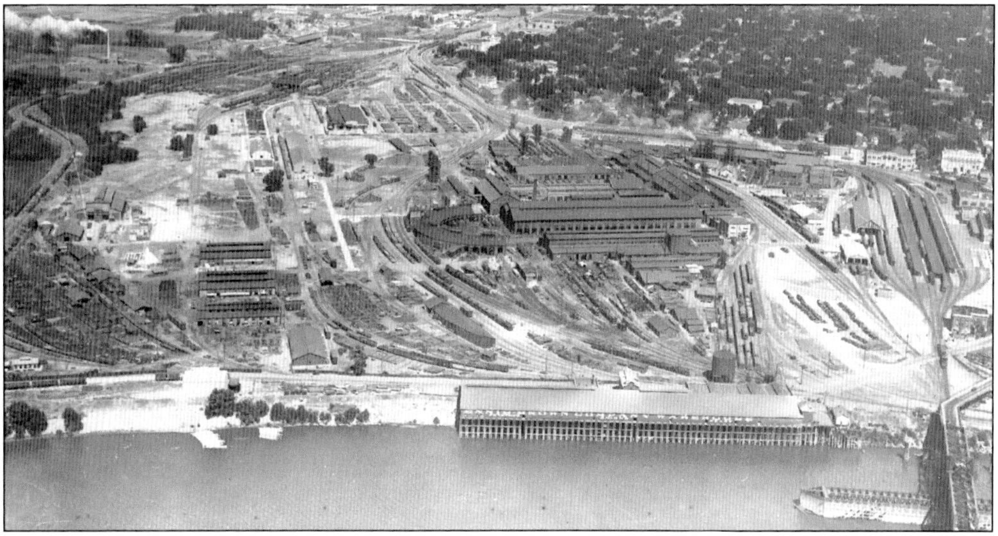

The Sacramento Shops complex is seen from the air around the 1930s. The depot tracks are at right; the I Street Bridge is at lower right. The SP for many years maintained, and in many cases built from scratch, locomotives and railcars at this facility. Only a few of these buildings remain standing. (Courtesy of the California State Railroad Museum Library.)

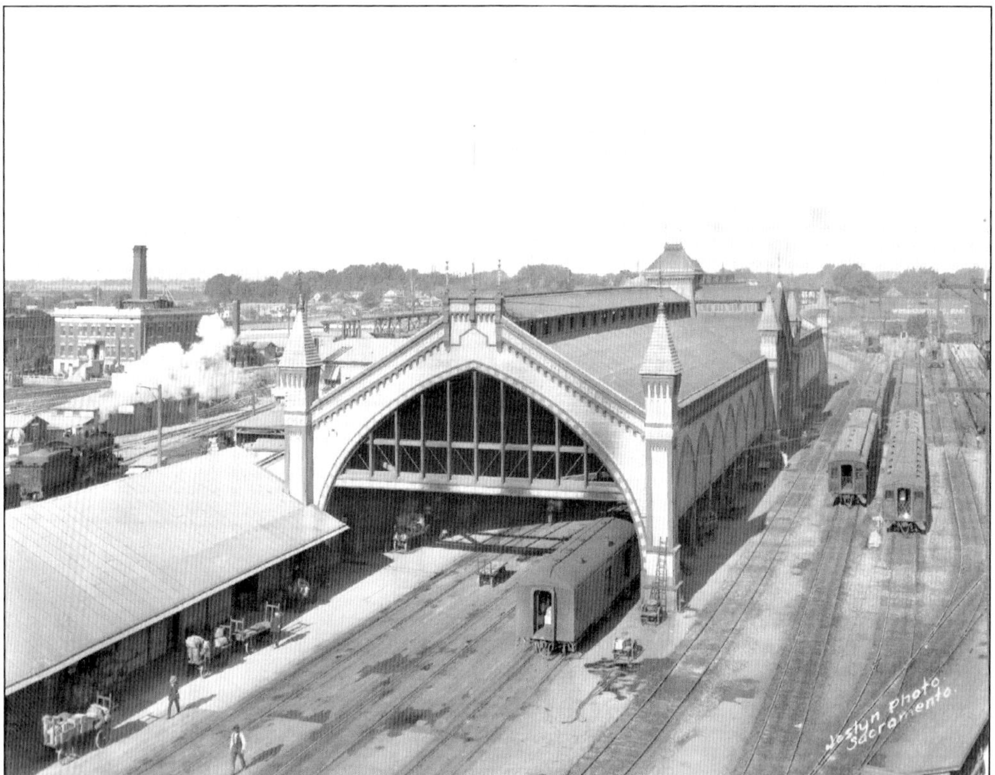

This depot, built by the Central Pacific in 1879, was still serving passengers when the Sacramento Southern opened. This building stood just east of the Sacramento River, north of I Street. (Courtesy of the California State Railroad Museum Library.)

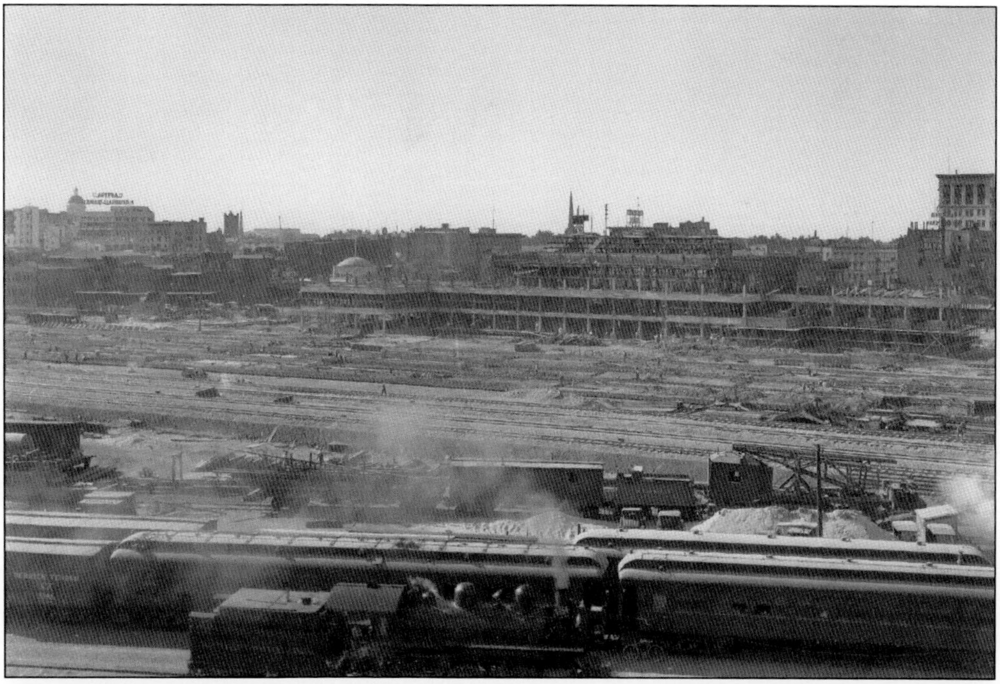

About 1925, the SP decided to build a new depot in Sacramento. David Joslyn's camera captured the new station under construction around 1925. (Courtesy of the Sacramento Archives and Museum Collection Center.)

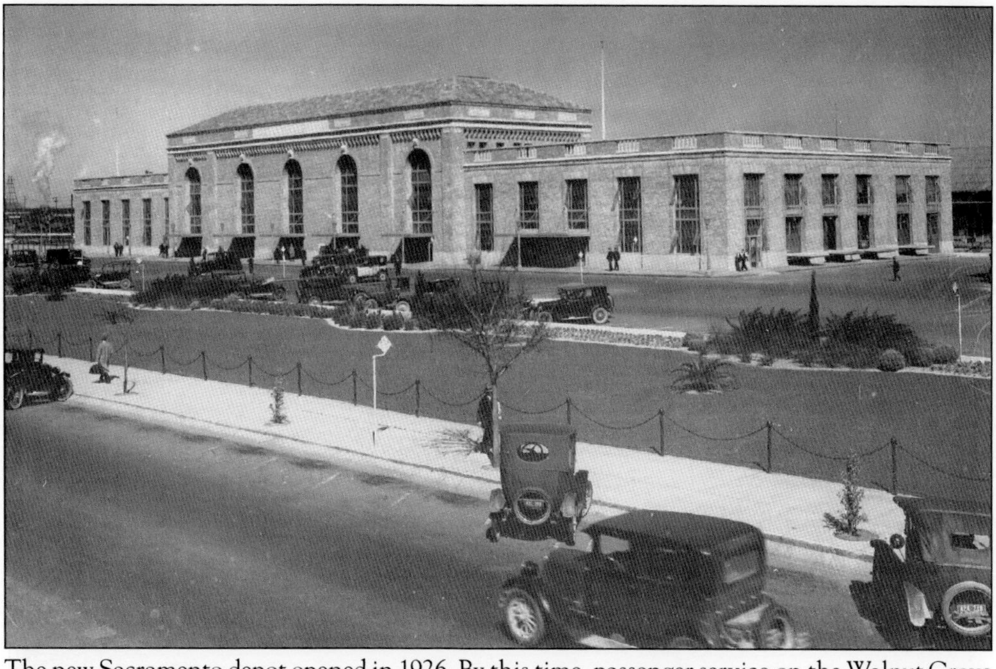

The new Sacramento depot opened in 1926. By this time, passenger service on the Walnut Grove Branch was down to a single mixed train. This building still stands, serving Amtrak's California Zephyr, Coast Starlight, San Joaquin, and Capitol Corridor routes as well as local buses and light-rail trains. (Courtesy of the California State Railroad Museum Library.)

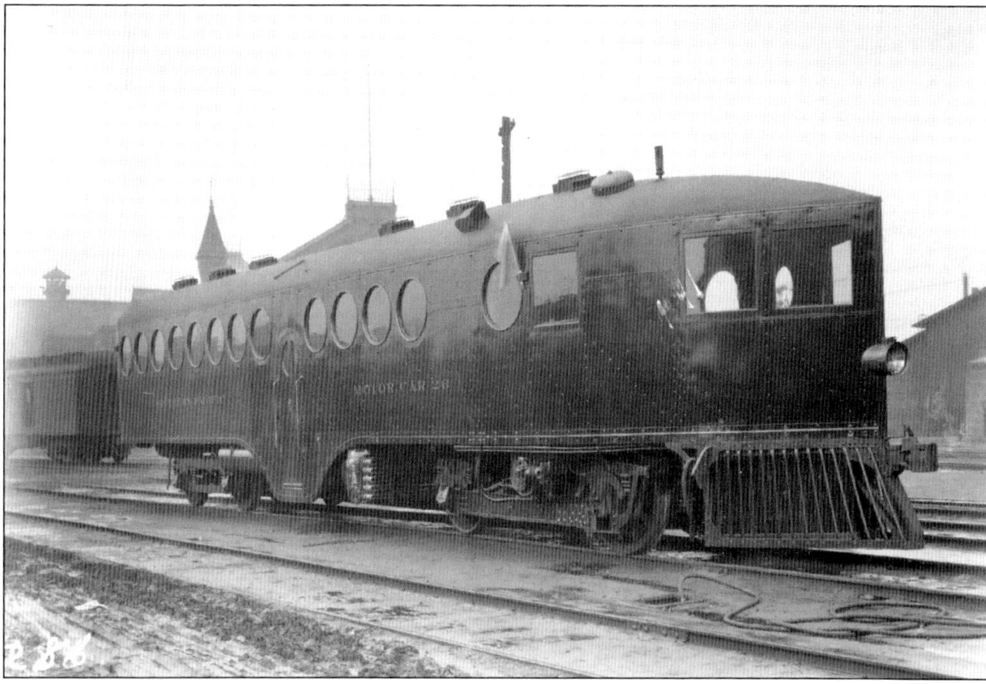

From 1909 to 1924, McKeen motorcars, such as this one seen in Sacramento, provided most of the passenger service on the Sacramento Southern/Walnut Grove Branch. This design was the brainchild of William McKeen, who came up with it while working for the Union Pacific early in the 20th century. The SP used these cars on several of its branch lines out of Sacramento. (Courtesy of the California State Railroad Museum Library.)

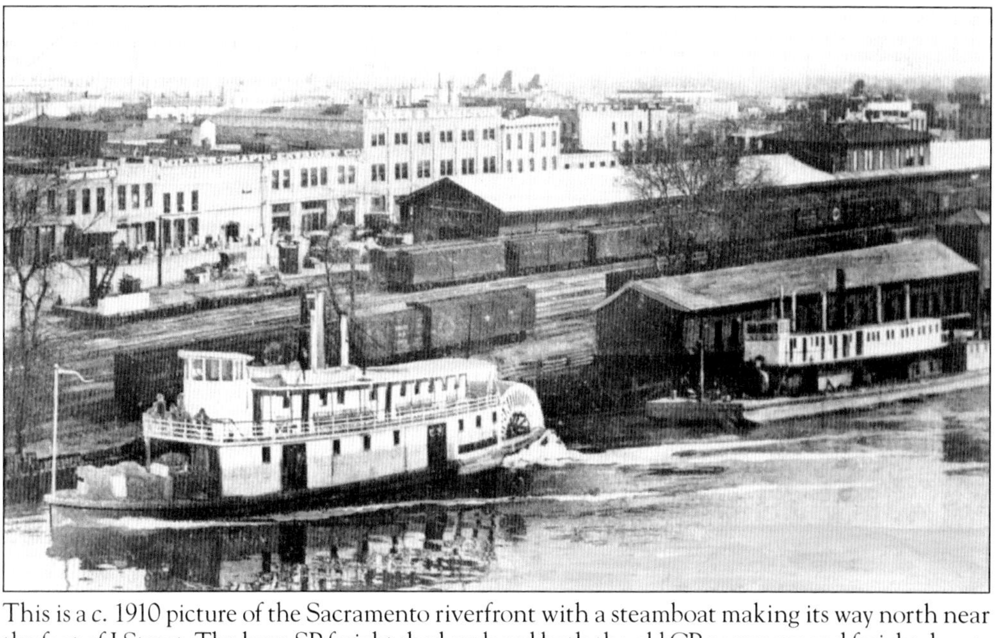

This is a c. 1910 picture of the Sacramento riverfront with a steamboat making its way north near the foot of I Street. The large SP freight shed replaced both the old CP passenger and freight depots and stretched two blocks along Front Street from I to K Streets. (Courtesy of the Sacramento Archives and Museum Collection Center.)

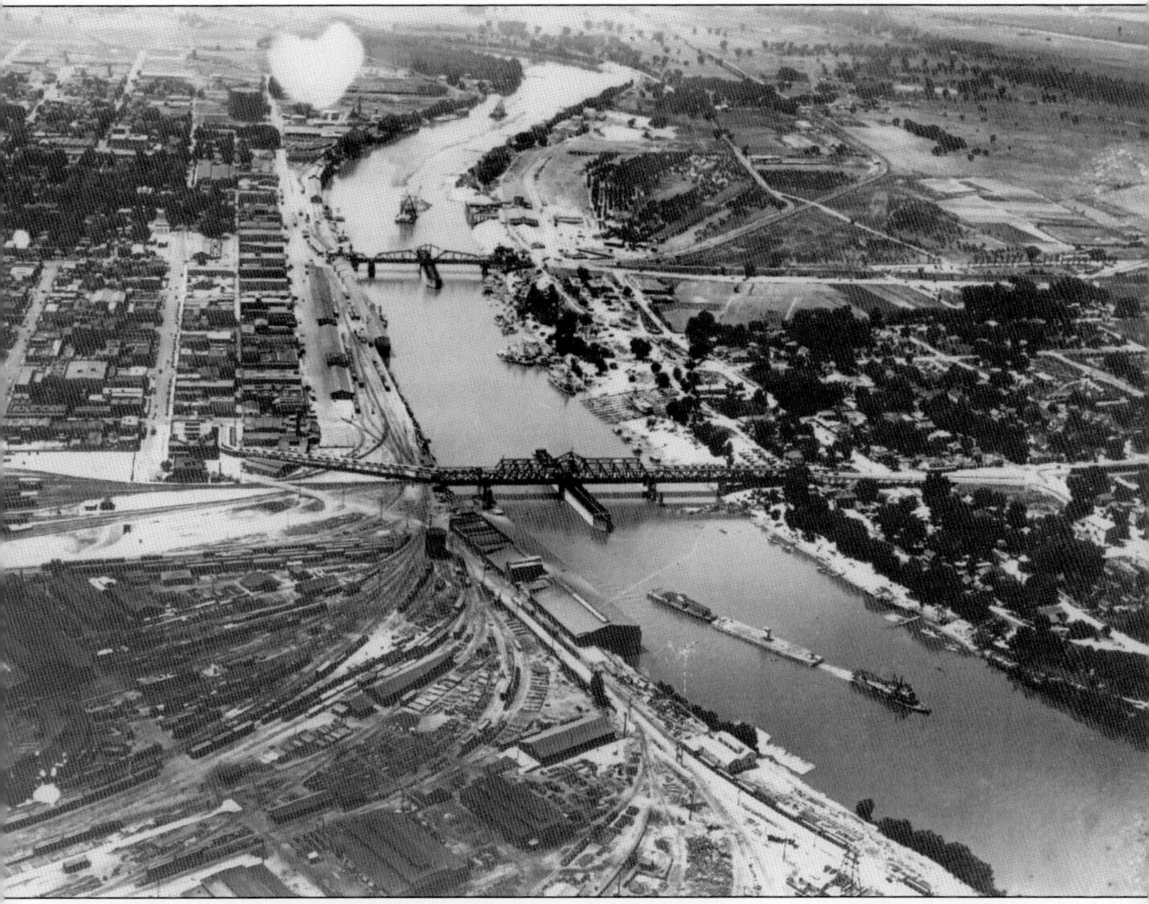

This 1920s view of Sacramento looks south along the Sacramento River, with the SP shops at lower left. On the riverfront, between the I Street and M Street Bridges, is the SP freight shed and yard. I Street Bridge (bottom) was built in 1911 and is still in service; M Street Bridge was built in 1913 and replaced by Tower Bridge in 1935. (Courtesy of the California History Room, California State Library.)

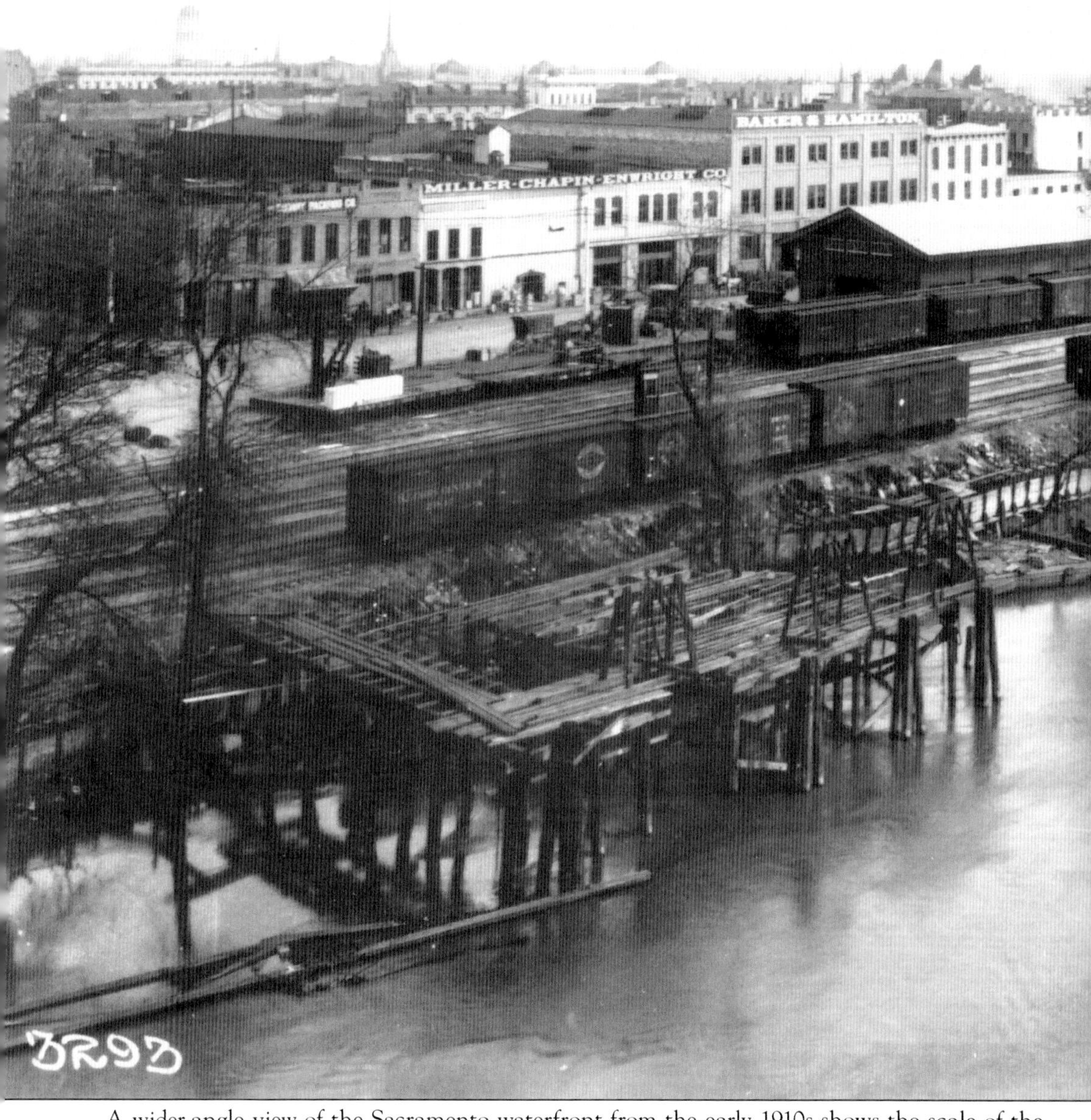

A wider-angle view of the Sacramento waterfront from the early 1910s shows the scale of the Southern Pacific's waterfront operations. Two large freight sheds and a steamboat wharf served

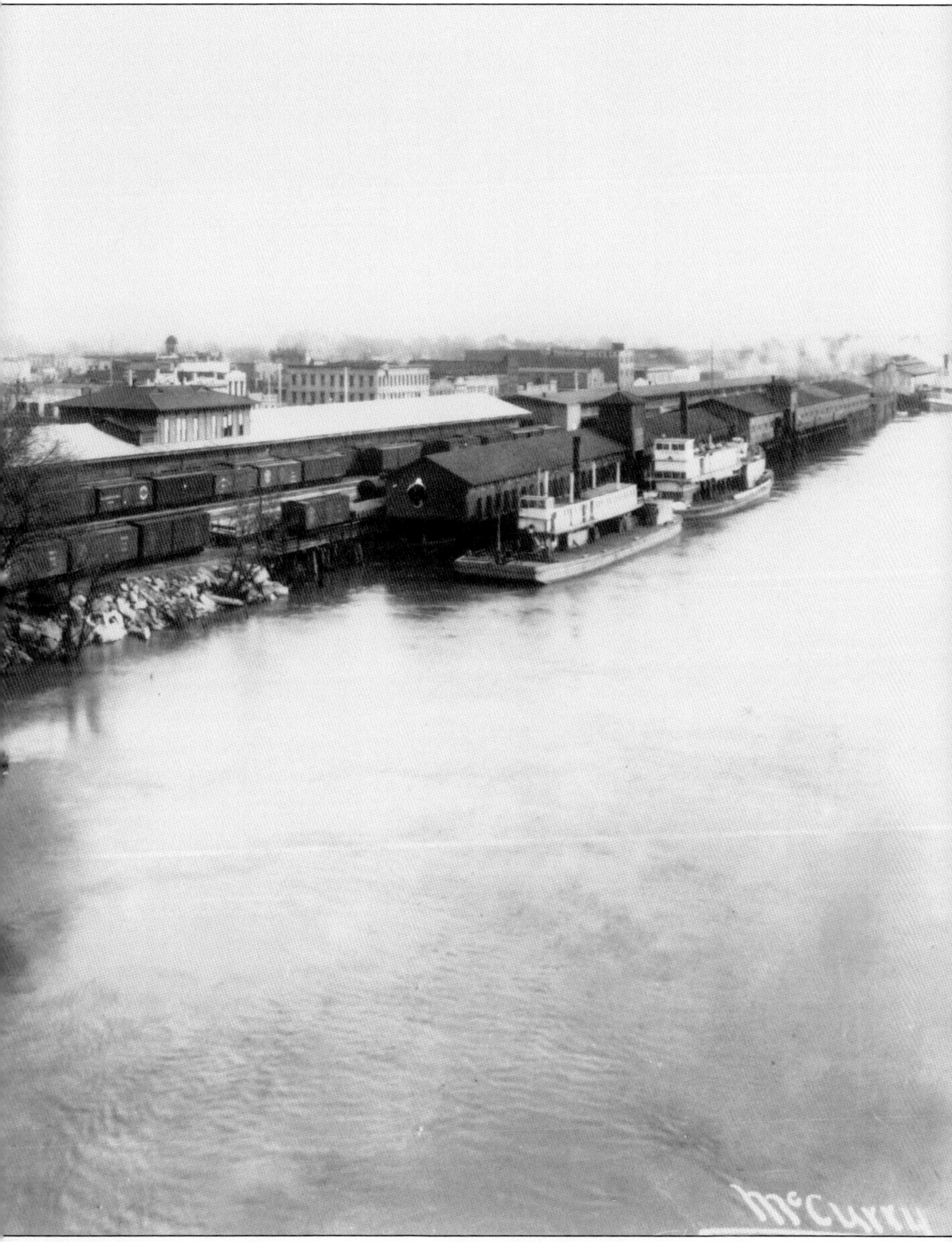

SP's freight operations. The capitol dome is visible at left. (Courtesy of the California History Room, California State Library.)

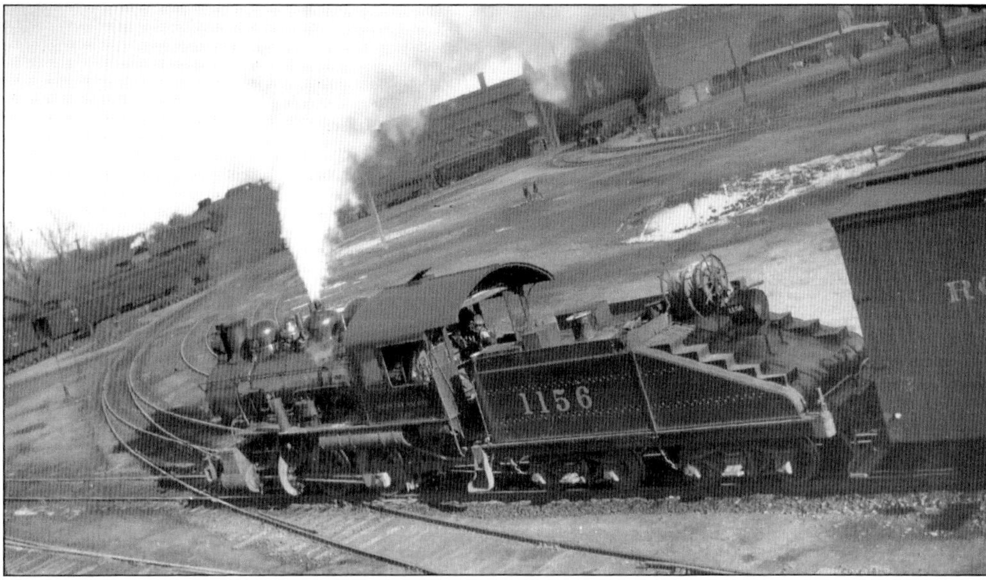

One of the many Southern Pacific switchers to work the Sacramento yards brings a freight train north from the waterfront toward the shops and the 1879-vintage passenger depot in the early 1920s. (Courtesy of the Sacramento Archives and Museum Collection Center.)

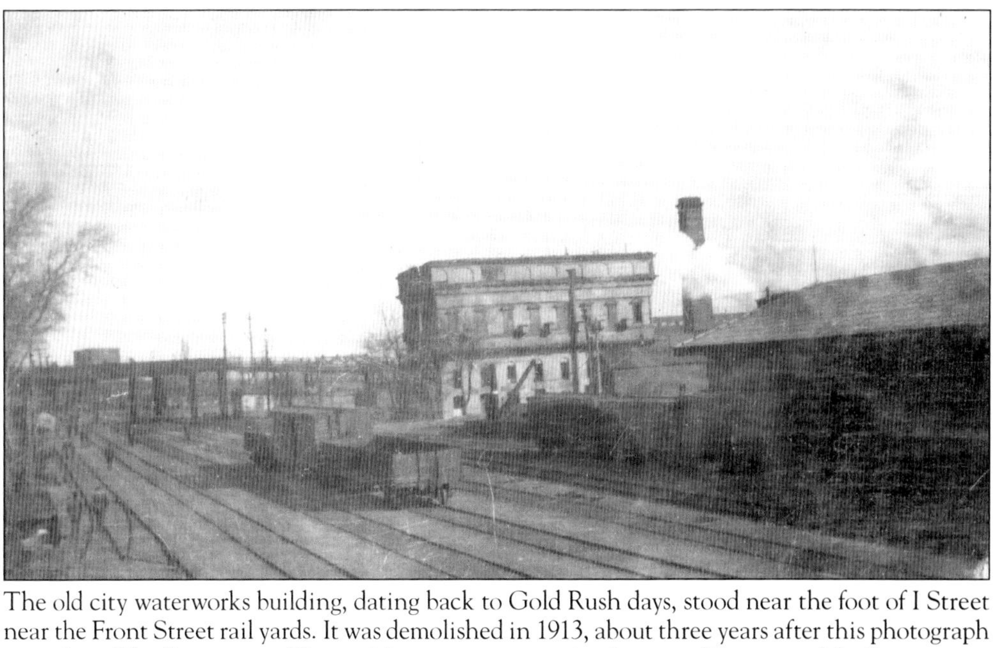

The old city waterworks building, dating back to Gold Rush days, stood near the foot of I Street near the Front Street rail yards. It was demolished in 1913, about three years after this photograph was taken. The Sacramento History Museum now occupies the spot. (Courtesy of the Sacramento Archives and Museum Collection Center.)

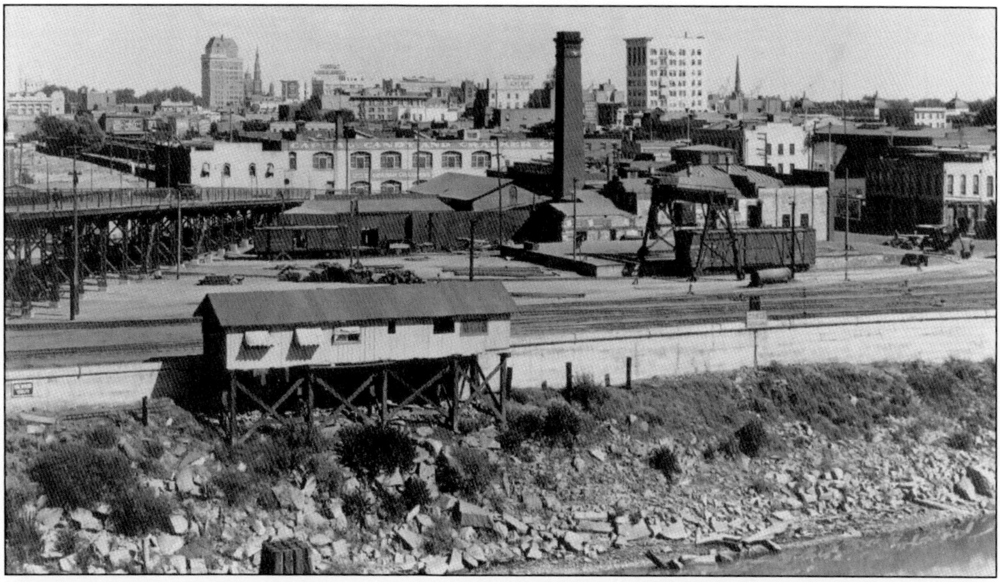

The Sacramento skyline is seen from the I Street Bridge in 1923, with the SP's tracks leading from the waterfront (at right) to the shops and depot. The building in the center is the Capital Candy and Cracker Company; the building with the smokestack in the foreground is about where the California State Railroad Museum stands today. (Courtesy of the Sacramento Archives and Museum Collection Center.)

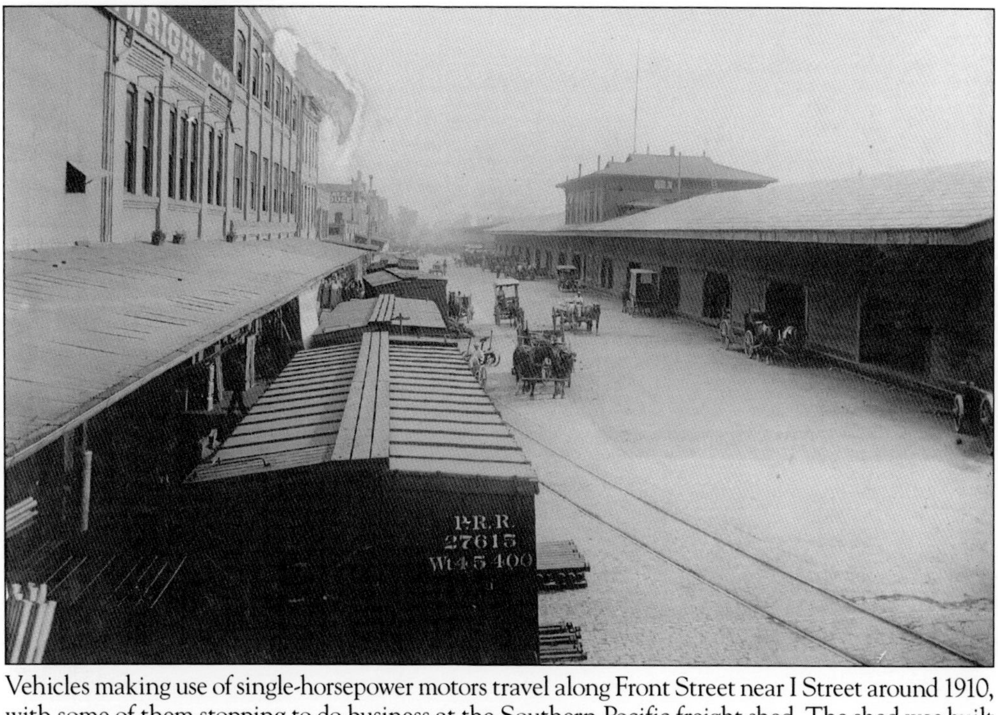

Vehicles making use of single-horsepower motors travel along Front Street near I Street around 1910, with some of them stopping to do business at the Southern Pacific freight shed. The shed was built about 1906 and stood until the early 1970s. Trackage on Front Street allowed SP to bring freight cars to customers' doors. The boxcar in the foreground is a long way from home rails—it belongs to the Pennsylvania Railroad. (Courtesy of the California History Room, California State Library.)

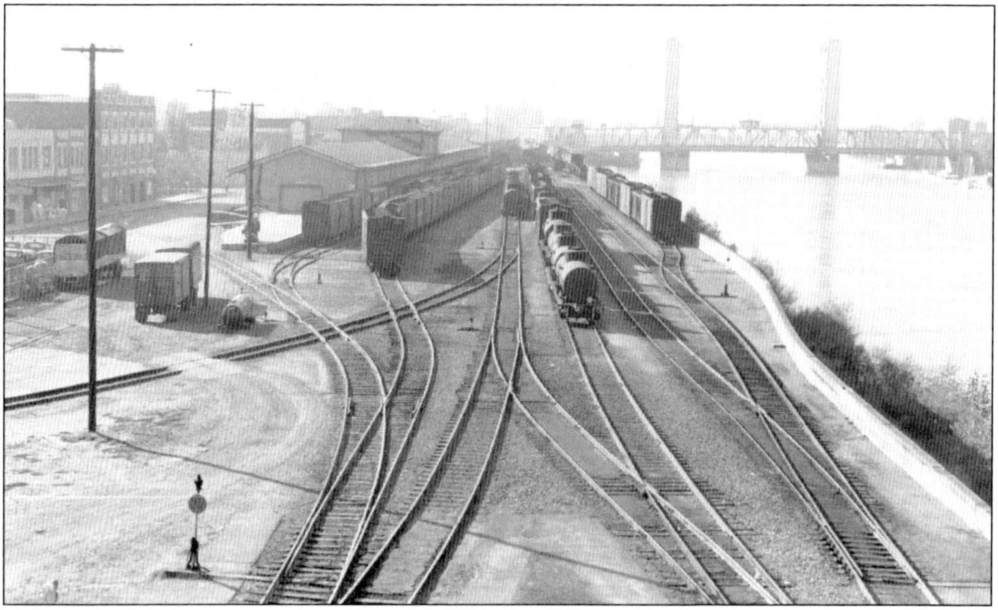

The SP's Front Street yard was a busy place in the 1940s, as seen from the approach to the I Street Bridge. Tower Bridge, at right, replaced M Street Bridge in 1935. It is still a Sacramento landmark. (Courtesy of the California State Railroad Museum Library.)

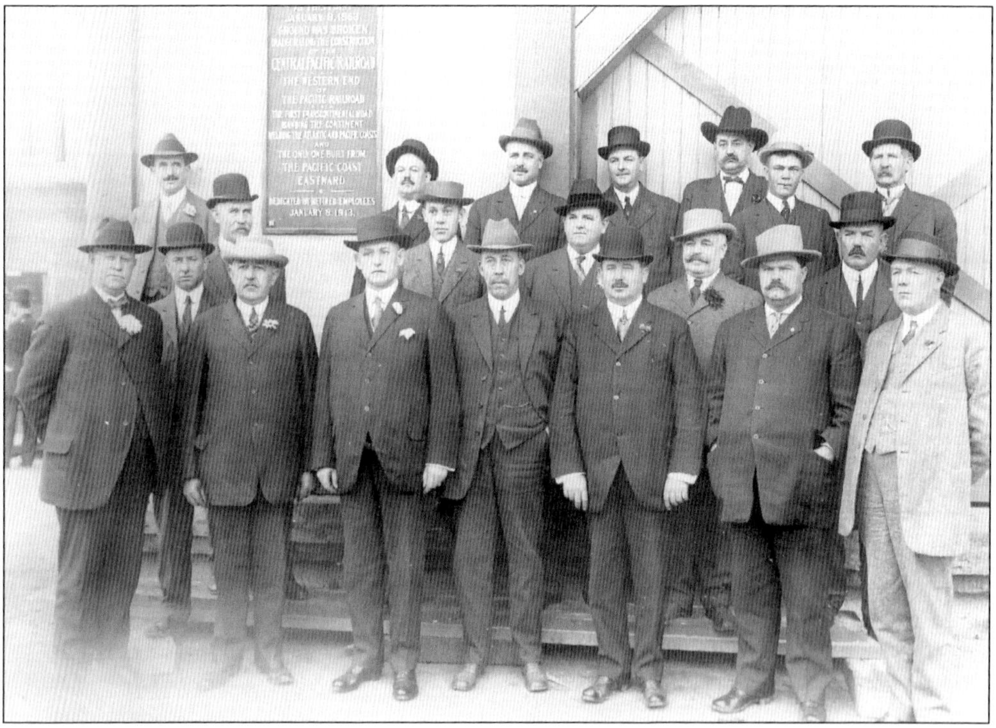

In 1913, a group of retired Southern Pacific employees dedicated a plaque on the south wall of the freight shed at the foot of Front and K Streets. The plaque marks the spot where the Central Pacific, a forerunner of the SP, broke ground in 1863 for the push east. (Courtesy of the Sacramento Archives and Museum Collection Center.)

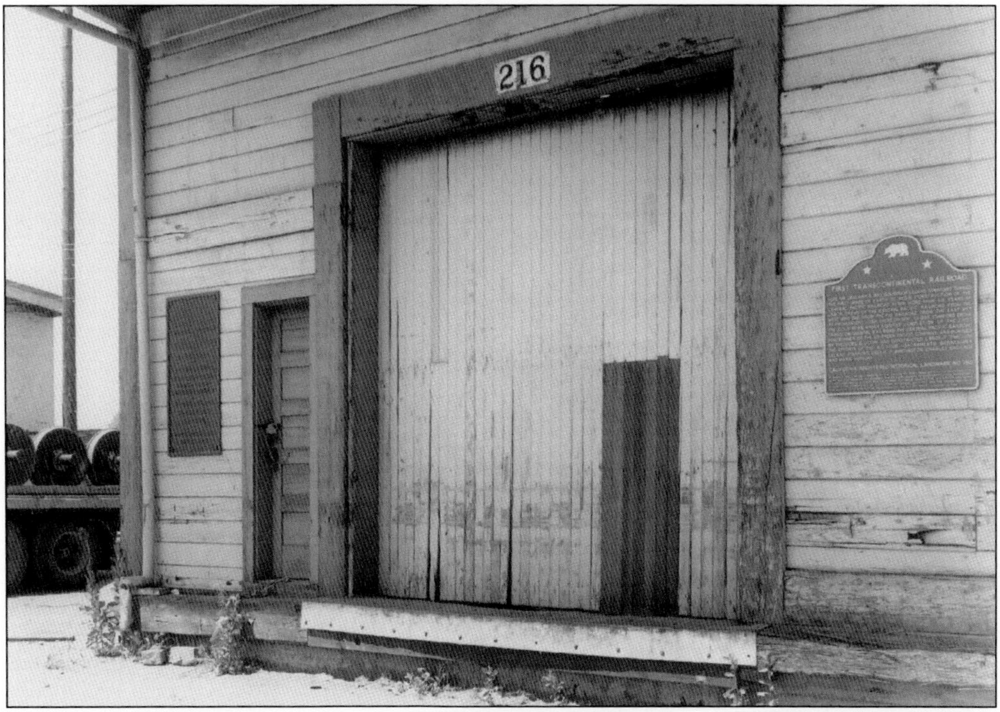

On January 8, 1963, the state of California added its own plaque marking the western birthplace of the first transcontinental railroad. The SP retirees' plaque is visible at left. Both plaques are now in the Transcontinental Gallery at the California State Railroad Museum. (Courtesy of the Sacramento Archives and Museum Collection Center.)

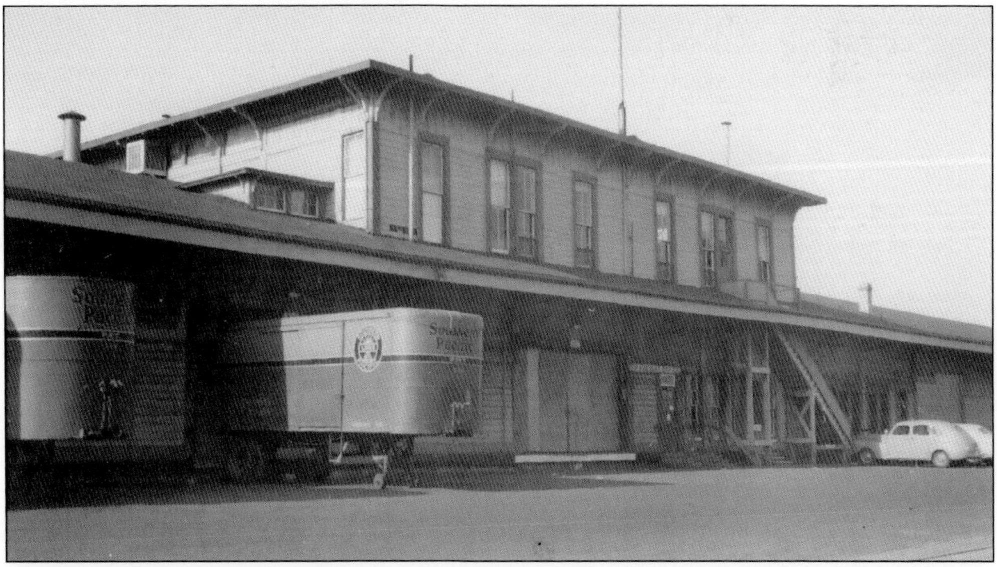

By 1951, the Front Street freight shed was looking a bit worse for wear. The freight office was across Front Street from the foot of J Street. The trailers at left belong to Pacific Motor Trucking, which was SP's trucking subsidiary. These trailers were painted red, orange, and black, the same colors used by the SP's legendary Daylight streamliners. (Courtesy of the Sacramento Archives and Museum Collection Center.)

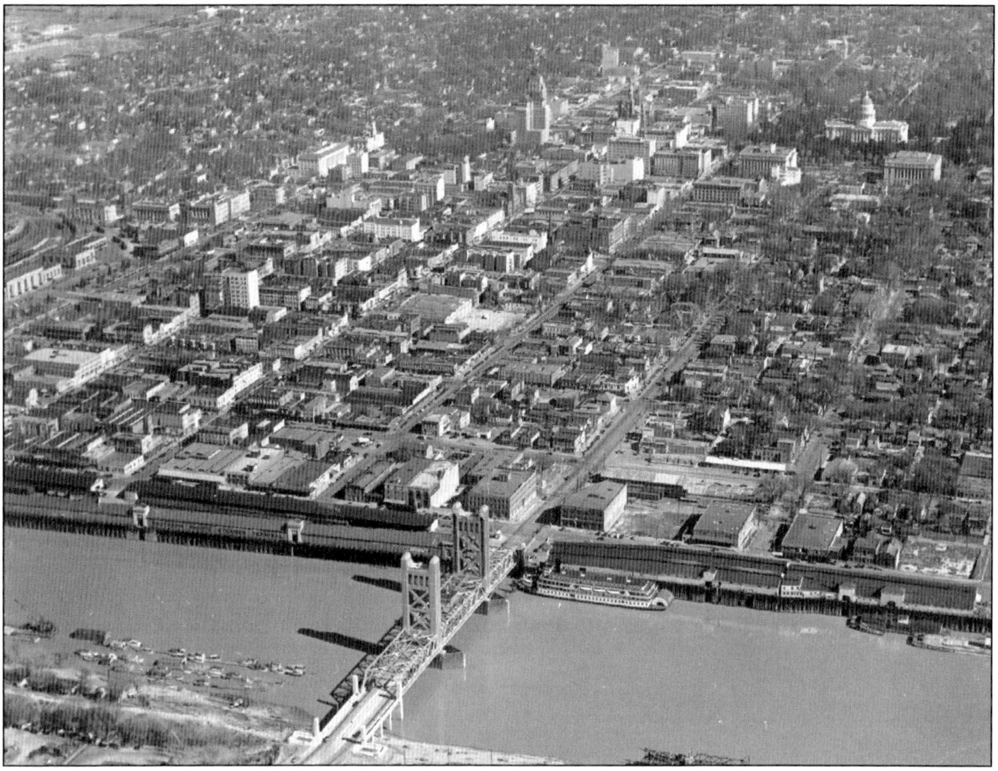

Sacramento in 1939 reflected a vibrant waterfront despite the decade-long Great Depression. To the left of Tower Bridge in the foreground is the Southern Pacific Steamer Terminal, where SP's riverboats would interchange freight traffic with the company's freight trains. To the right of Tower Bridge is the River Lines shed, which served as homeport for the *Delta King* and *Delta Queen*. These were in service between Sacramento and San Francisco. (Courtesy of the Sacramento Archives and Museum Collection Center.)

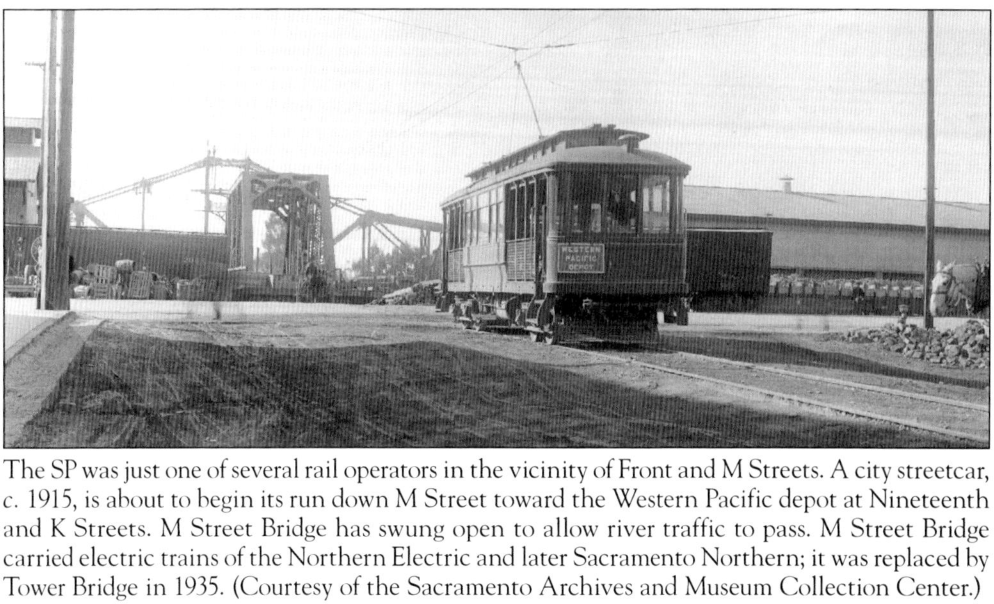

The SP was just one of several rail operators in the vicinity of Front and M Streets. A city streetcar, c. 1915, is about to begin its run down M Street toward the Western Pacific depot at Nineteenth and K Streets. M Street Bridge has swung open to allow river traffic to pass. M Street Bridge carried electric trains of the Northern Electric and later Sacramento Northern; it was replaced by Tower Bridge in 1935. (Courtesy of the Sacramento Archives and Museum Collection Center.)

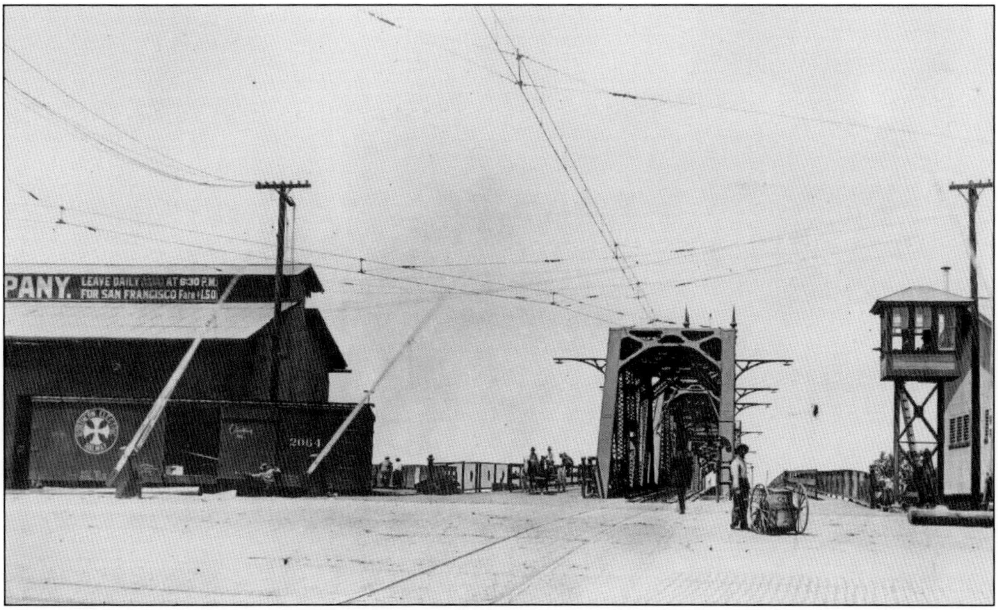

This is how the intersection of the Southern Pacific and Northern Electric lines at Front and M Streets appeared in the mid-1910s. The interlocking tower at right was manned by SP personnel who controlled train movements through the area. To this day, Sacramento Southern trains have to stop short of Capitol Mall (formerly M Street) and await a clear signal before proceeding. (Courtesy of the BAERA Archives Collection/Western Railway Museum.)

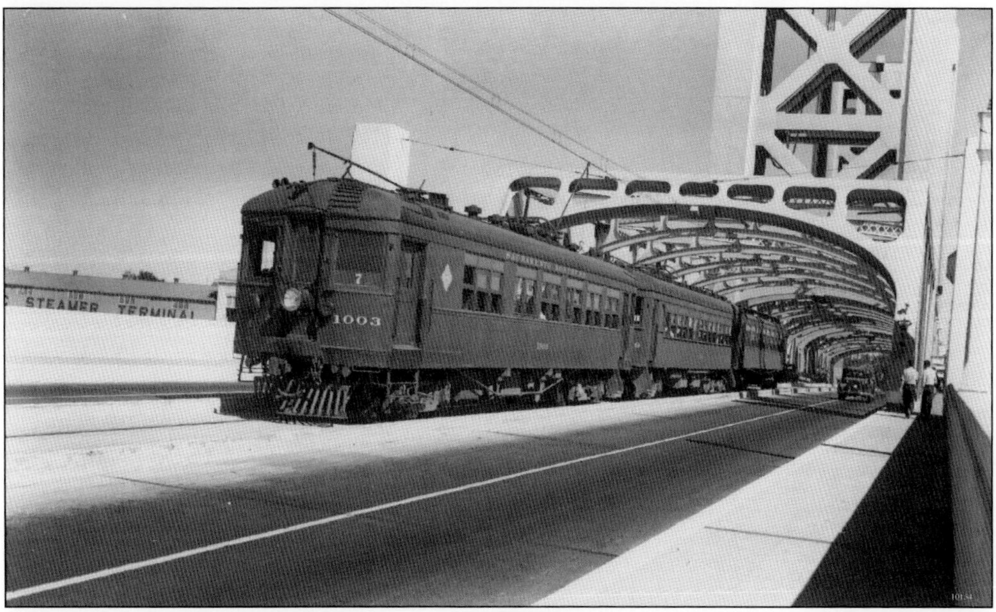

Tower Bridge was built in 1935 to accommodate rubber-tired and steel-wheeled vehicles. Sacramento Northern interurban trains traveled from San Francisco and Oakland to Marysville and Chico via Sacramento. SN trains last traveled over Tower Bridge in 1962; today plans are afoot to restore streetcar service between Sacramento and West Sacramento via Tower Bridge. The Southern Pacific Steamer Terminal is visible at left. (Courtesy of the BAERA Archives Collection/Western Railway Museum.)

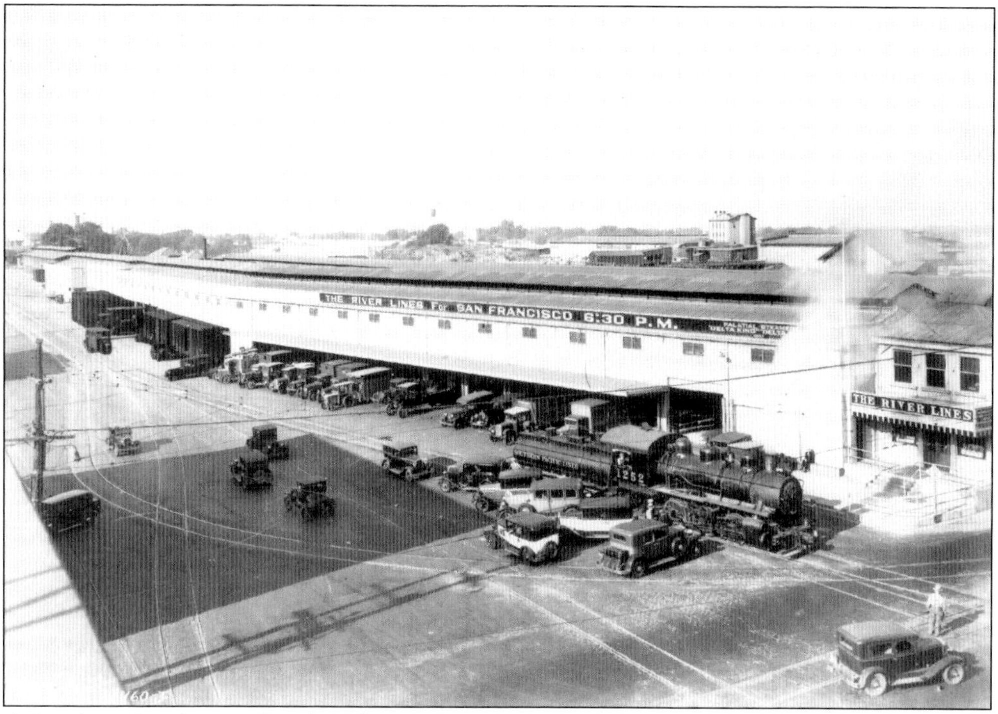

A Southern Pacific switcher threads its way past some cars parked perilously close to the tracks on Front Street just south of M Street around 1934. The River Lines shed is doing good business in freight, judging from all the trucks and boxcars. The track curving from left to right carried Sacramento Northern electric-powered freight trains to and from M Street Bridge, out of the picture to the right. (Courtesy of the Sacramento Archives and Museum Collection Center.)

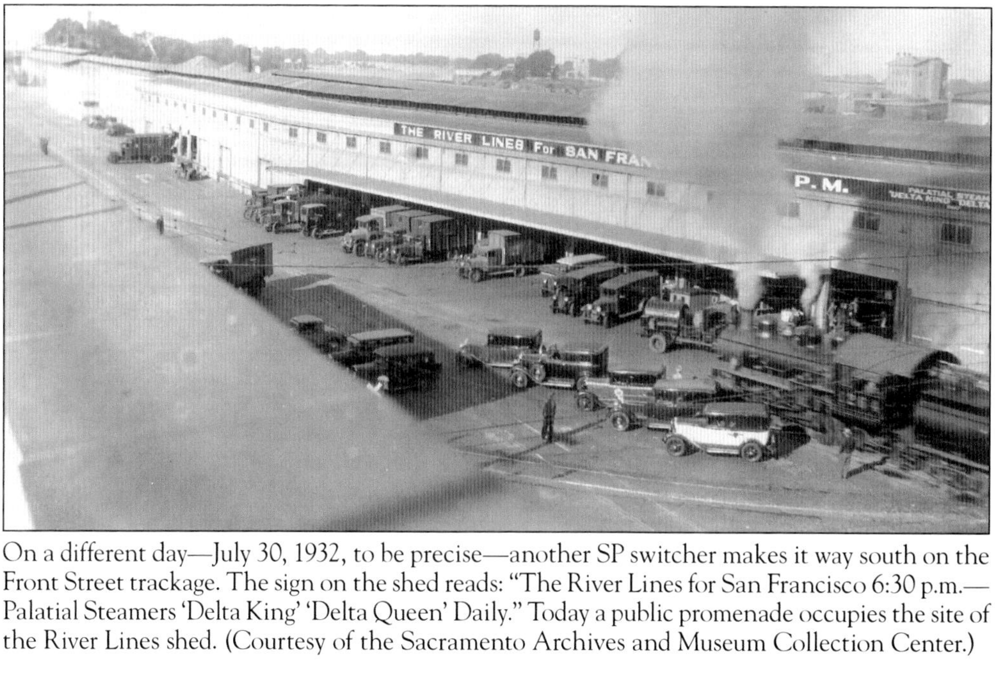

On a different day—July 30, 1932, to be precise—another SP switcher makes it way south on the Front Street trackage. The sign on the shed reads: "The River Lines for San Francisco 6:30 p.m.—Palatial Steamers 'Delta King' 'Delta Queen' Daily." Today a public promenade occupies the site of the River Lines shed. (Courtesy of the Sacramento Archives and Museum Collection Center.)

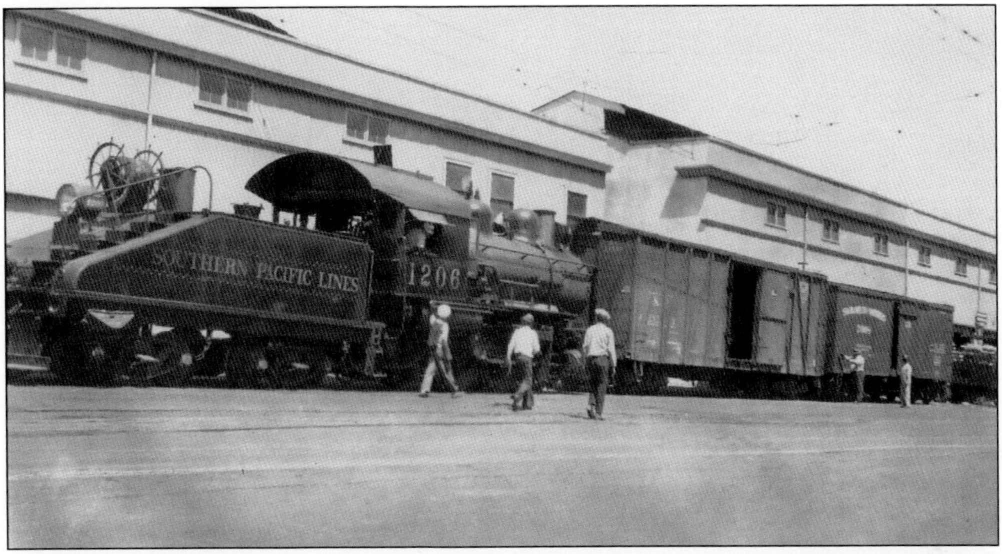

On July 30, 1932, SP switcher No. 1206 spots a couple of boxcars next to the River Lines shed. Note the electric wires overhead; these are for the Sacramento Northern's electric locomotives. (Courtesy of the Sacramento Archives and Museum Collection Center.)

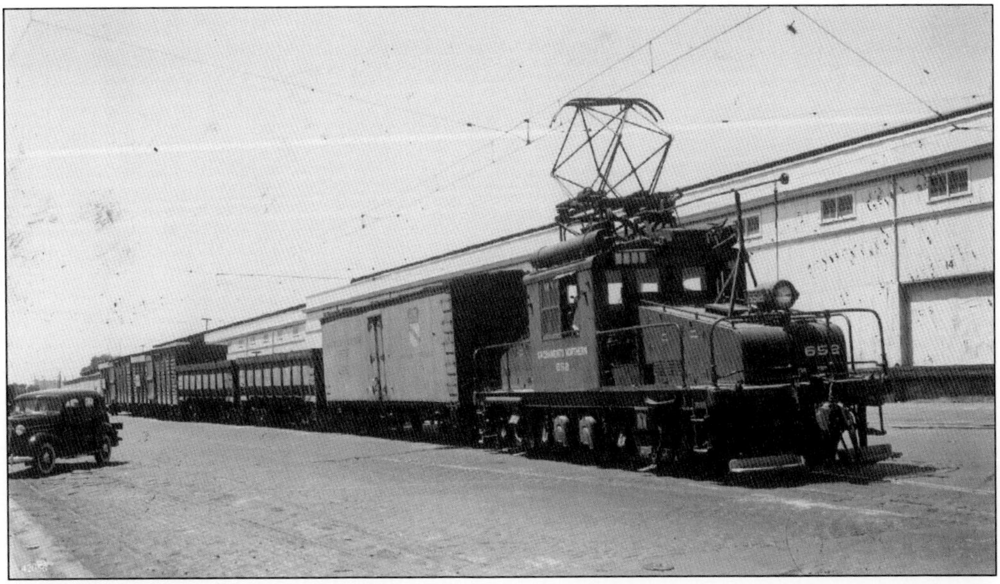

Speaking of the Sacramento Northern, here is one of their electrics hauling several freight cars on the SN's Front Street trackage. (Courtesy of the BAERA Archives Collection/Western Railway Museum.)

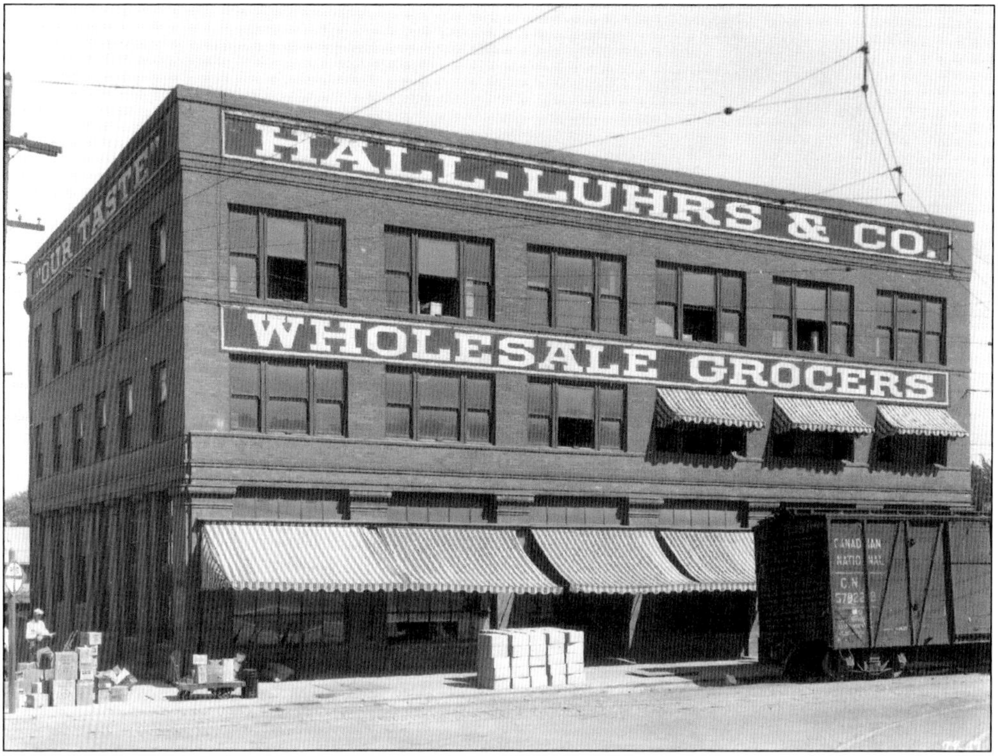

The Hall-Luhrs wholesale grocery business once stood at the southeast corner of Front and M Streets, where the Embassy Suites Hotel is now. This 1920s view finds a Canadian National Railway boxcar next to the business. Note the overhead wire for Sacramento Northern trains. (Courtesy of the Sacramento Archives and Museum Collection Center.)

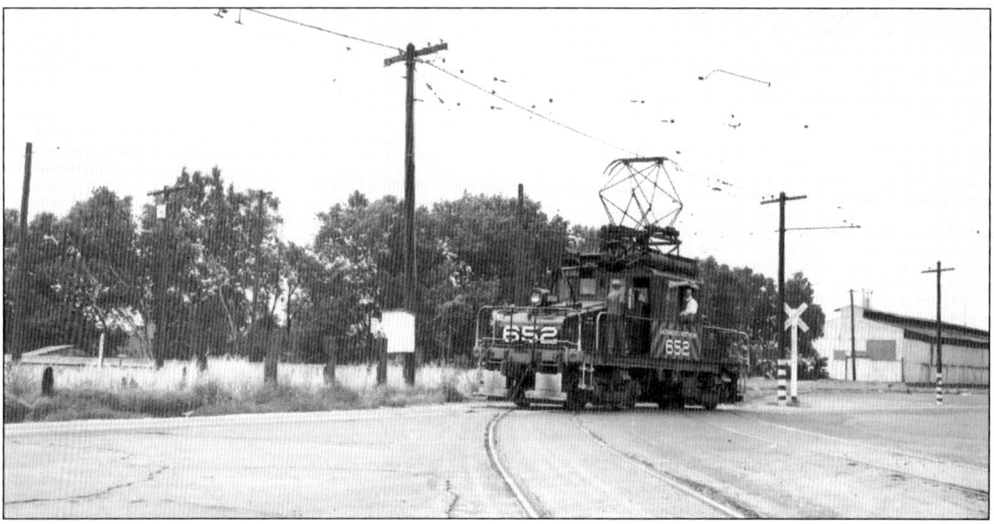

A Sacramento Northern locomotive makes its way down Front Street around the 1940s. Behind the locomotive is SP's Walnut Grove Branch. The crossbuck to the right of the locomotive bears the name of Western Pacific, which was SN's corporate parent. The WP tracks here led to the company's Sacramento River wharf. (Courtesy of the BAERA Archives Collection/Western Railway Museum.)

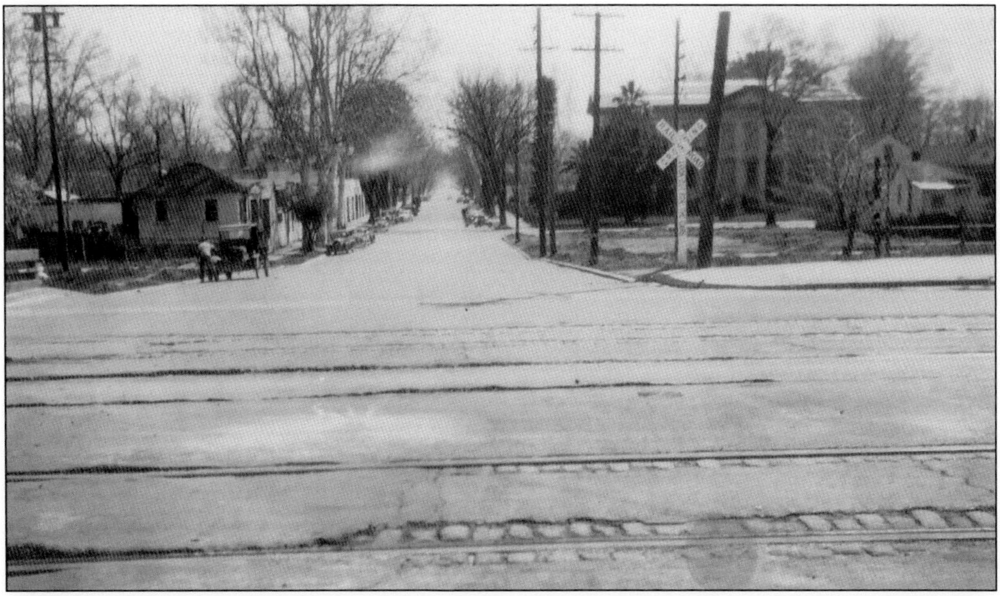

O Street crossed the SP tracks at grade near Front Street. Behind the crossbuck is the Crocker Art Museum. This museum was originally the home of Judge Edwin Bryant Crocker, older brother of "Big Four" principal Charles Crocker. His widow donated the family home and attached art gallery, together with its contents, to the city of Sacramento in 1885. (Courtesy of the Sacramento Archives and Museum Collection Center.)

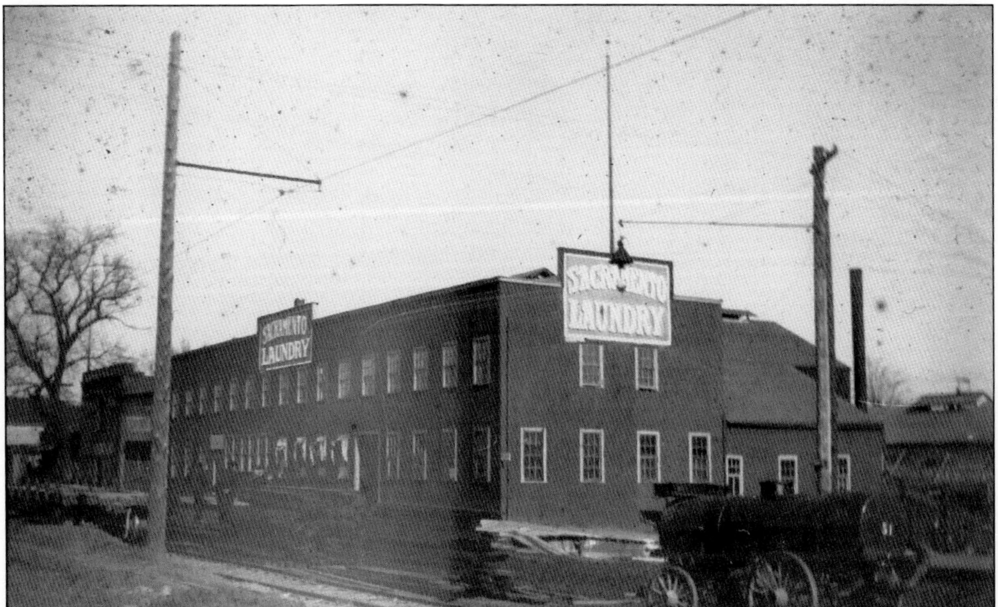

Between N and O Streets stood Sacramento Laundry and, just to the south, Union Iron Works, around 1919. The SP line leading to the Walnut Grove Branch is on the other side of this building; the electrified track in the foreground is for Sacramento Northern trains. (Courtesy of the Sacramento Archives and Museum Collection Center.)

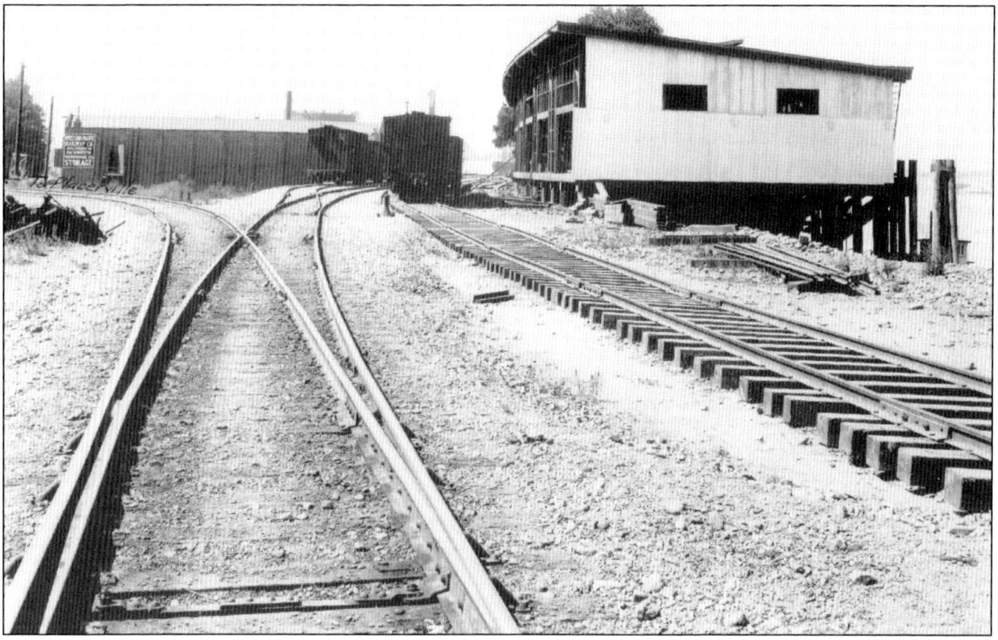

The WP wharf stood on the riverbank between P and R Streets, right next to the Sacramento Southern. The WP reached its wharf via a spur from its main line, between Nineteenth and Twentieth Streets. The WP warehouse at left was the former Clunie warehouse, owned by the family of Thomas J. Clunie. The tracks at left lead to SP's line down R Street and eventually to Folsom and Placerville. (Courtesy of the California State Railroad Museum Library.)

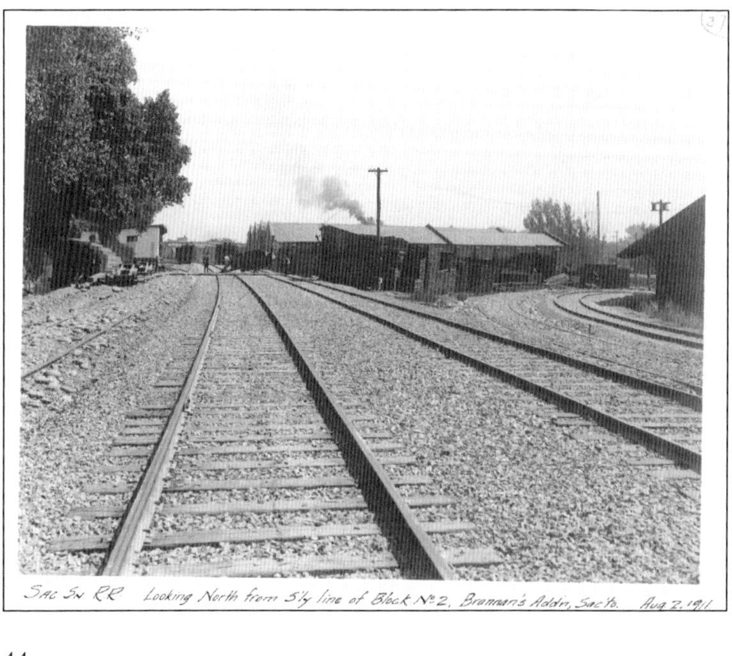

This is the scene along the Sacramento Southern on August 2, 1911. The tracks curving to the right (east) lead to R Street. In the background can be seen the Western Pacific's wharf (left) and warehouse, next to the present-day Clunie siding. (Courtesy of the California State Railroad Museum Library.)

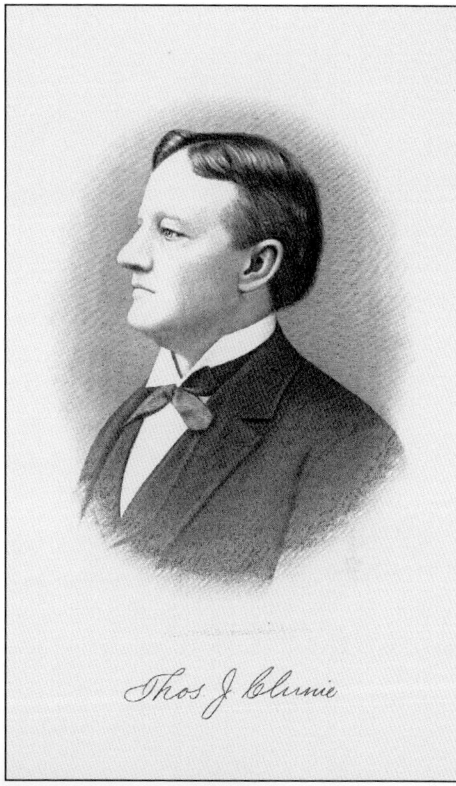

The siding next to the Clunie/WP warehouse on page 44 is now called Clunie in honor of the building that used to stand here. The warehouse was named after its original proprietor, Thomas J. Clunie (1852–1903). Clunie, born at sea off Newfoundland, came to Sacramento as a boy. He earned the right to practice law at 18 and soon became a highly successful lawyer and businessman. Clunie, a Democrat, was elected to the state legislature in 1875 and to Congress in 1888, serving a single term in D.C. before losing his reelection bid and returning to private life. When Clunie died, his widow, Florence, took over his businesses; when she died in 1934, she left Sacramento $150,000 to construct a clubhouse and pool (Clunie Pool) in McKinley Park. (Right, courtesy of the Sacramento Room, Sacramento Public Library; below, photograph by author.)

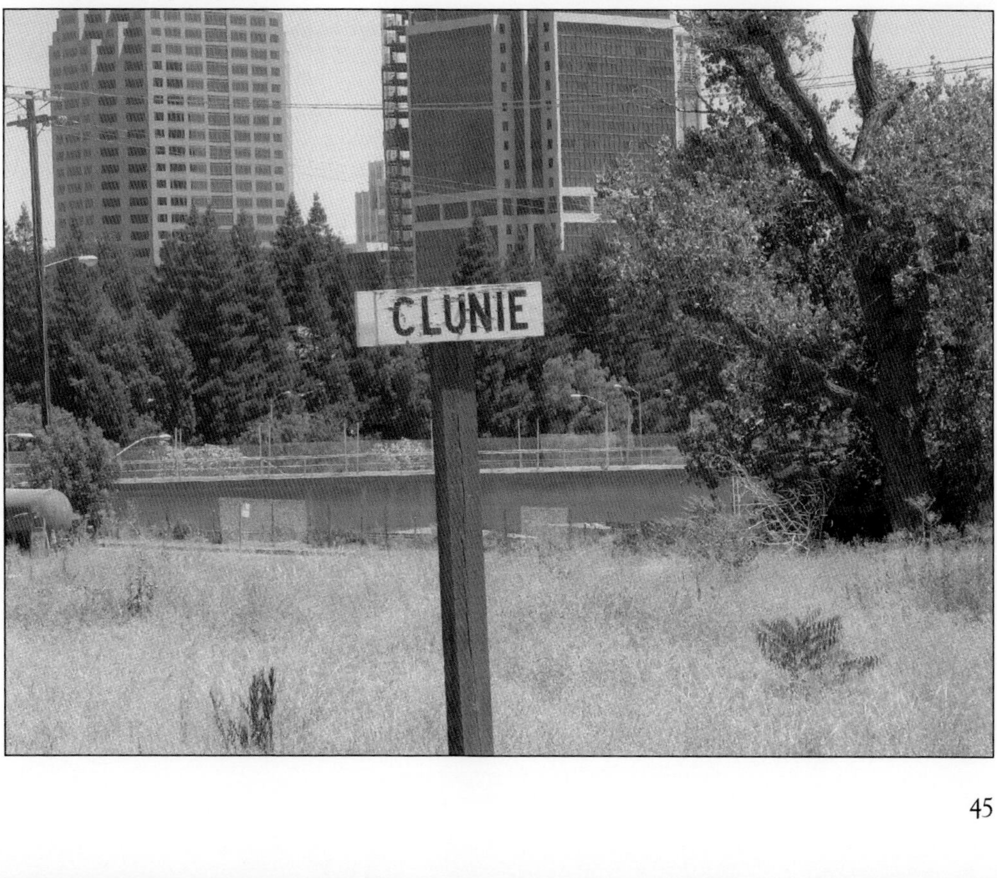

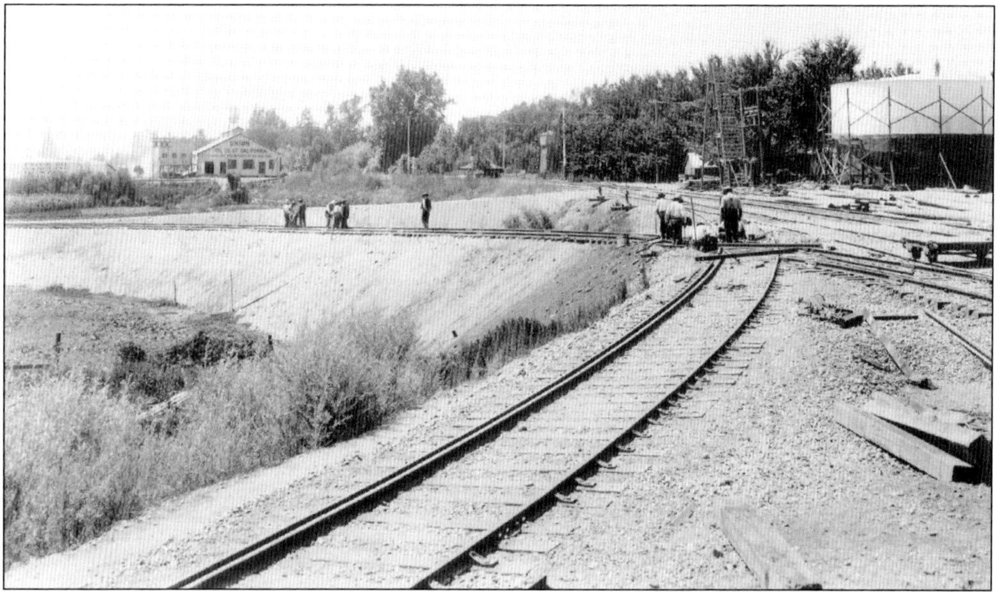

The Western Pacific and Southern Pacific connections to the wharf and Walnut Grove Branch near Front and R Streets were receiving some attention from track workers in 1911. In the background is a Union Oil tank farm, a facility that still exists today, albeit rebuilt. (Courtesy of the California State Railroad Museum Library.)

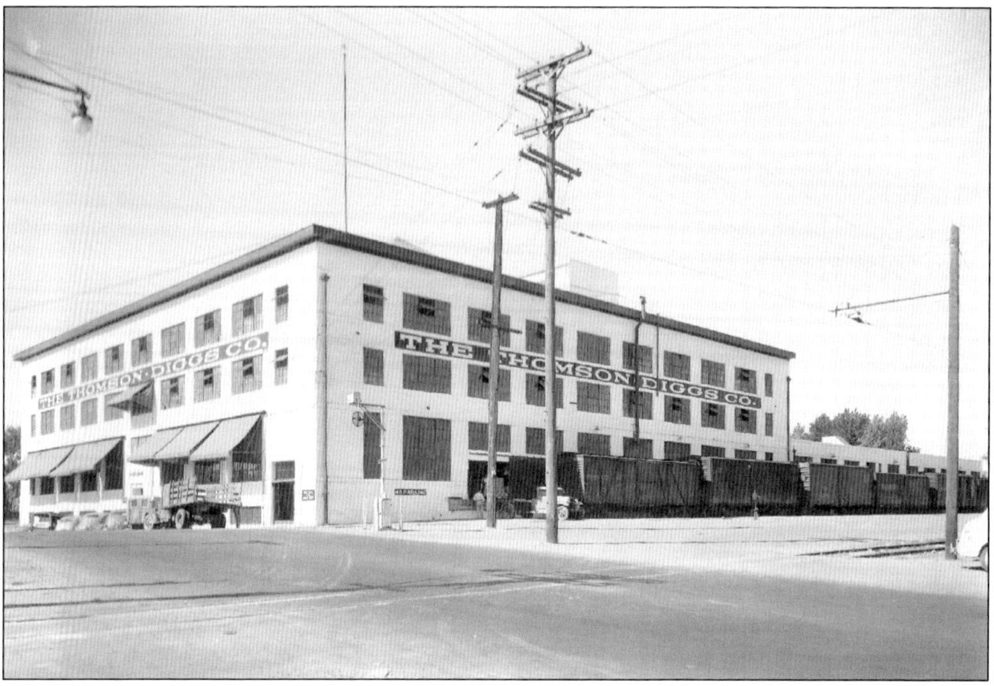

At the corner of Third and R Streets, where the Sacramento Valley Railroad's passenger depot once stood, the Thomson-Diggs Company had a warehouse served from the SP's line along the riverfront. Thomson-Diggs, incorporated in 1900, was long in the hardware and sporting-goods wholesaling business. This building still stands; it now contains offices for companies such as Accenture. (Courtesy of the Sacramento Room, Sacramento Public Library.)

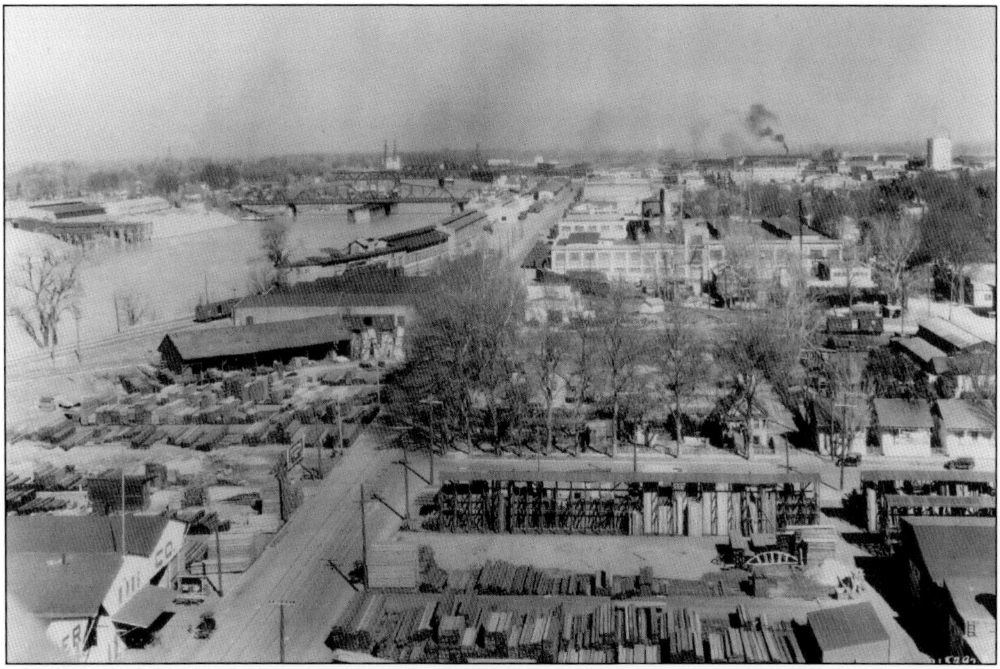

This bird's-eye view of the Sacramento waterfront around the mid-1920s finds an area teeming with economic activity. The *Sacramento Bee* reported on March 1, 1930, that 41 businesses, mainly wholesale distributors and manufacturers, had set up shop on Front Street, between I and Y Streets, to take advantage of easy transportation by rail and/or water. (Courtesy of the California History Room, California State Library.)

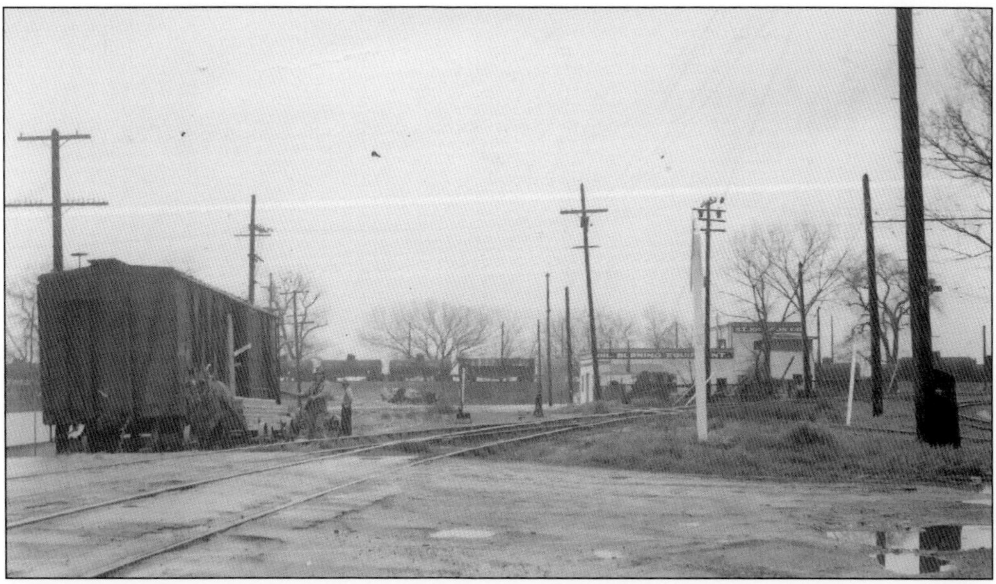

At Second and R Streets *c.* 1938, a couple of workers unload a boxcar. In the background is S. T. Johnson Company, which specialized in oil burners. Also note the tank cars in the background. Associated, Standard, and Union Oil all had facilities near the foot of Y Street (now Broadway), generating substantial tank-car traffic for the SP. (Courtesy of the Sacramento Archives and Museum Collection Center.)

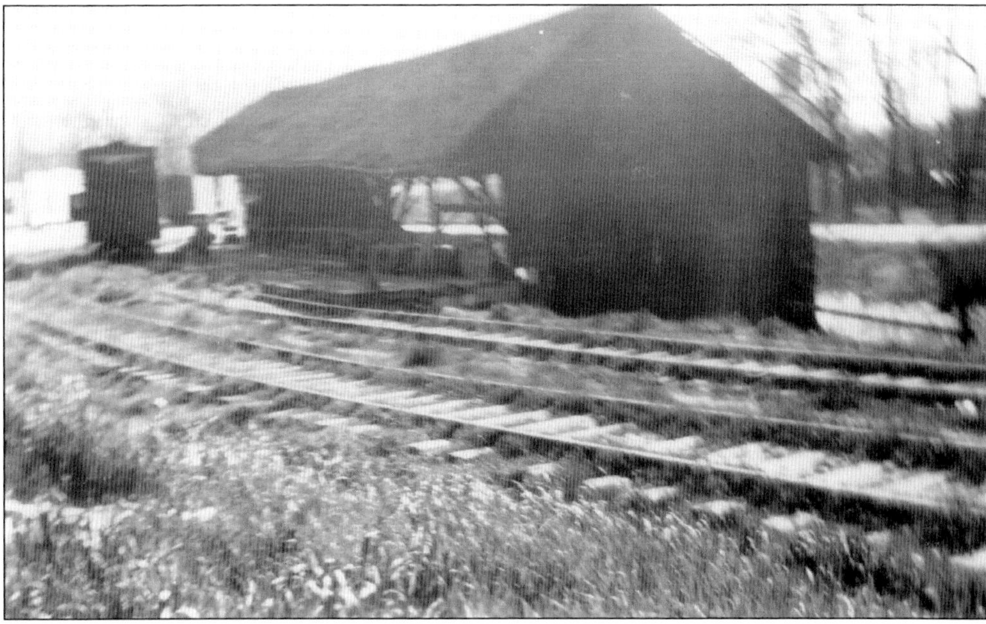

The Sacramento Valley Railroad's old woodshed was still standing at Front and R Streets in 1922. This was used to store the vast amounts of wood consumed as fuel by early steam locomotives. By the time of this picture, SP steam locomotives were using oil or coal for fuel, rendering the shed surplus. (Courtesy of the Sacramento Archives and Museum Collection Center.)

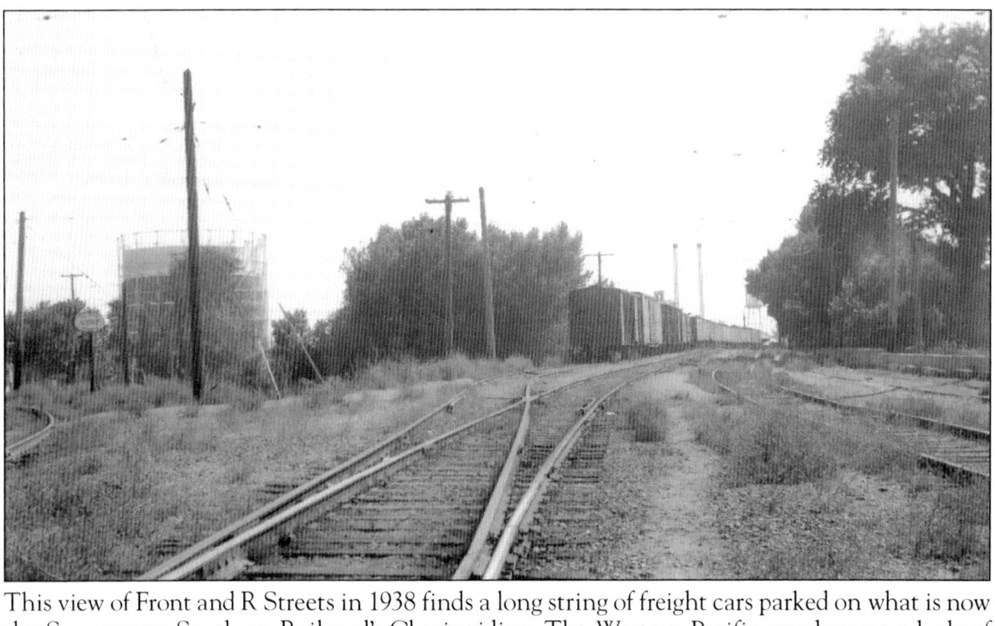

This view of Front and R Streets in 1938 finds a long string of freight cars parked on what is now the Sacramento Southern Railroad's Clunie siding. The Western Pacific warehouse and wharf are gone. (Courtesy of the Sacramento Archives and Museum Collection Center.)

Even in 1940, with so much history still to be made, historical markers were going up in town. This one marks the spot of the Sacramento Valley Railroad's freight depot at Front and R Streets. (Courtesy of the Sacramento Archives and Museum Collection Center.)

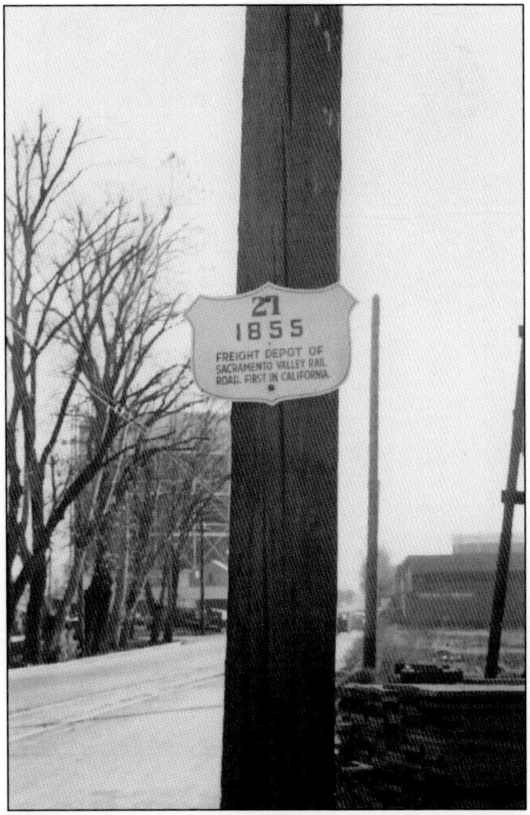

Southern Pacific interchanged freight cars with two electric roads, the Northern Electric/Sacramento Northern and California Traction, near Front and X Streets at the southwestern edge of town. The refrigerator cars, or "reefers," at right are kept cool with large blocks of ice and are typical of those used to haul fresh fruits and vegetables on the Walnut Grove Branch, which runs from left to right in the background. (Courtesy of the BAERA Archives Collection/Western Railway Museum.)

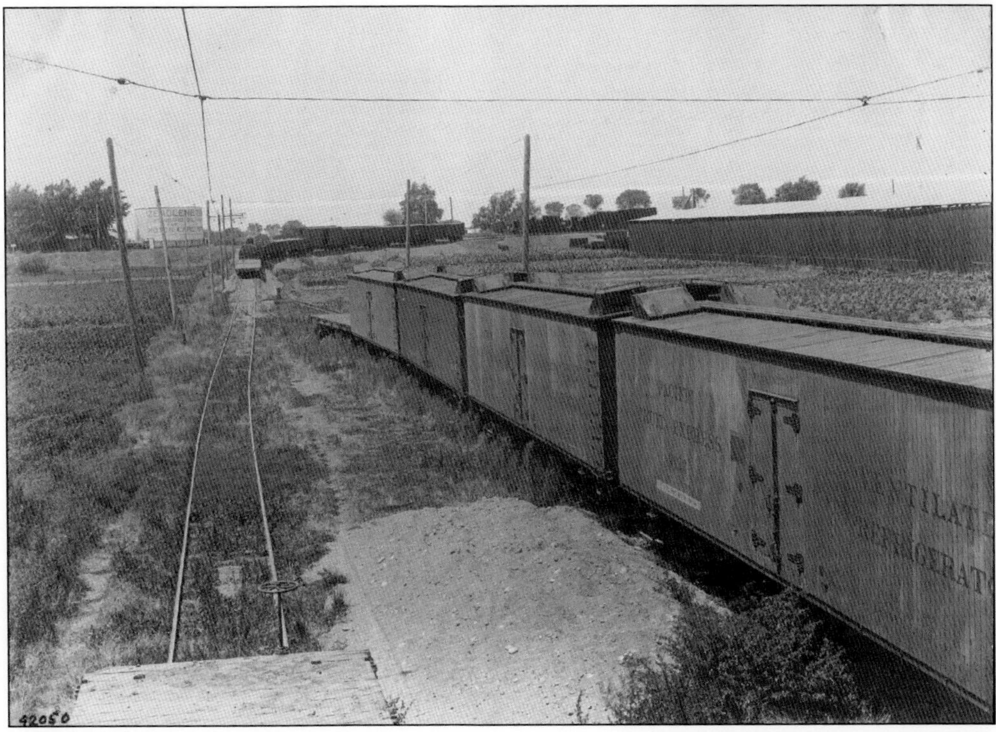

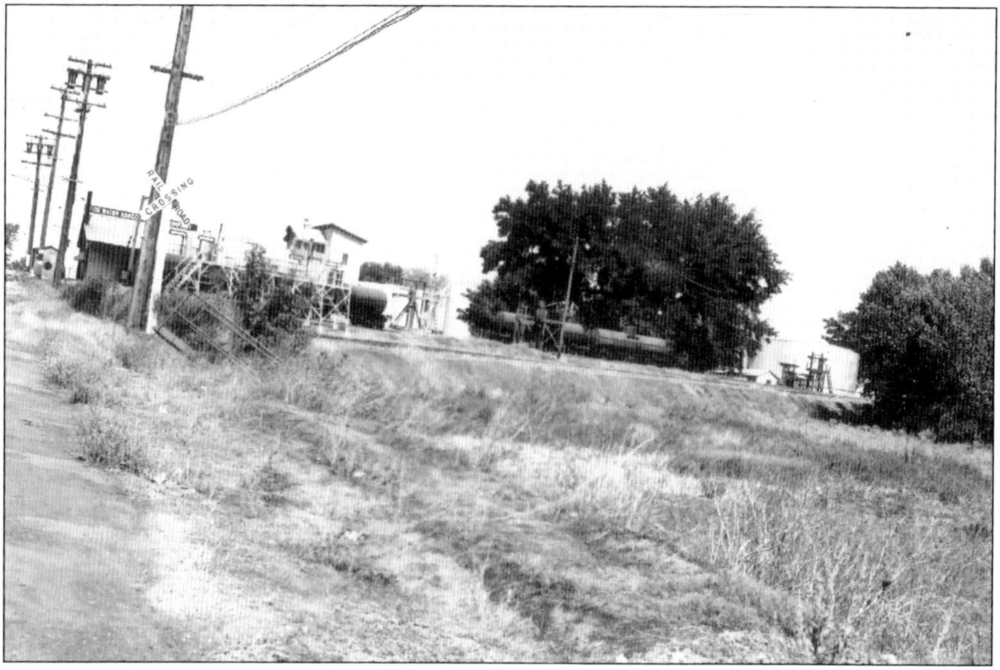

The tank farm near Front and Y Streets at the city limits resulted in SP moving scores of tank cars over the northernmost stretch of the Walnut Grove Branch. Several of these cars are visible here. The tank farm is still in place today. (Courtesy of the Sacramento Archives and Museum Collection Center.)

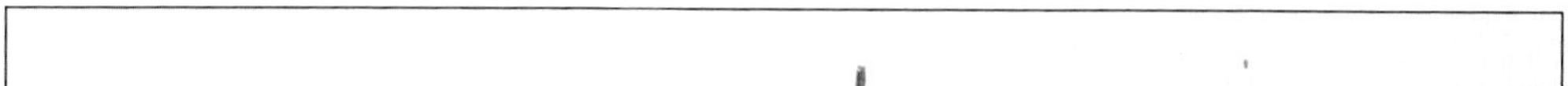

Setzer Forest Products was founded in 1927 by Curt Setzer to make wooden boxes for agricultural products. At one time, this plant manufactured Presto-Logs, the logo of which is still visible on the factory roof. The business, seen here in 1942, is still in family hands today. Setzer is the modern Sacramento Southern's major freight customer, receiving shipments of wood products brought to Sacramento by the Union Pacific and forwarded to the plant by Sacramento Southern crews. (Courtesy of the Sacramento Archives and Museum Collection Center.)

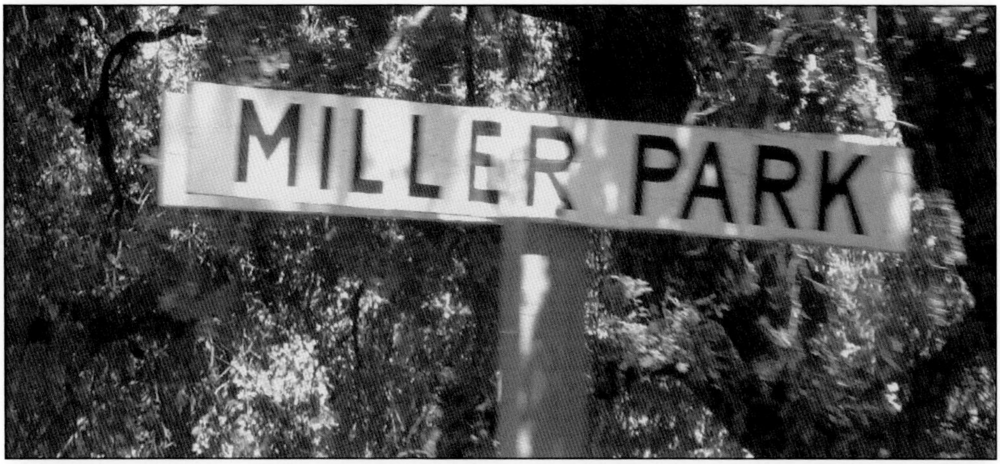

F. A. Miller, who once fought the Sacramento Southern Railroad over a right-of-way through his property, has a park next to the railroad named in his honor thanks to his sister. When Alice Miller, the last living member of her immediate family, died in 1942, she bequeathed 38 acres of family property to the city of Sacramento with a request to use it as a public park and marina and name it after her brother. The marina opened in 1958 and today has 551 boat slips. (Above, photograph by author; below, courtesy of the Sacramento Archives and Museum Collection Center.)

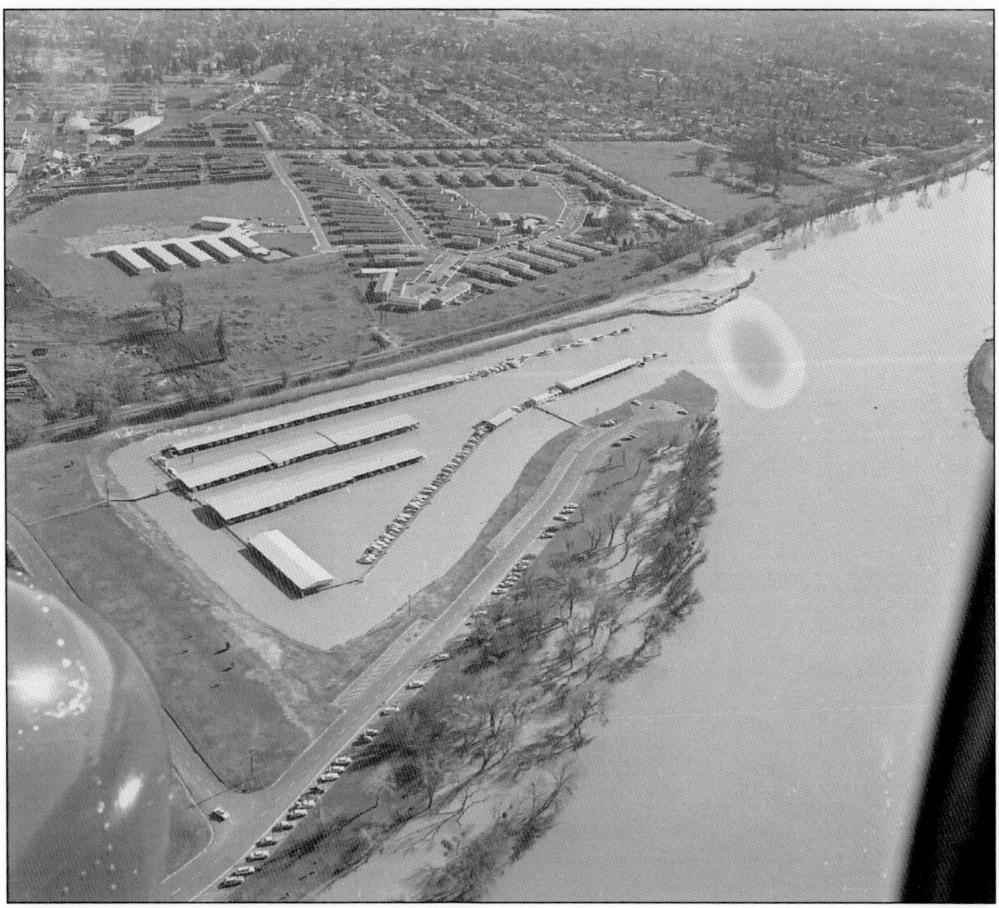

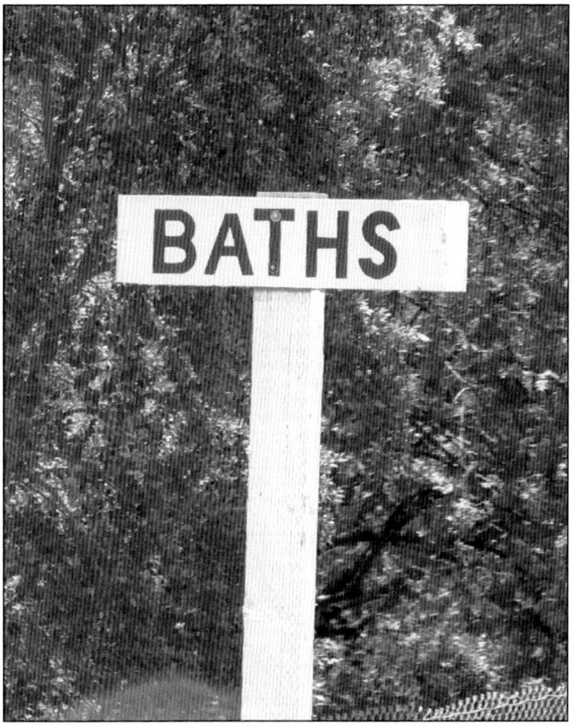

The Sacramento Southern built this truss bridge, below, over Riverside Boulevard in 1907. The main line is at left in this 1911 view; the track at right is a siding built to accommodate meets. Nearby industries that kept the SP busy included Richfield Oil and Pratt Rock and Gravel. At left is the sign for Riverside Baths, the popular local swimming pool that gave the nearby Sacramento Southern station its name. When Interstate 5 was constructed in 1973, this bridge was removed and the line relocated in an S curve just to the south. The tracks now cross I-5 and Riverside Boulevard on a narrow concrete bridge. The Baths station is still in Sacramento Southern's timetable; it is presently the southernmost point of operations. (Left, photograph by author; below, courtesy of the California State Railroad Museum Library.)

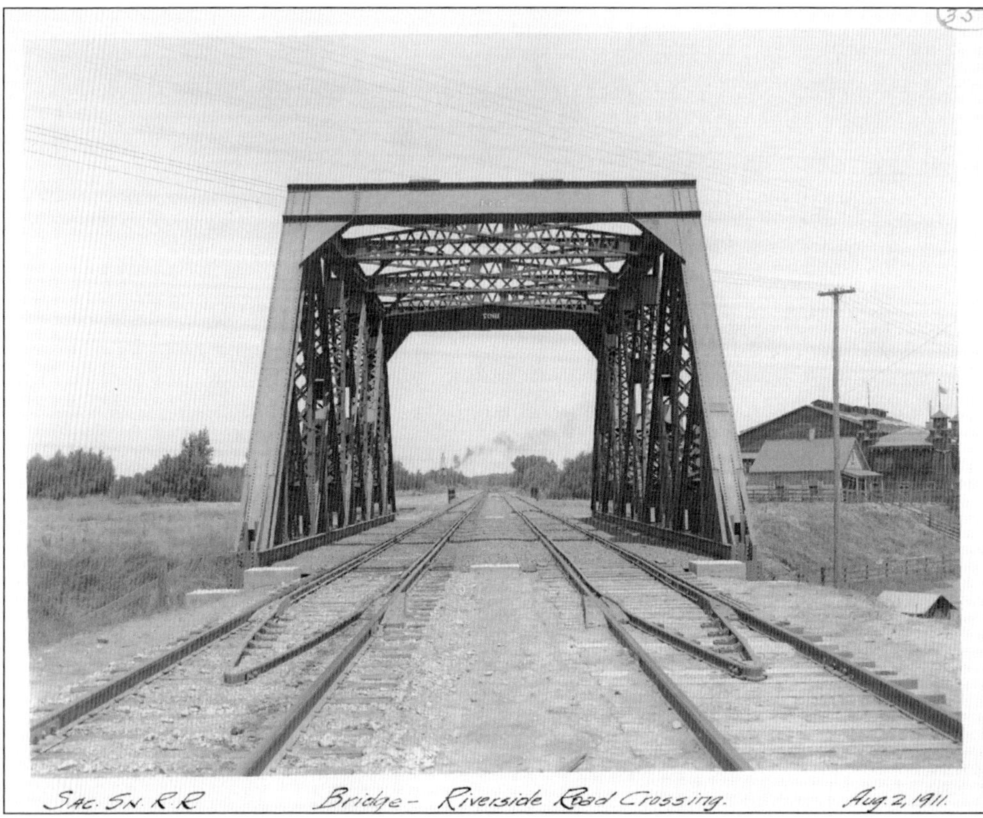

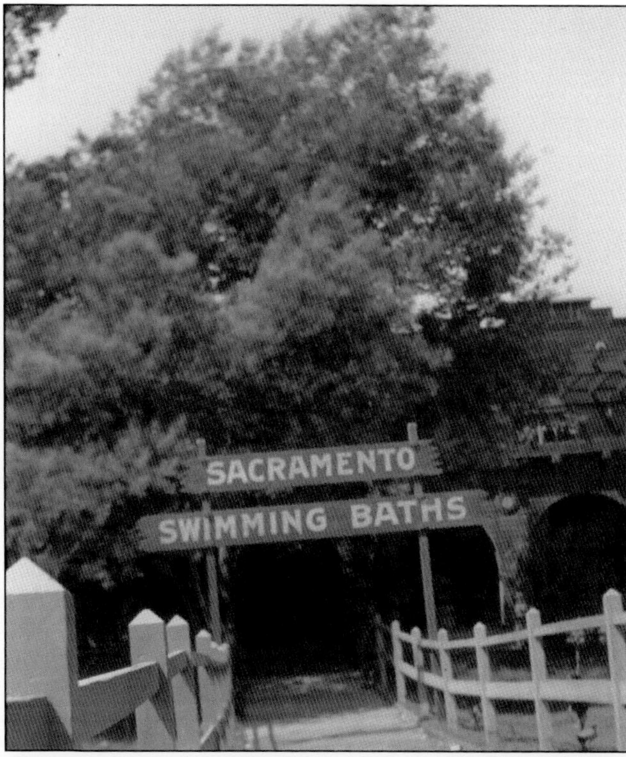

In 1909, Riverside Baths opened alongside Riverside Boulevard, just south of Sacramento. Initially the pool was enclosed; by the 1930s, the roof had been removed. The pool was later renamed Land Park Plunge. Generations of Sacramentans came to the baths to cool off on a hot day. The catch was they had to be white—the pool barred everyone else from entering. The "Baths" station name remained in SP's timetable until the abandonment of the branch. The Riverside Baths property is now partly occupied by the B'nai Israel synagogue and partly by Interstate 5. (Right, courtesy of the Sacramento Archives and Museum Collection Center; below, the Sacramento Room, Sacramento Public Library.)

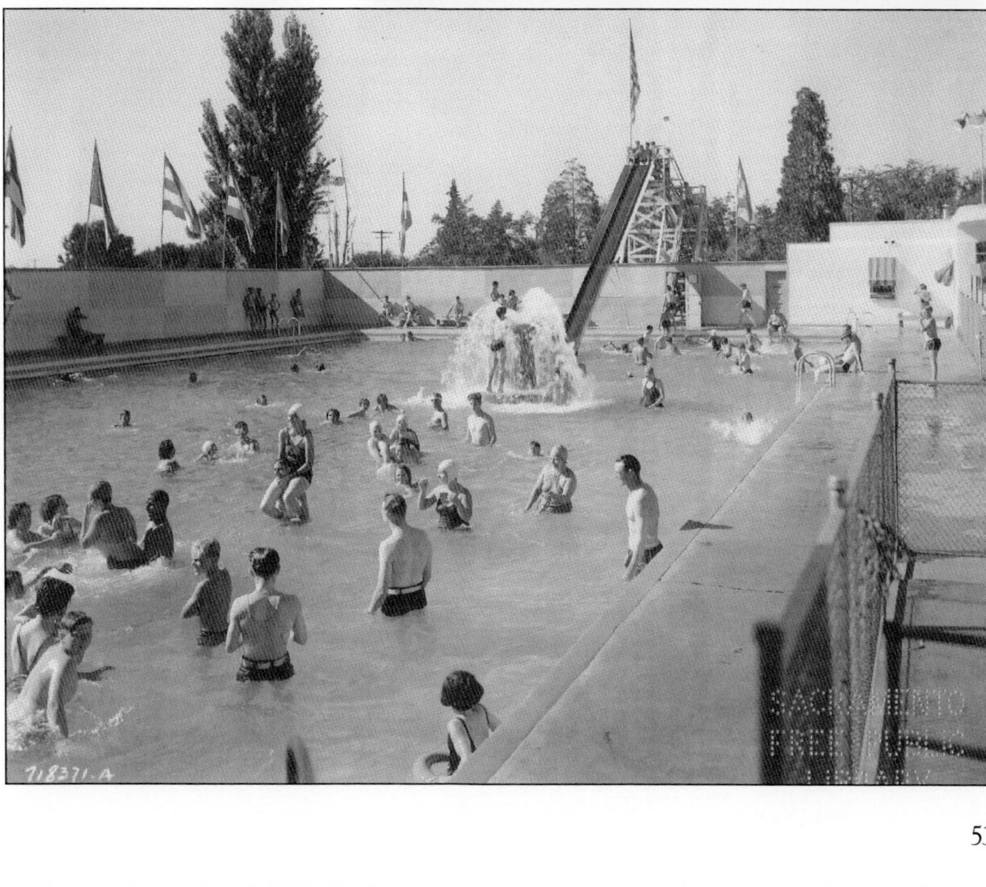

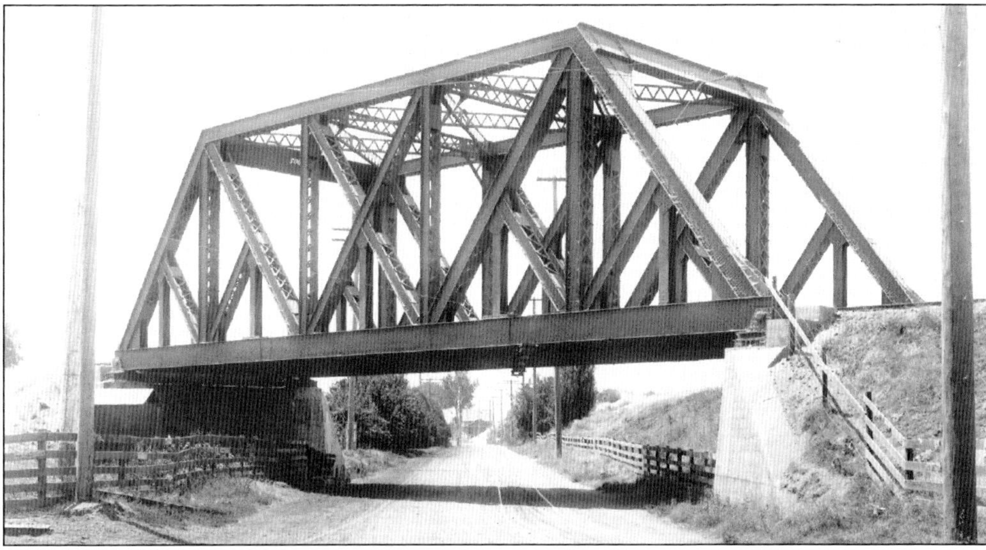

This bridge is seen from Riverside Boulevard. The construction of Interstate 5 in the early 1970s led to the replacement of this bridge with a concrete structure just to the south. The tracks, originally laid straight, were realigned in an S curve. Pacific Gas and Electric Railway had a streetcar line from the city that terminated here near Riverside Baths and later William Land Park. (Courtesy of the California State Railroad Museum Library.)

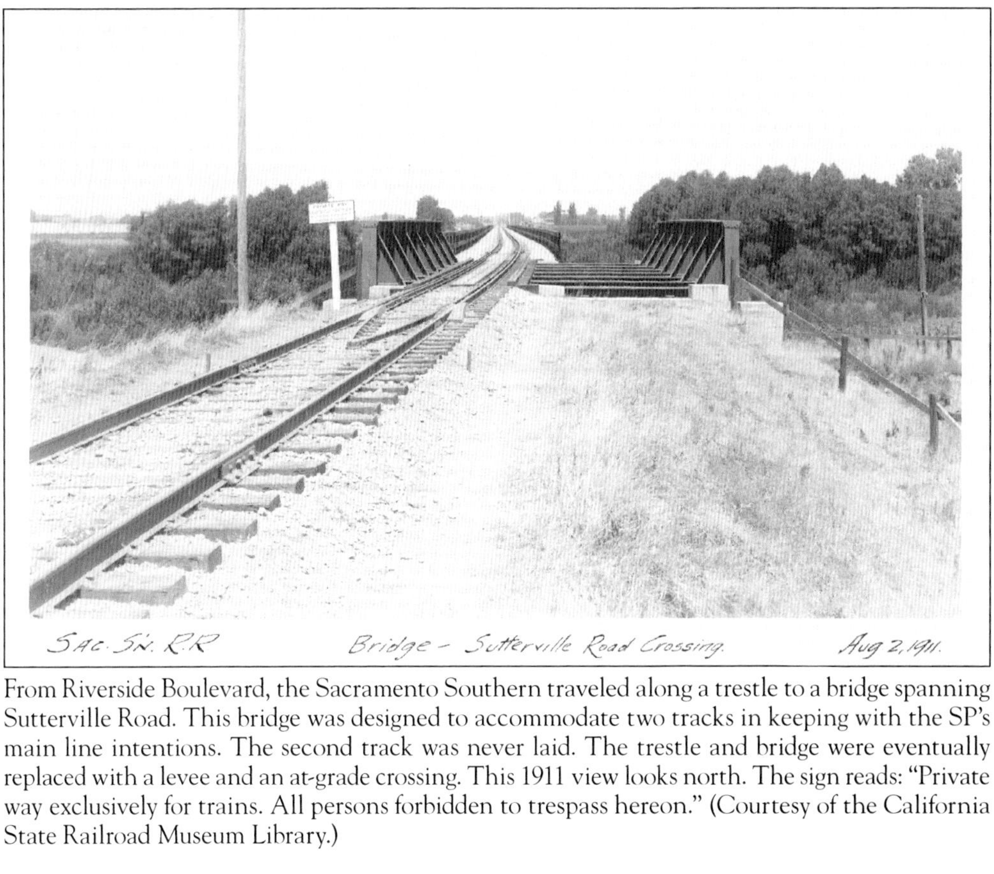

From Riverside Boulevard, the Sacramento Southern traveled along a trestle to a bridge spanning Sutterville Road. This bridge was designed to accommodate two tracks in keeping with the SP's main line intentions. The second track was never laid. The trestle and bridge were eventually replaced with a levee and an at-grade crossing. This 1911 view looks north. The sign reads: "Private way exclusively for trains. All persons forbidden to trespass hereon." (Courtesy of the California State Railroad Museum Library.)

Four

FREEPORT

Freeport was born of the Sacramento Valley Railroad's desire to avoid paying a tax. According to rail historian David Joslyn, the SVRR's line from Third and R Streets up Front Street to the wharf at K Street cost Sacramento a good deal of money, as stage companies moved their termini from the waterfront to Folsom, the SVRR's eastern terminus. To compensate for lost business, Sacramento levied a tax on goods transferred from steamboat to rail at the city wharf. In case that was not enough, the city also pulled up the SVRR's tracks on Front Street under the premise that the railroad did not have a franchise to operate in a city street. SVRR retaliated by joining forces with the Sacramento and Placerville Railroad, which was busy building from Folsom to Placerville, and creating a new western terminus, a spot on the Sacramento River just south of the city. This terminus was intended as a "free port," where goods could be exchanged without taxes.

The SVRR did not last long in Freeport; in 1865, the wannabe transcontinental railroad was taken over by the Central Pacific and the line to Freeport taken up. Not until the Sacramento Southern arrived in 1909 would Freeport have a railroad again. Freeport—current population 125—does have a bit of a place in Hollywood history; the depot and branch in town were used in the filming of the 1928 Buster Keaton silent comedy *Steamboat Bill Jr.* The depot was disguised as River Junction for the movie, and the Sacramento River was a stand-in for the mighty Mississippi.

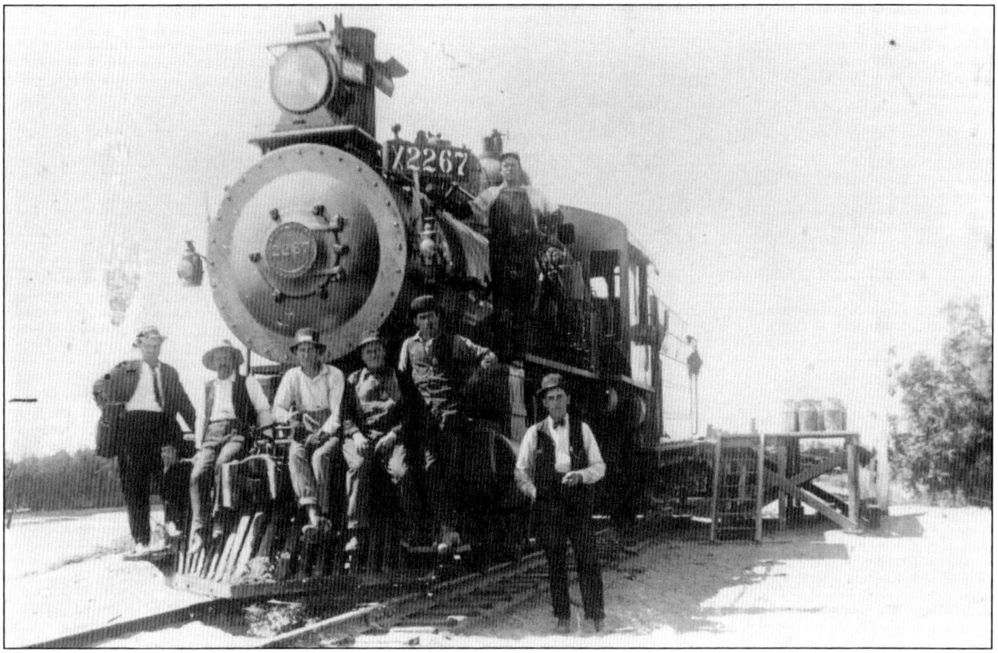

The crew of a Walnut Grove Branch freight train gathers on the locomotive at Freeport c. 1915. Freight regularly picked up at this station included milk cans, such as those seen on the platform. Second from left on the locomotive is Joseph Contente, who was among the many Portuguese immigrants to settle down in the Sacramento area. Contente worked for the SP for several years in the early 1910s as part of a section gang. (Courtesy of the Portuguese Historical and Cultural Society, Sacramento.)

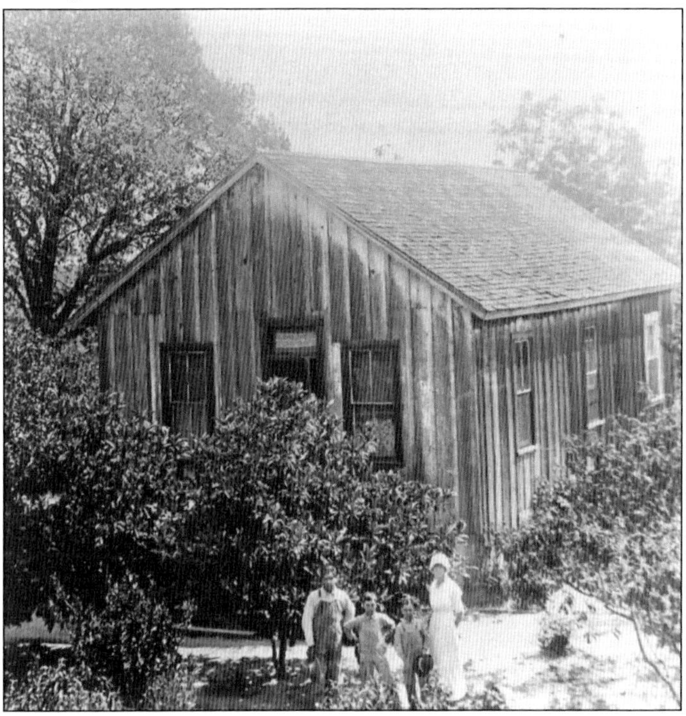

This was the Contente family residence, about a mile and a half south of Freeport, around 1914. Out front are four of Joseph's children, who are from left to right: William, Alfred, Clarence, and Emily. Freight trains would often stop near the Contente residence to pick up freight, and Joseph Contente would sometimes ride along. Neighbors took to calling this stop Contente Station, and the SP even added the station to its timetable (albeit misspelled Content). (Courtesy of the Portuguese Historical and Cultural Society, Sacramento.)

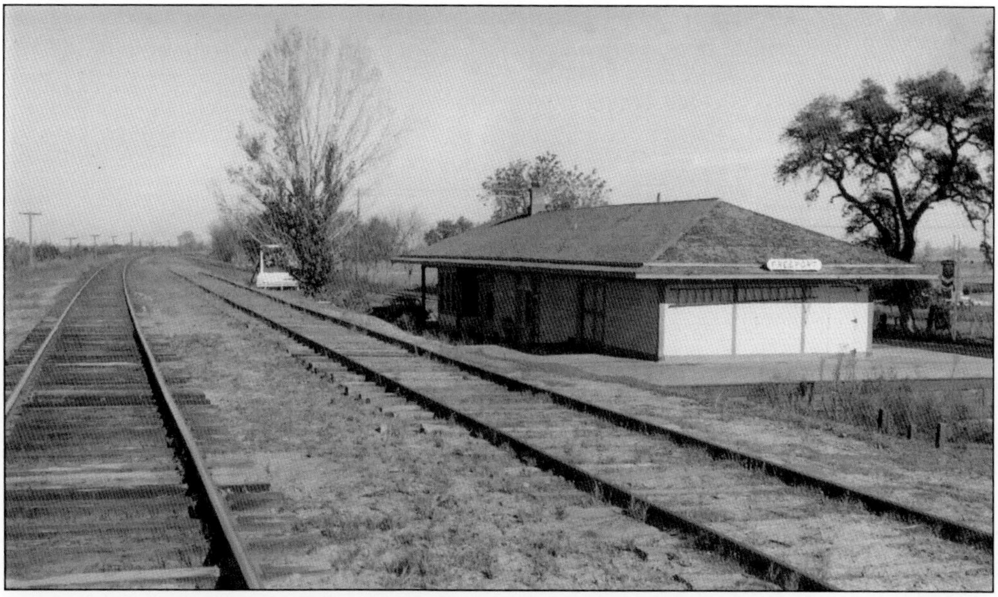

The Freeport depot stood to the east of the embankment carrying the Sacramento Southern main line through town. This view looks north; the Sacramento River is out of view to the left. (Courtesy of the Roy Graves Collection, Bancroft Library, University of California, Berkeley.)

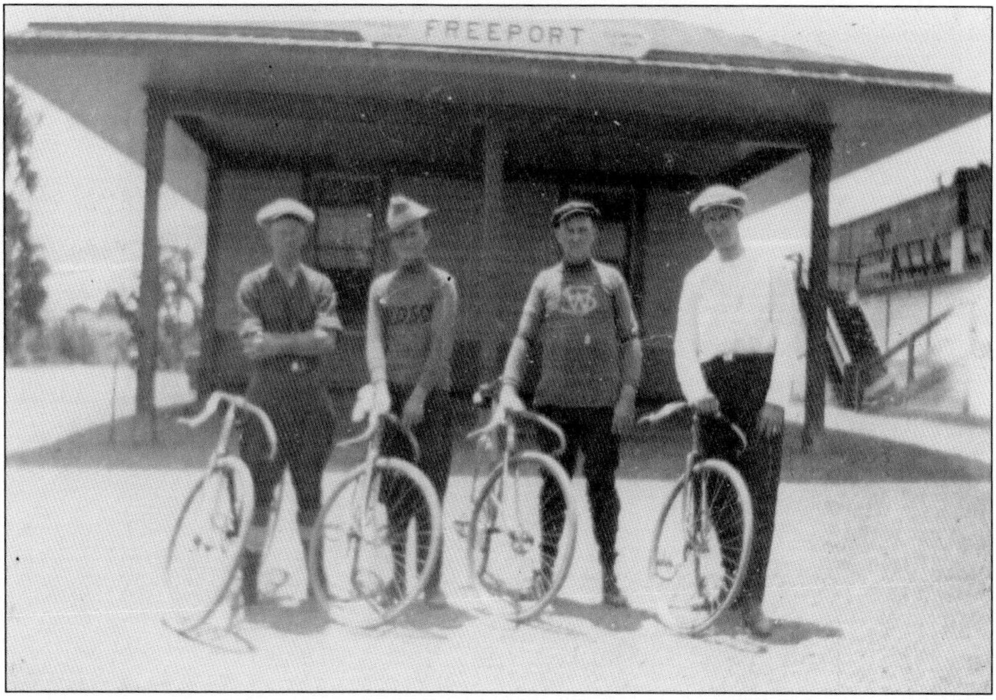

Four bicyclists, whose names have been lost to history, gather at the Freeport depot about 1921. The stairs at right lead to the tracks on the embankment, where a couple of refrigerator cars can be seen. (Courtesy of the Sacramento Archives and Museum Collection Center.)

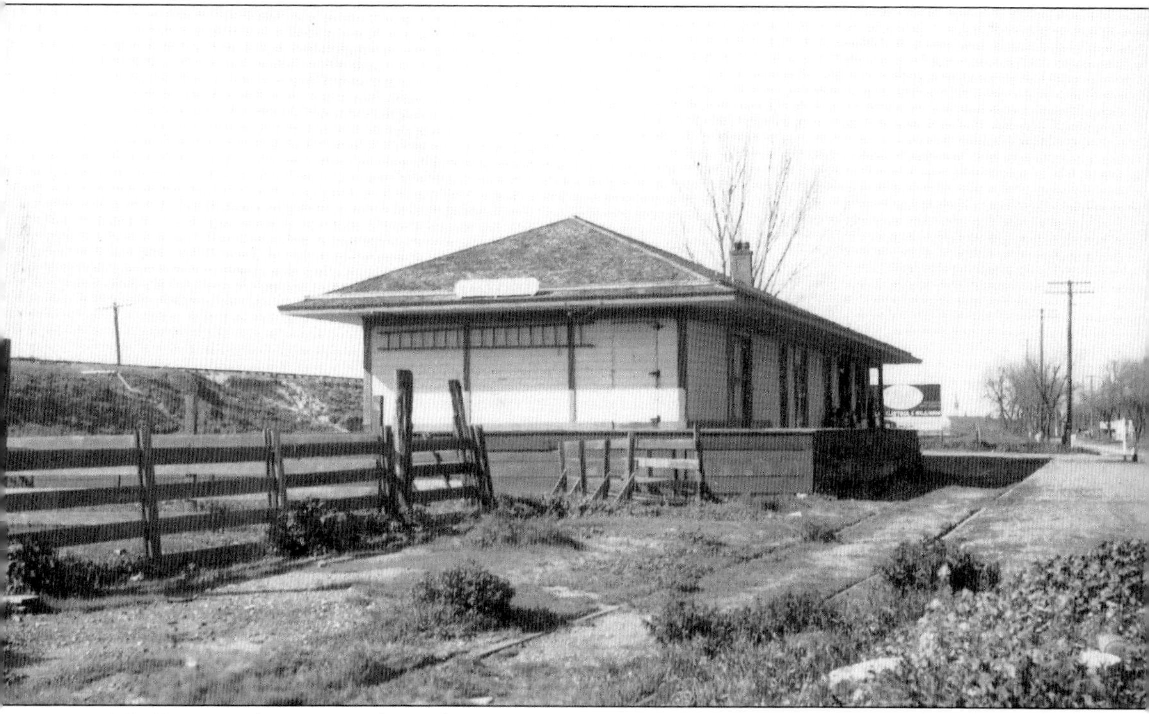

The Freeport depot is seen here about 1940. A short time later, the passenger portion of this depot was sold and removed. This building does have a minor role in Hollywood history: it was used as the River Junction depot in the 1928 Buster Keaton silent movie *Steamboat Bill Jr.* (Courtesy of the Sacramento Archives and Museum Collection Center.)

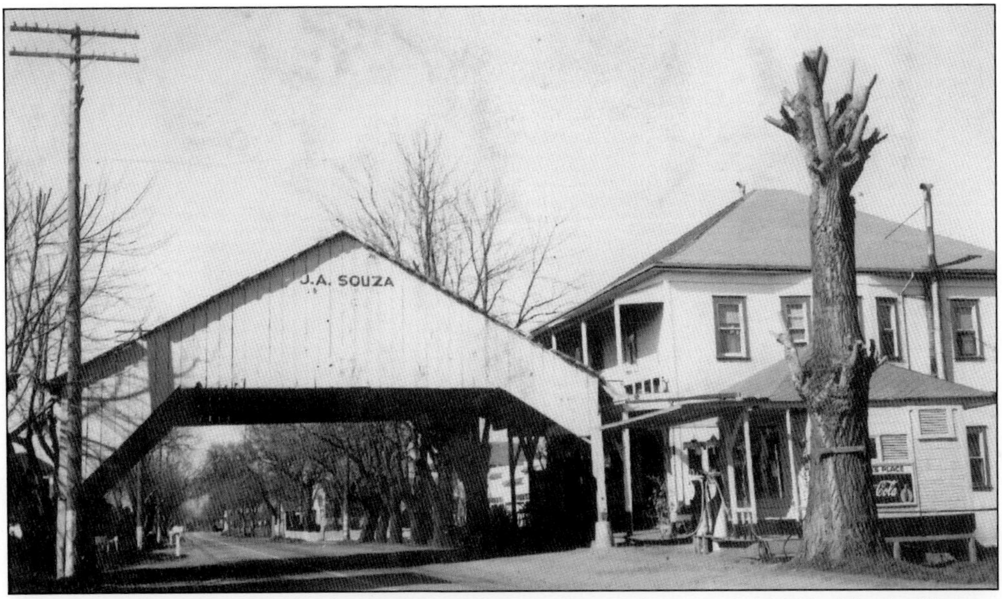

River Road, also known as Highway 160, in Freeport is seen here in the 1920s. The building at right, which is on the east side of the road, still stands, though the canopy over the roadway is long gone. (Courtesy of the Sacramento Archives and Museum Collection Center.)

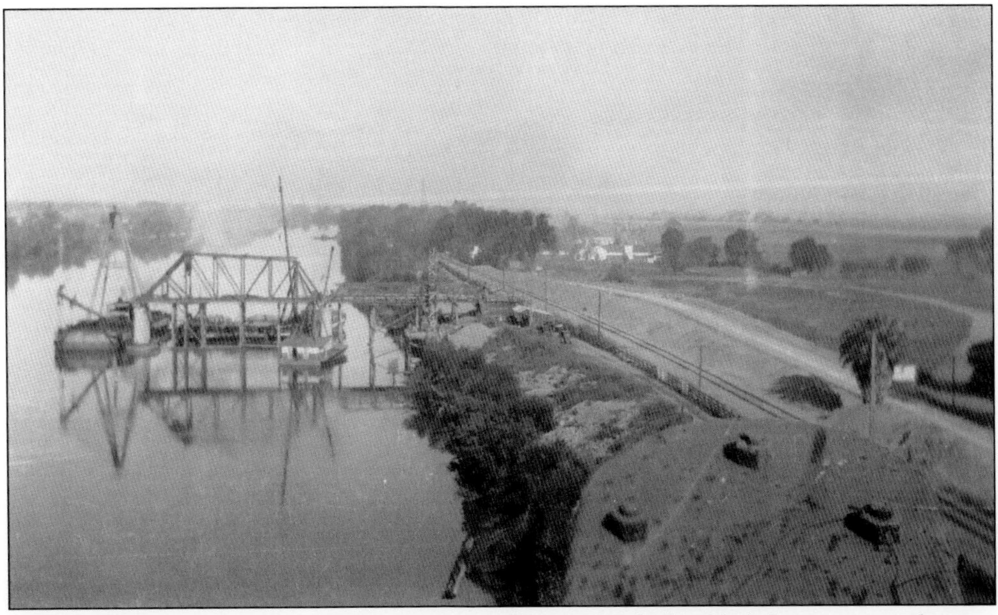

Freeport Bridge was built to connect its namesake town with the Clarksburg area on the west side of the Sacramento River. The drawbridge, seen under construction in 1926, is still in use today. The Walnut Grove Branch is at right. (Courtesy of the Sacramento Archives and Museum Collection Center.)

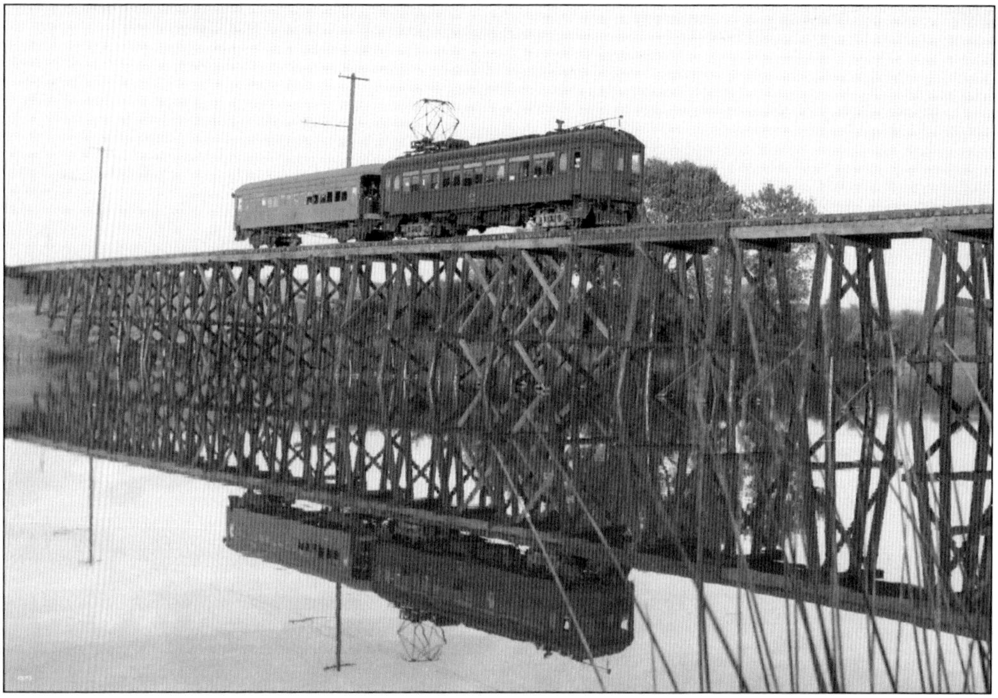

The Walnut Grove Branch's nearest rail competition was the Sacramento Northern's Holland Branch, which opened in 1927. This branch extended from Riverview, on SN's main line to Oakland, to Oxford, west of the Sacramento River. As with the Walnut Grove Branch, agriculture was the line's main reason for existence. (Courtesy of the BAERA Archives Collection/ Western Railway Museum.)

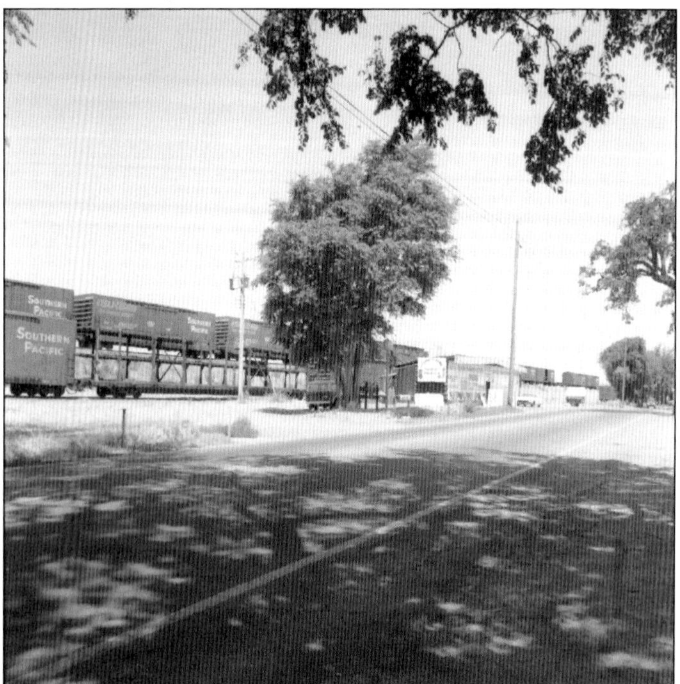

Freeport's depot was gone by the mid-1970s, but plenty of Southern Pacific freight cars can still be seen. Some of these cars are parked on a track that came down to street level from the levee. (Photograph by Marilyn Sommerdorf, courtesy of the California State Railroad Museum Library.)

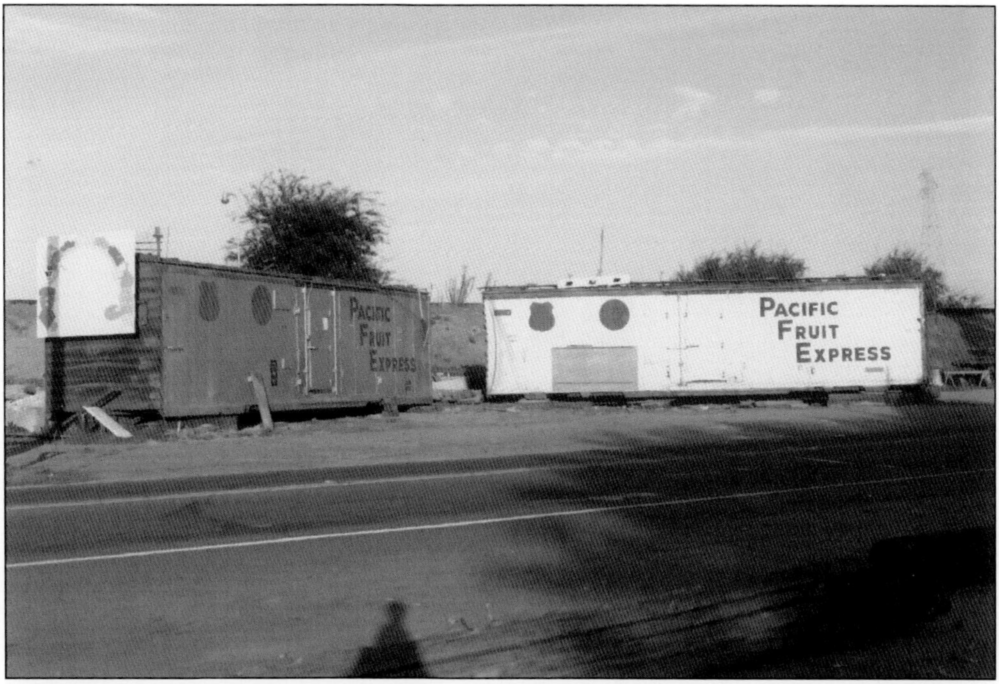

In the 1970s, two retired Pacific Fruit Express reefers were brought to the site of the demolished Freeport depot, where they served as a family produce stand. (Photograph by Marilyn Sommerdorf, courtesy of the California State Railroad Museum Library.)

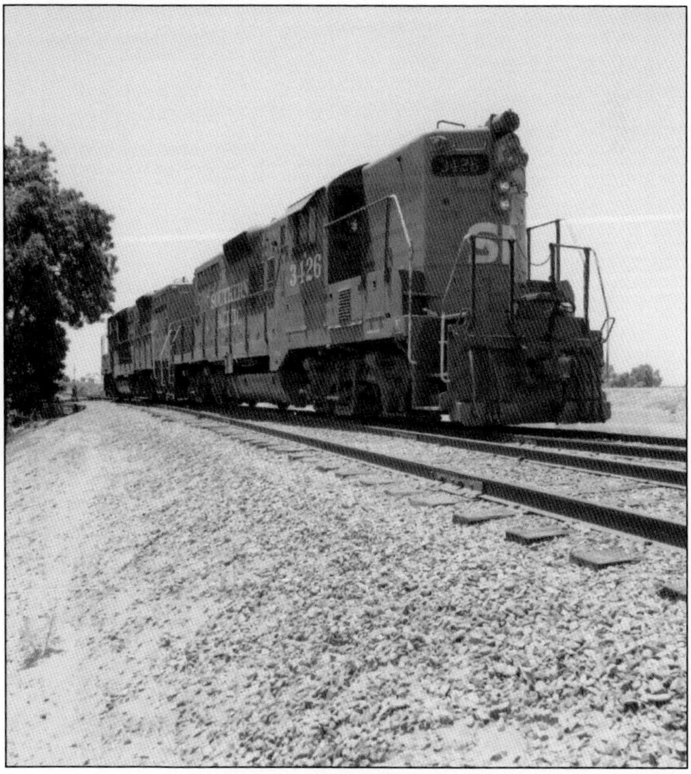

Two Southern Pacific GP9 diesel locomotives work in Freeport around 1977, the last full year of Walnut Grove Branch service. The GP9 was a product of the Electro-Motive Division of General Motors. GP stands for General Purpose; as with the military vehicle, it did not take long for people to start calling these locomotives "Geeps." (Photograph by Marilyn Sommerdorf, courtesy of the California State Railroad Museum Library.)

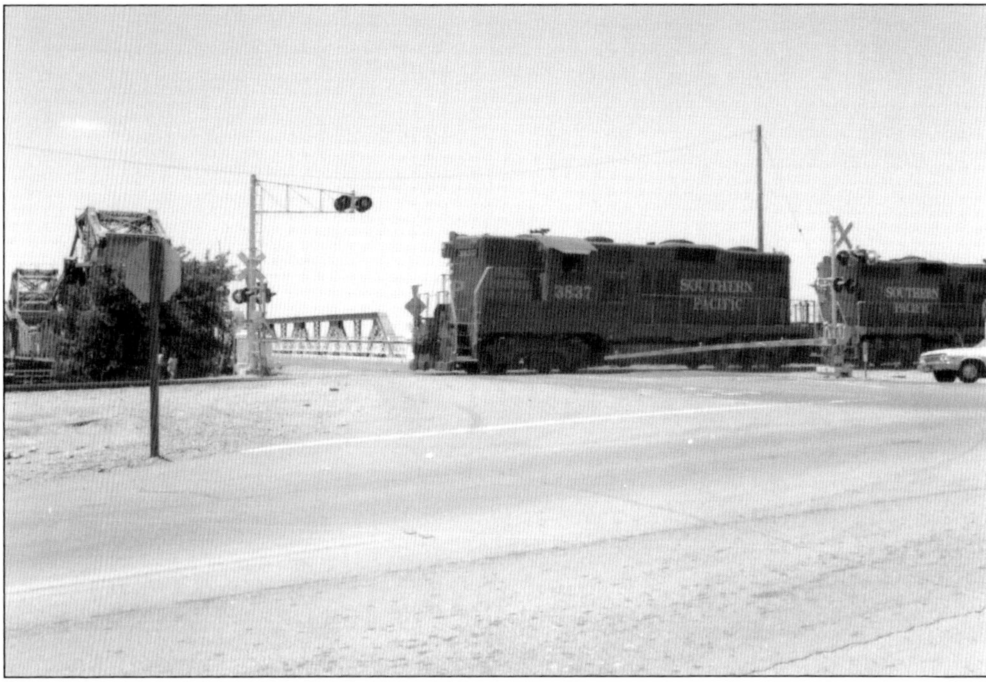

A Walnut Grove Branch freight train trundles south past Freeport Bridge in 1977. Trains moved at a leisurely pace; by this time, the speed limit south of Baths was 10 miles per hour. (Photograph by Marilyn Sommerdorf, courtesy of the California State Railroad Museum Library.)

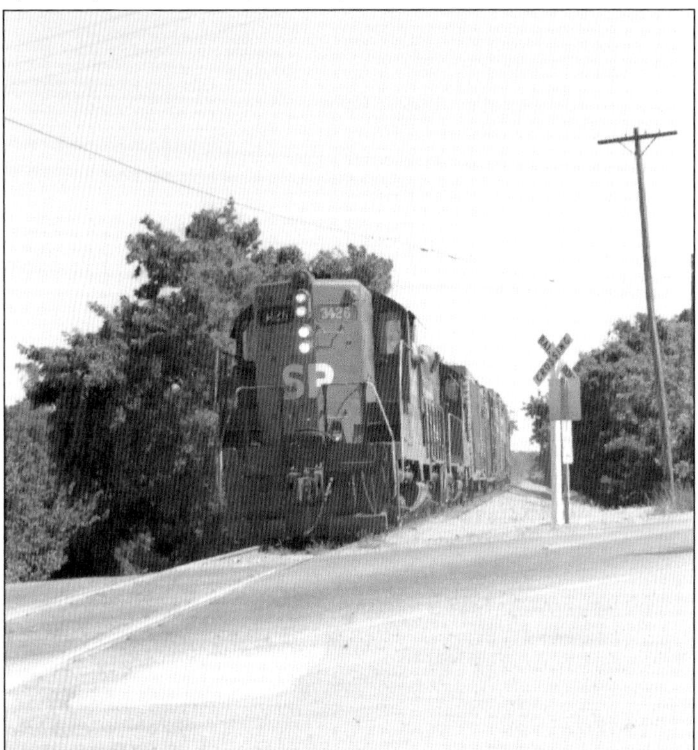

Returning to Sacramento later the same day, the two Geeps bring a short freight train across River Road/Highway 160 near Cliff's Marina at the southern edge of Freeport. (Photograph by Marilyn Sommerdorf, courtesy of the California State Railroad Museum Library.)

Five
Hood

Originally named Richland, this river hamlet's name was changed to Hood in 1909 in honor of one William Hood. Hood (1846–1926), a Civil War veteran, put his Dartmouth engineering degree to good use helping the Central Pacific Railroad build its line through the Sierra Nevada. During his long and distinguished career with the CP, and later the SP, he oversaw the design and construction of many projects, including the famous Tehachapi Loop in Southern California in the mid-1870s. (This line is still heavily used by Union Pacific and Burlington Northern Santa Fe trains.) Hood eventually rose to chief engineer of the Southern Pacific in 1900 and held the office until he retired in 1921.

Trains reached the wharf at Hood on a spur from Hood Junction, just south of Hood-Franklin Road. A large packing shed at the wharf was maintained at various times by the California Fruit Exchange, D. J. Elliot, and Stillwater Orchards. An American Fruit Growers packing shed also stood at Hood Junction until 1943, when it was dismantled and moved to Walnut Grove as an extension of the company's packing shed there.

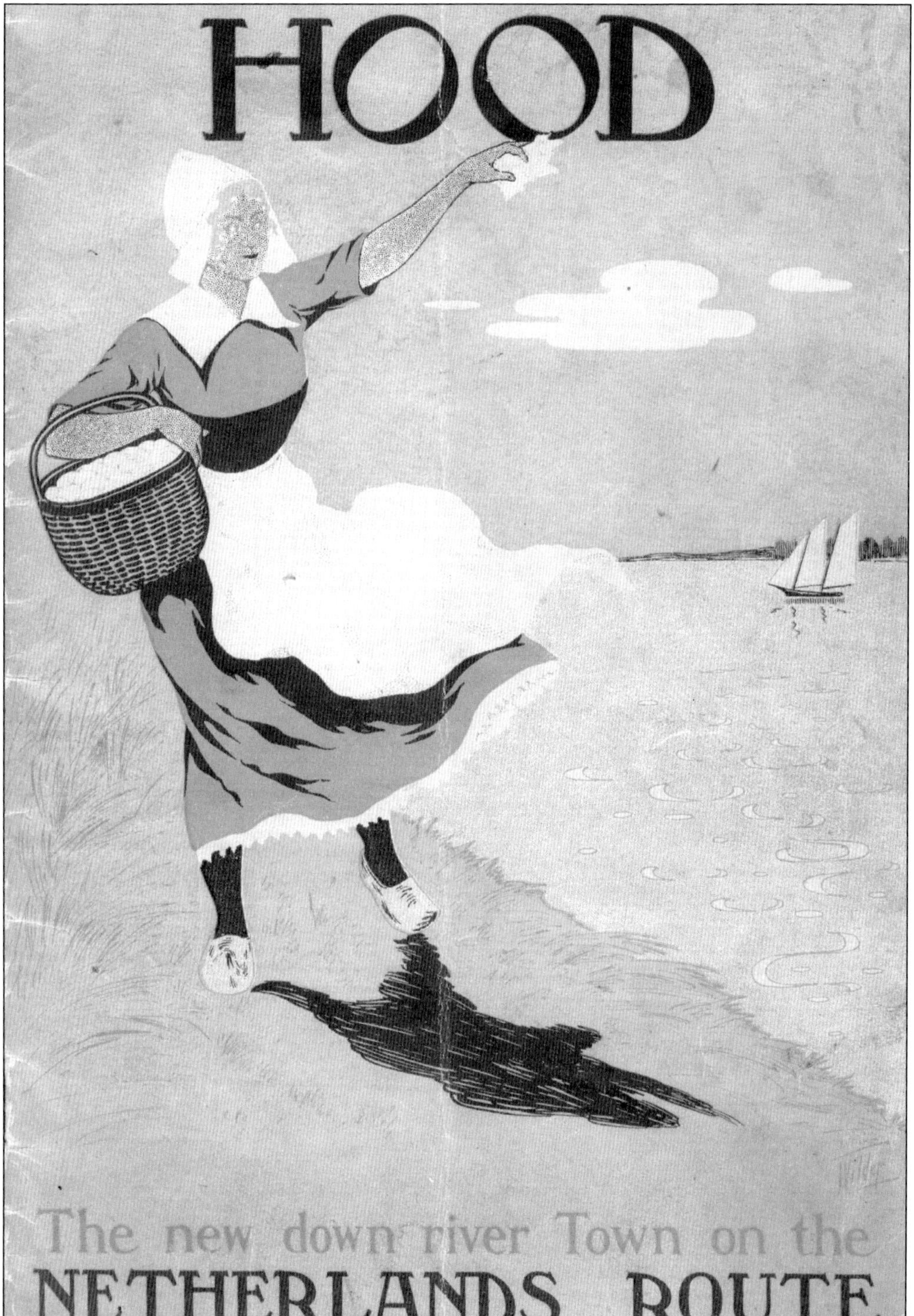

This booklet was part of an attempt made in the 1920s to market Hood as a real estate venture and vacation destination. That never happened; the town's population is now about 100, and businesses are virtually nonexistent. (Courtesy of the Sacramento River Delta Historical Society.)

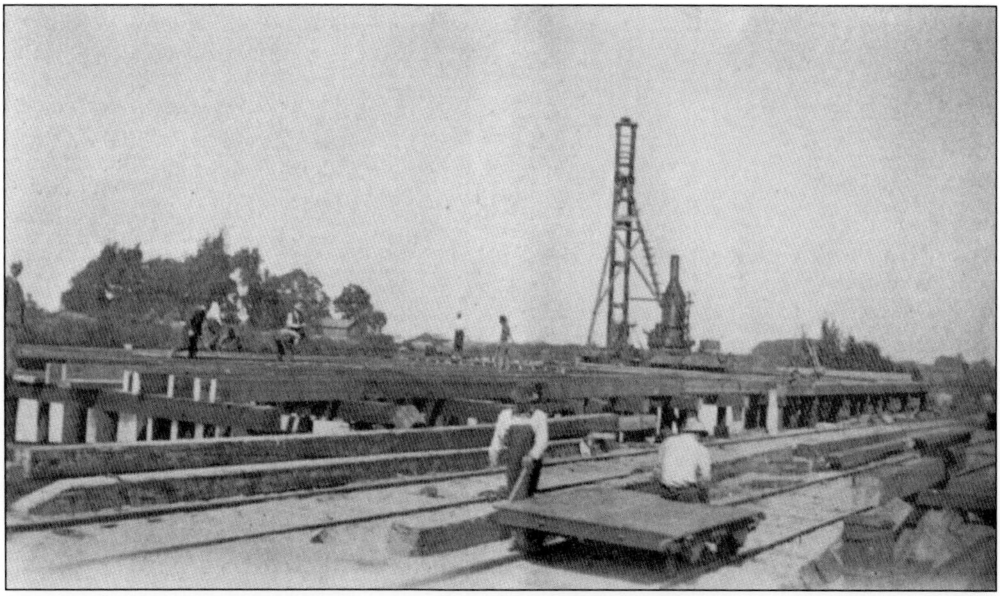

The Hood wharf is pictured here under construction. The anonymous marketer responsible for the booklet wrote of this wharfage: "Upon investigation I learned that these docks were being constructed by the Southern Pacific Company, and that they owned an additional 119 feet adjoining them on the north. However, I learned that these docks are open to every boat that operates on the river in this section, regardless of the company to whom it belongs." (Courtesy of the Sacramento River Delta Historical Society.)

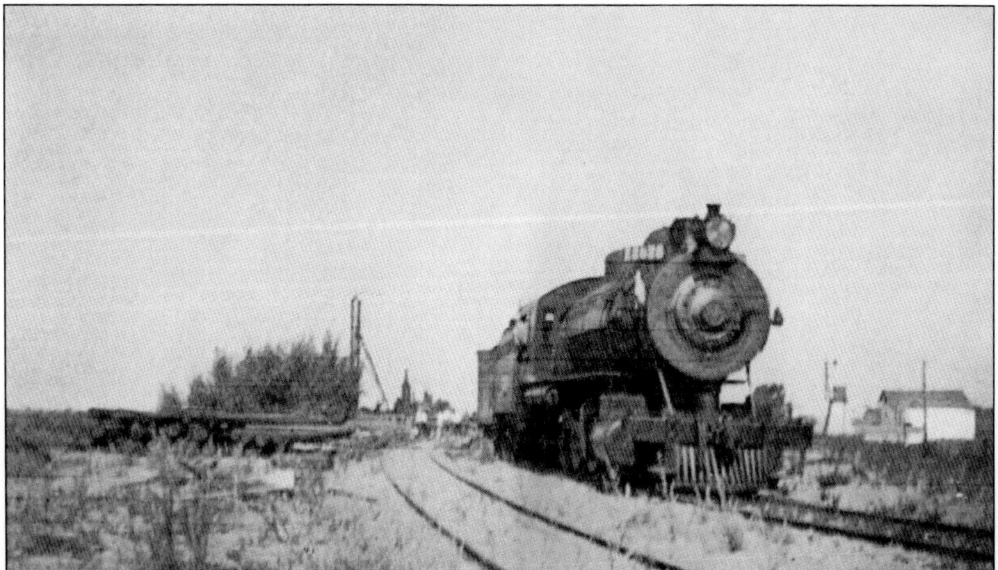

A Southern Pacific construction train backs onto the Hood wharf. "I was told that these docks represented concrete evidence of what the Southern Pacific Company—the builders of these docks—thought of the Hood's future," the unnamed marketer wrote, going on to compare Hood's seemingly rapid rise with that of Roseville, then as now the site of a major rail yard and shops complex. (Courtesy of the Sacramento River Delta Historical Society.)

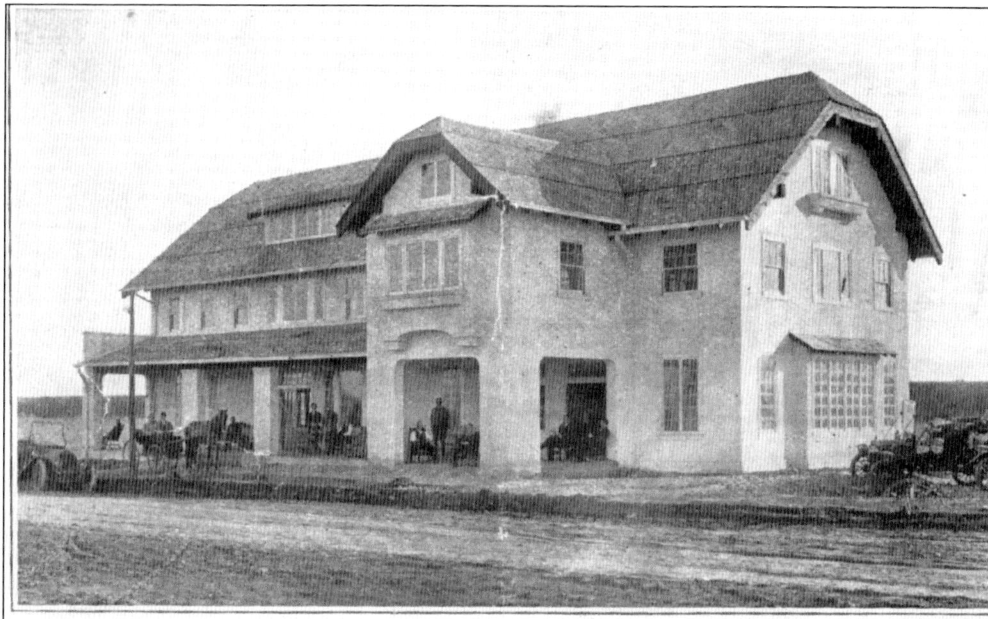

Hotel Netherlands at Hood--on the Netherlands Route

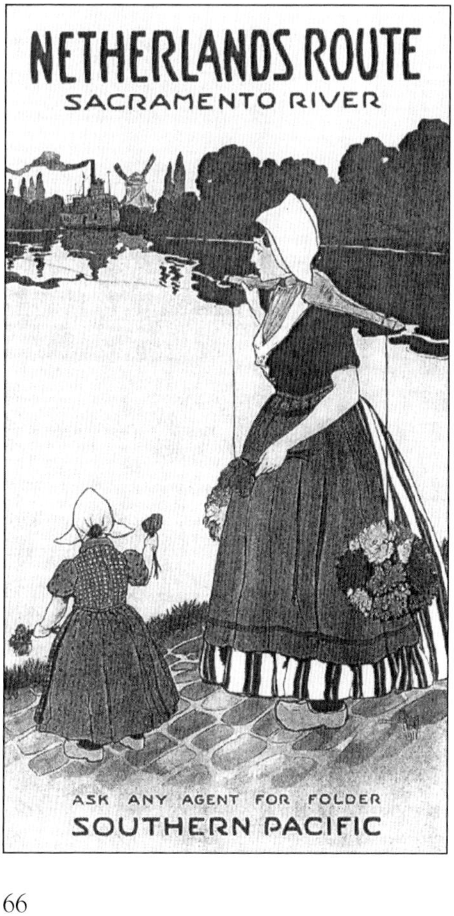

As part of the venture, a rather spectacular hostelry known as the Hotel Netherlands was built in Hood. Any Dutch-inspired ambience was, of course, completely intentional. (Courtesy of the Sacramento River Delta Historical Society.)

The Hotel Netherlands fit in nicely with the theme of Southern Pacific's Sacramento River steamboat service. According to *Southern Pacific Water Lines* by David F. Myrick, it was SP assistant passenger traffic manager F. E. Batturs who labeled the Sacramento River Delta the "Netherlands of America" after the levees and the agricultural activity taking place behind them. The SP discontinued passenger riverboat service around 1930. (Courtesy of the Sacramento River Delta Historical Society.)

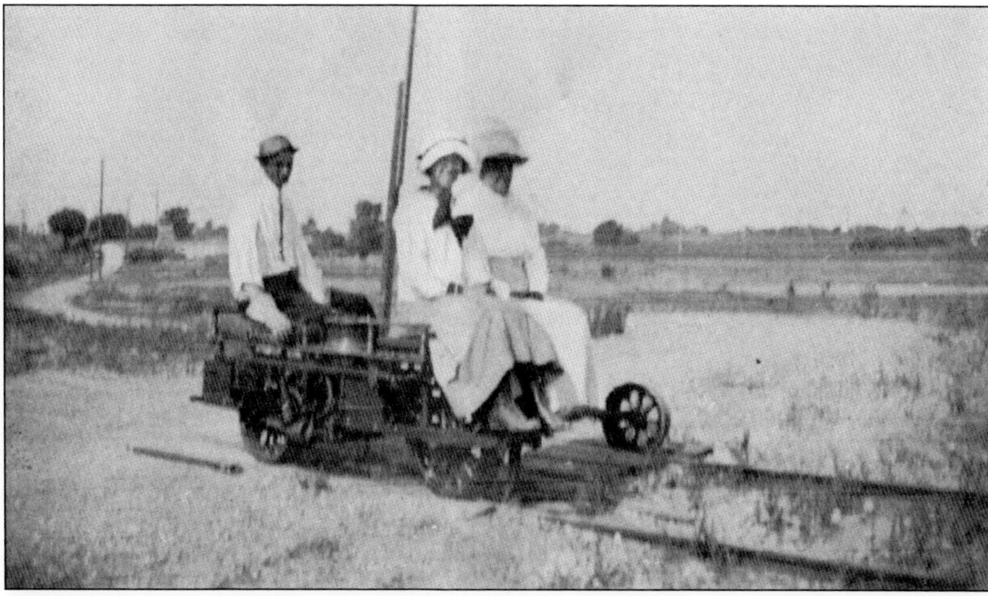

This, the brochure declares, is a "'President Special'—P. T. Robinson in Charge." (Courtesy of the Sacramento River Delta Historical Society.)

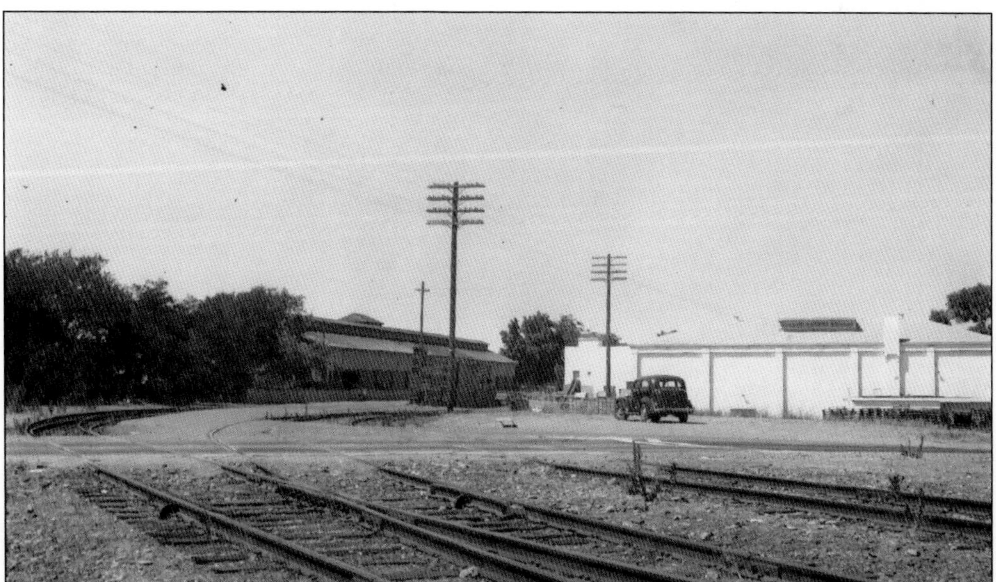

The wharf and packing shed on Hood's riverfront were reached via a spur from the Walnut Grove Branch beginning at Hood Junction. The tracks led west over River Road to the wharf. (Courtesy of the Roy Graves Collection, Bancroft Library, University of California, Berkeley.)

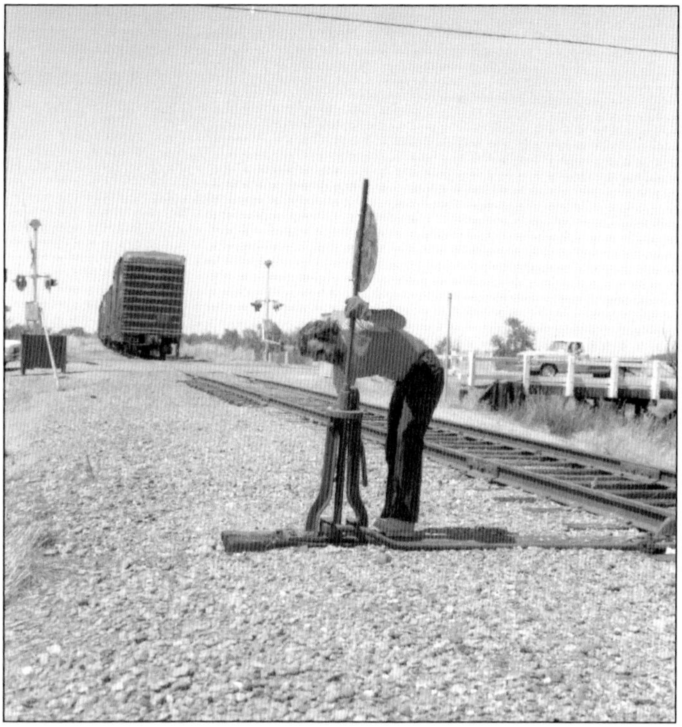

A freight train out of Sacramento has arrived at Hood Junction in 1977. The conductor is preparing to throw the switch that leads from the main line to the spur to the Hood wharf. The train is stopped just to the north of Hood-Franklin Road. (Photograph by Marilyn Sommerdorf, courtesy of the California State Railroad Museum Library.)

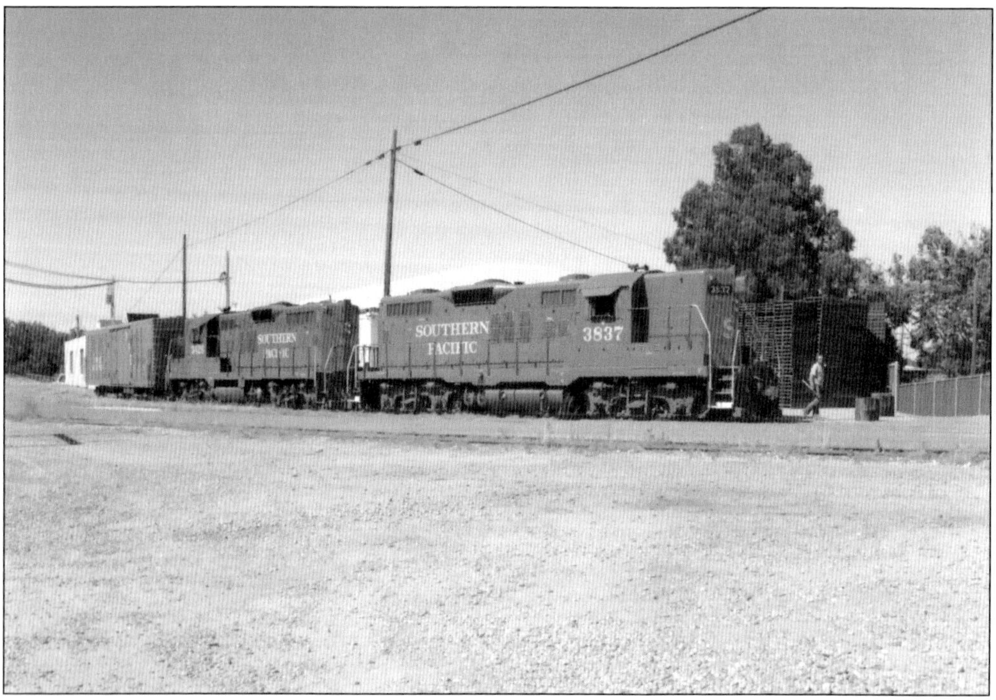

Today's train has one Pacific Fruit Express reefer for the still-active California Fruit Exchange packing shed on the Hood wharf. The crew has backed down the spur from Hood Junction and across River Road to reach the wharf. (Photograph by Marilyn Sommerdorf, courtesy of the California State Railroad Museum Library.)

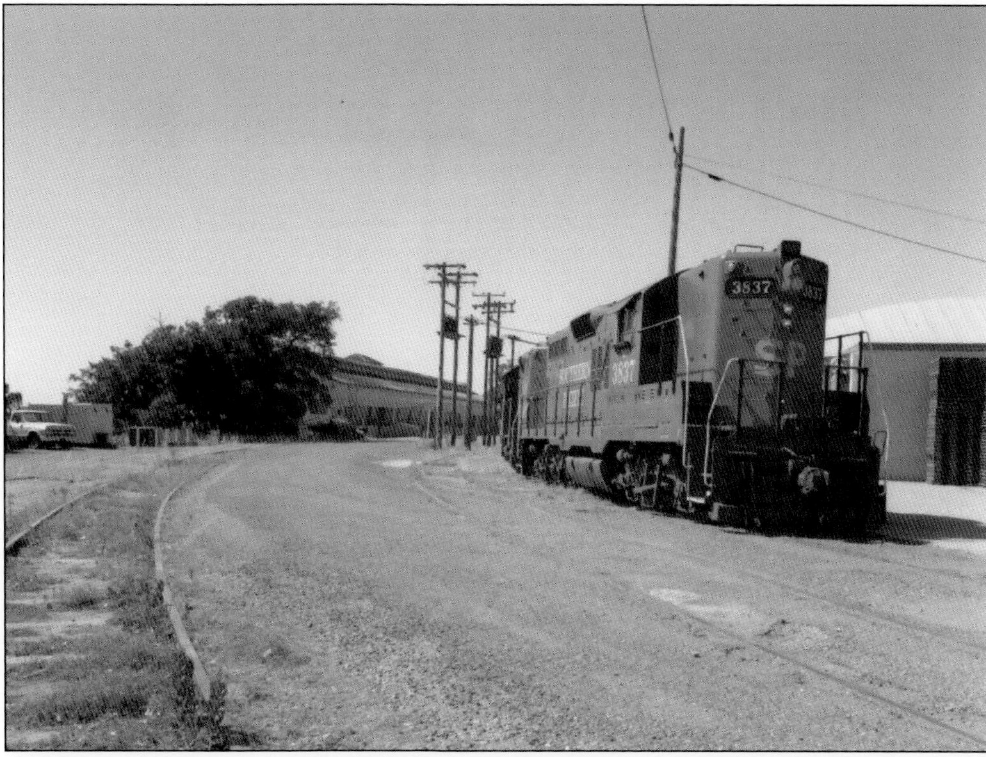

Another view of the freight train at Hood shows the wharf at left, now somewhat disused. (Photograph by Marilyn Sommerdorf, courtesy of the California State Railroad Museum Library.)

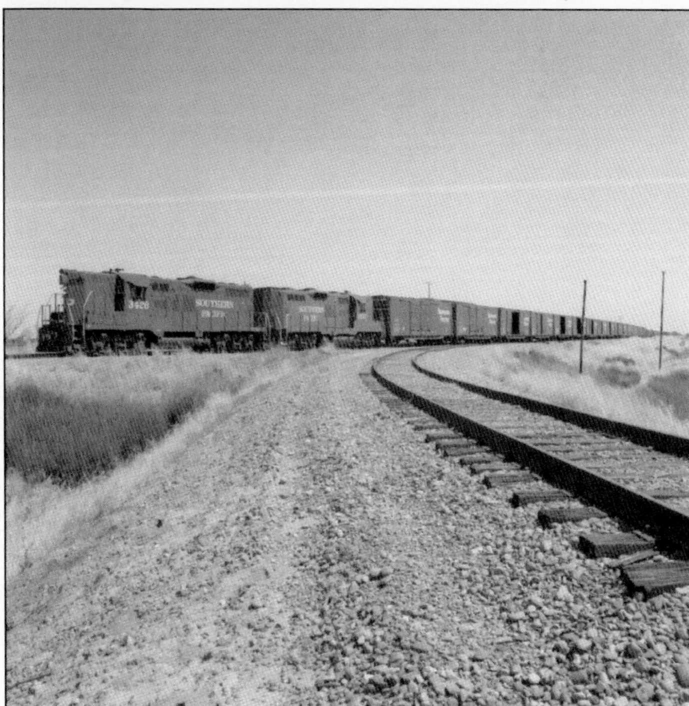

The train prepares to return to Sacramento. The track at right is the spur leading to the wharf. The train is standing just south of Hood-Franklin Road. (Photograph by Marilyn Sommerdorf, courtesy of the California State Railroad Museum Library.)

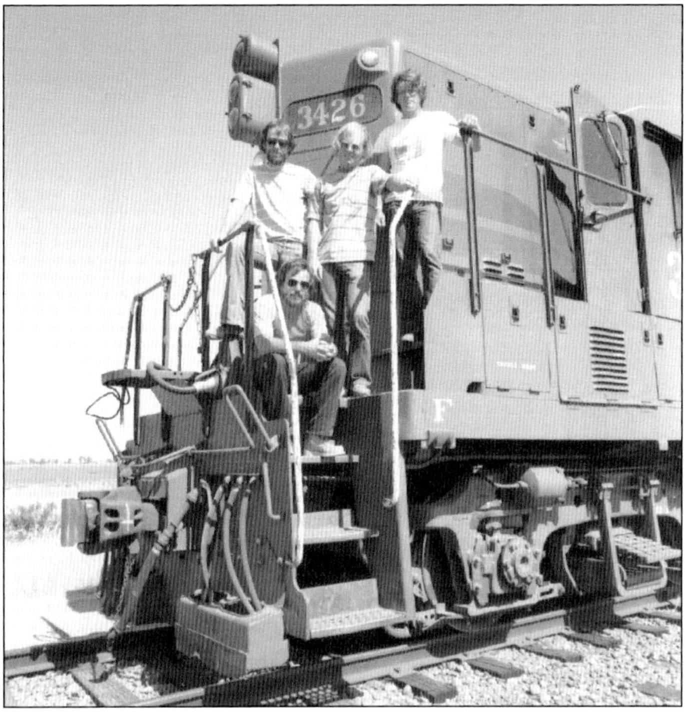

Before leaving Hood, the train crew posed aboard SP Geep No. 3426 for Marilyn Sommerdorf's camera. The year was 1977, and the Walnut Grove Branch was not long for the world. (Photograph by Marilyn Sommerdorf, courtesy of the California State Railroad Museum Library.)

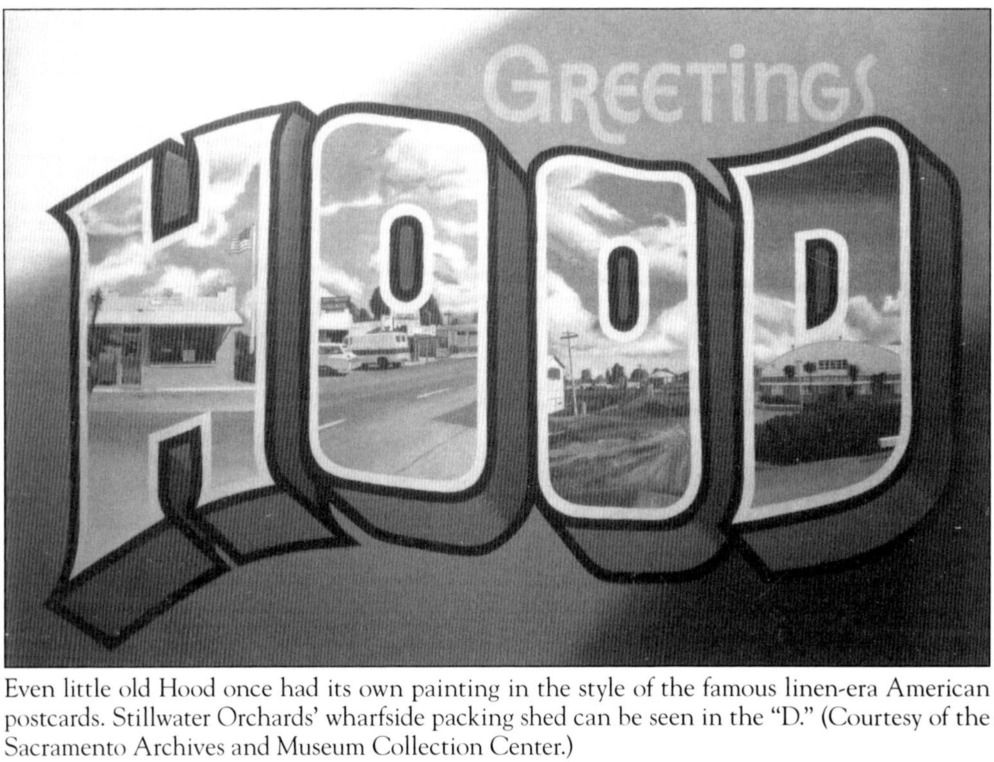

Even little old Hood once had its own painting in the style of the famous linen-era American postcards. Stillwater Orchards' wharfside packing shed can be seen in the "D." (Courtesy of the Sacramento Archives and Museum Collection Center.)

Six

Locke and Walnut Grove

The town that eventually gave the Walnut Grove Branch its name was founded in 1850 by John Sharp, who had brought his family west from Ohio. Twenty years later, it was a bustling town with shops and businesses as well as the obligatory steamboat landing. When Sharp died in 1880, Agnes Brown and her son Alex bought a large portion of the Sharp estate. The Browns, especially Alex, would go on to play large roles in Walnut Grove history. Among other business enterprises, Alex Brown at one time operated an asparagus-packing plant in town as well as the locally well-known Bank of Alex Brown (the bank building still stands on River Road).

Walnut Grove at one time had large Chinese and Japanese communities; indeed, Walnut Grove's Chinatown at one time was said to be the largest such establishment in California outside San Francisco. A disastrous fire in 1915 prompted many of the Chinese residents to relocate to Locke, just up the river, while the Japanese neighborhood was rebuilt and prospered until World War II.

Locke (pronounced "lock") featured a sizable Southern Pacific wharf built in 1909. When the Walnut Grove Branch arrived in its namesake town in 1912, the SP built a spur from the branch to serve the wharf and packing shed. Nearby, Chinese laborers displaced by the Walnut Grove fire of 1915 took up residence on land owned by local pear farmer George Locke. (State law at the time forbade Chinese immigrants from owning land.) Businesses, legal and otherwise, were soon set up, and the town flourished until post–World War II years, when a declining need for farm labor prompted many Chinese Americans to seek their fortunes elsewhere. Besides Alex Brown's asparagus operation, fruit and vegetable packers active in Walnut Grove included Earl Fruit Company, California Fruit Exchange, and American Fruit Growers. All four were served by spur tracks from the Walnut Grove Branch main line, which traveled through town on an embankment. In Locke, Libby, McNeill, and Libby maintained a large produce-packing plant, also served by the SP.

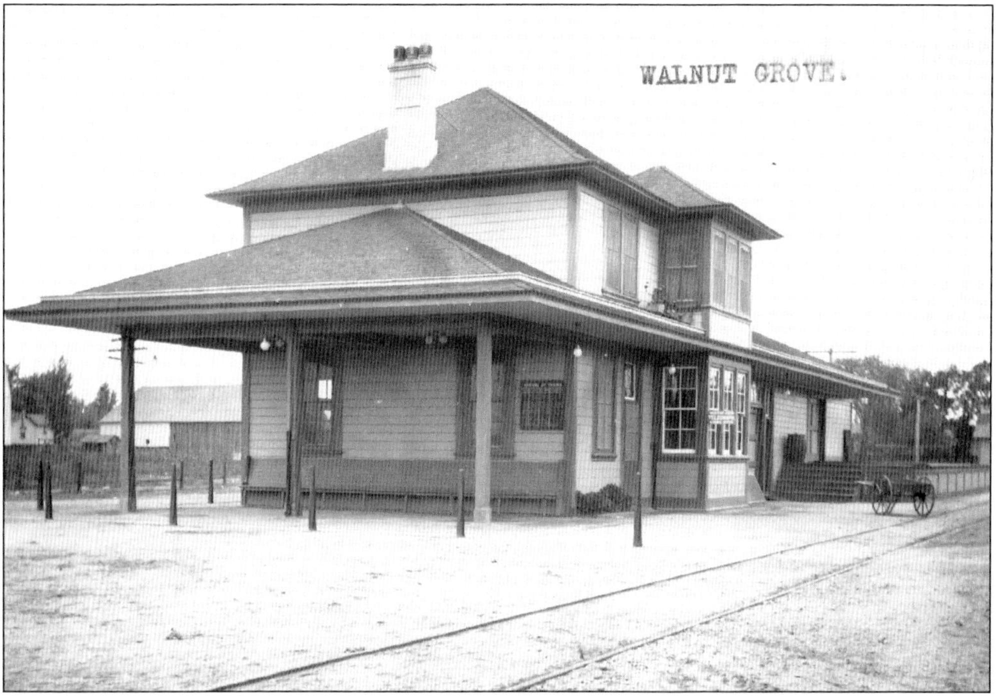

Walnut Grove's depot was built around 1912 by contractor A. F. Graff for the then-princely sum of $6,500. The depot was a two-story Common Standard No. 22, one of many depot plans in SP's files. Whenever a depot needed to be built, SP would pull the appropriate size plan from the files and get to work. (Courtesy of the California State Railroad Museum Library.)

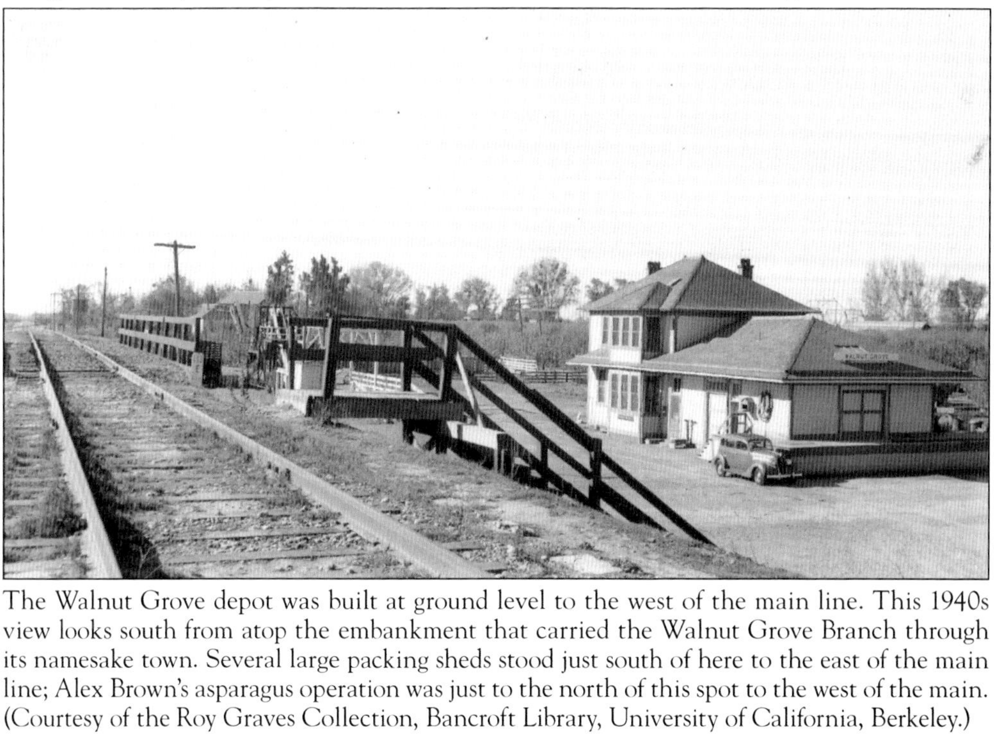

The Walnut Grove depot was built at ground level to the west of the main line. This 1940s view looks south from atop the embankment that carried the Walnut Grove Branch through its namesake town. Several large packing sheds stood just south of here to the east of the main line; Alex Brown's asparagus operation was just to the north of this spot to the west of the main. (Courtesy of the Roy Graves Collection, Bancroft Library, University of California, Berkeley.)

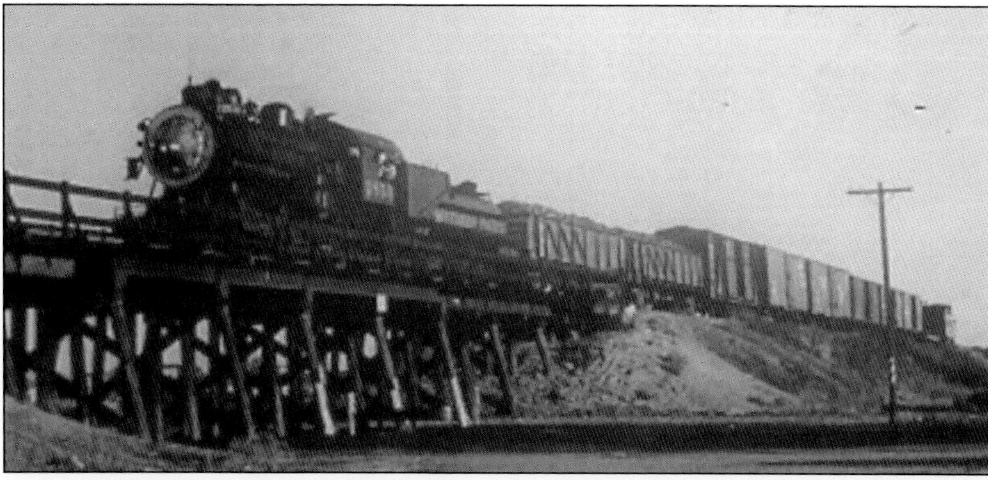

A short Walnut Grove Branch freight train rumbles through town, likely in the 1940s. The two freight cars immediately behind the locomotive appear to be loaded with sugar beets, one of the prime commodities carried on the branch. (Courtesy of the Sacramento River Delta Historical Society.)

EASTWARD					Time Table No. 120 January 13, 1924	WESTWARD			11
Capacity of Sidings in Car Lengths	SECOND CLASS 238 Local Freight Leave Wed. and Sat. Only	FIRST CLASS 534 Sacramento Walnut Grove MOTOR Leave Daily	FIRST CLASS 532 Sacramento Walnut Grove MOTOR Leave Daily	Distance from San Francisco	STATIONS	Distance from Walnut Grove	FIRST CLASS 533 Walnut Grove Sacramento MOTOR Arrive Daily	FIRST CLASS 535 Walnut Grove Sacramento MOTOR Arrive Daily	THIRD CLASS 239 Local Freight Arrive We !. and Sat. Only
Terminal Yard WFTYPBK	6.30AM	4.15PM	7.40AM	88.8	TO-R SACRAMENTO 0.5	24.6	s 10.45AM	s 6.50PM	11.30AM
Yard				89.3	S. N. R. R. Crossing 0.3	24.1			
Yard P	6.40	4.20	7.45	89.6	JCT. SWITCH R STREET 2.2	23.8	10.39	6.43	11.20
Yard	6.50	f 4.26	f 7.51	91.8	BATHS 2.4	21.6	f 10.34	f 6.38	11.10
60	7.00	f 4.33	f 7.58	94.2	DEL RIO 3.3	19.2	f 10.28	f 6.32	11.00
60	7.15	s 4.42	s 8.07	97.5	FREEPORT 7.8	15.9	s 10.20	s 6.23	10.50
66 P	7.50	s 5.02	s 8.27	105.3	HOOD 4.0	9.5	s 10.00	s 6.03	10.20
55	8.00	f 5.15	f 8.40	107.9	LAMBERT 3.3	5.5	f 9.47	f 5.50	10.00
No Siding	8.10	f	f	111.2	MOFUBA 2.2	2.2	f	f	9.50
61 PWY	8.20AM	s 5.30PM	s 8.55AM	113.4	TO-R WALNUT GROVE	0.0	9.30AM	5.35PM	9.40AM
	Arrive Wed. and Sat. Only	Arrive Daily	Arrive Daily		(24.6)		Leave Daily	Leave Daily	Leave Wed. and Sat. Only
	(1.50) 13.41	(1.15) 19.68	(1.15) 19.68		Time over District Average speed per hour		(1.15) 19.68	(1.15) 19.68	(1.50) 13.41

Exception: No. 532 is superior to No. 533.
Exception: No. 534 is superior to No. 535.

ADDITIONAL FLAG STOPS TO RECEIVE OR DISCHARGE PASSENGERS:—First class trains at Front and M Street Sacramento, Charles, Pocket, Content, Cronin, Mosher, Acacia, Locke and Rosebud.

ADDITIONAL STATIONS:—Charles Mile Post 93.0; Pocket 96.4; Content 98.9; Cronin 100.1; Mosher 100.9; Acacia 102.6; Rosebud 103.3; Locke and Walnut Grove Wharf 112.6.

In early 1924, the Walnut Grove Branch saw two daily McKeen motorcar trips for passengers and twice-weekly freight trips. When harvest seasons were at their peak, additional freight trains, known as "extras," would be called. (Courtesy of the California State Railroad Museum Library.)

Capacity of Sidings in Car Lengths		EASTWARD SECOND CLASS 532 Sacramento Walnut Grove MIXED	Distance from San Francisco	Time Table No. 122 May 3, 1925 STATIONS	Distance from Walnut Grove	WESTWARD SECOND CLASS 533 Walnut Grove Sacramento MIXED	11
		Leave Daily				Arrive Daily	
Terminal Yard WFTYPBK		8.30AM	88.8	TO R SACRAMENTO	24.6	s 5.50PM	
				0.5			
Yard			89.3	S. N. R. R. Crossing	24.1		
				0.3			
Yard P		8.35	89.6	JCT. SWITCH R STREET	23.8	5.42	
				2.2			
Yard		f 8.41	91.8	BATHS	21.6	f 5.36	
				2.4			
60		f 8.48	94.2	DEL RIO	19.2	f 5.30	
				3.3			
60		s 8.57	97.5	FREEPORT	15.9	s 5.20	
				7.8			
66 P		s 9.17	105.3	HOOD	9.5	s 5.00	
				4.0			
55		f 9.30	107.9	LAMBERT	5.5	f 4.47	
				3.3			
44		f	111.2	MOFUBA	2.2	f	
				2.2			
61 PWY		s 9.45AM	113.4	TO-R WALNUT GROVE	0.0	4.30PM	
		Arrive Daily		(24.6)		Leave Daily	
		(1.15)		Time over District		(1.20)	
		19.68		Average speed per hour		18.45	

ADDITIONAL FLAG STOPS TO RECEIVE OR DISCHARGE PASSENGERS: — Nos. 532 and 533 at Front and M Street Sacramento, Charles, Pocket, Content, Cronin, Mosher, Acacia, Locke and Rosebud.

ADDITIONAL STATIONS:—Charles Mile Post 93.0; Pocket 96.4; Content 98.9; Cronin 100.1; Mosher 100.9; Acacia 102.6; Rosebud 103.3; Locke and Walnut Grove Wharf 112.6.

By 1925, the passenger business was cut back to this once-daily mixed train. A mixed train would carry passengers and freight; paying customers would usually be accommodated in a coach carried in lieu of a caboose. A flag stop is a station where a train would stop only if passengers were seen to be waiting on the platform, or passengers on the train had notified the conductor of their intentions to disembark. (Courtesy of the California State Railroad Museum Library.)

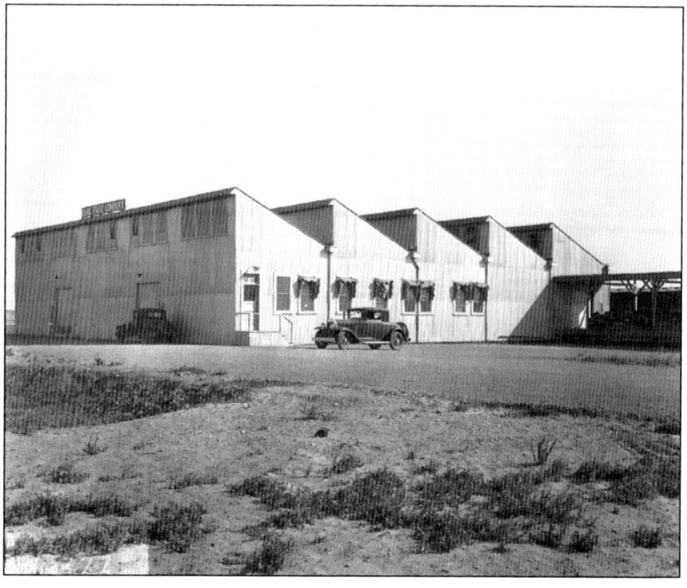

Earl Fruit Company was one of three produce companies with packing sheds just southeast of the Walnut Grove depot. Earl's shed was sandwiched between those of American Fruit Growers (to the south) and Pacific Fruit Exchange (to the north). All three were served via spurs from the Walnut Grove Branch. A Southern Pacific boxcar is barely visible at right in this 1929 view. (Courtesy of the California History Room, California State Library.)

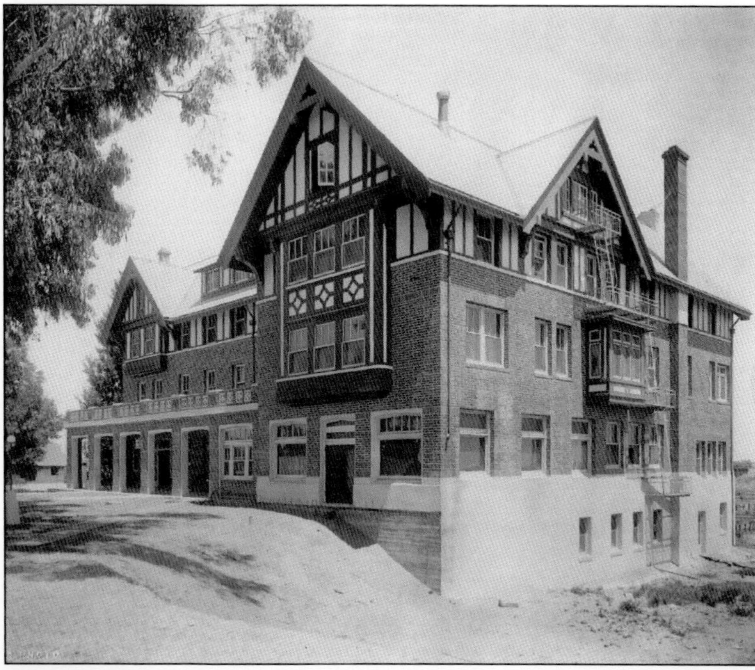

The palatial Walnut Grove Hotel is nearing completion in 1918. This hotel, built by Alex Brown's family, was of mock Tudor design and featured three stories and a basement. One of its residents was Kate Brown, widow of Alex. This hotel burned down in 1969; the Boon Dox Liquor Store now occupies the site. (Courtesy of the Sacramento River Delta Historical Society.)

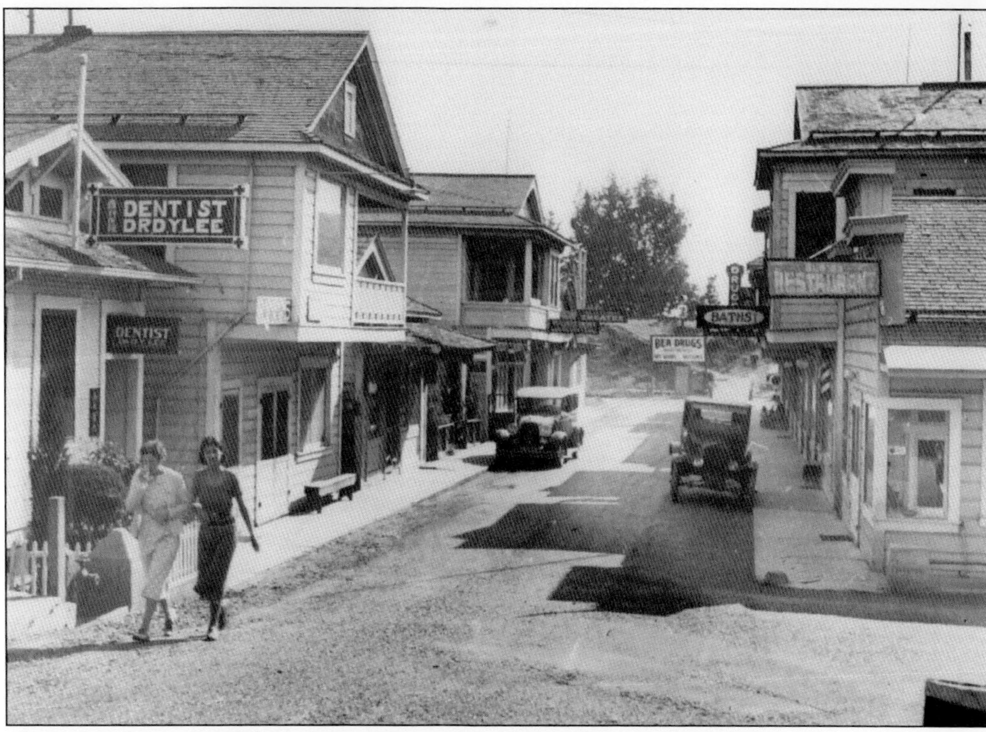

This is A Street in Walnut Grove's Japanese section. This *c.* 1926 view looks east from near River Road toward the Walnut Grove Branch embankment in the background. The building at left, housing the dental offices of Dr. D. Y. Lee, is still standing today, albeit remodeled. The embankment in the background has been leveled and the space used for parking. (Courtesy of the California History Room, California State Library.)

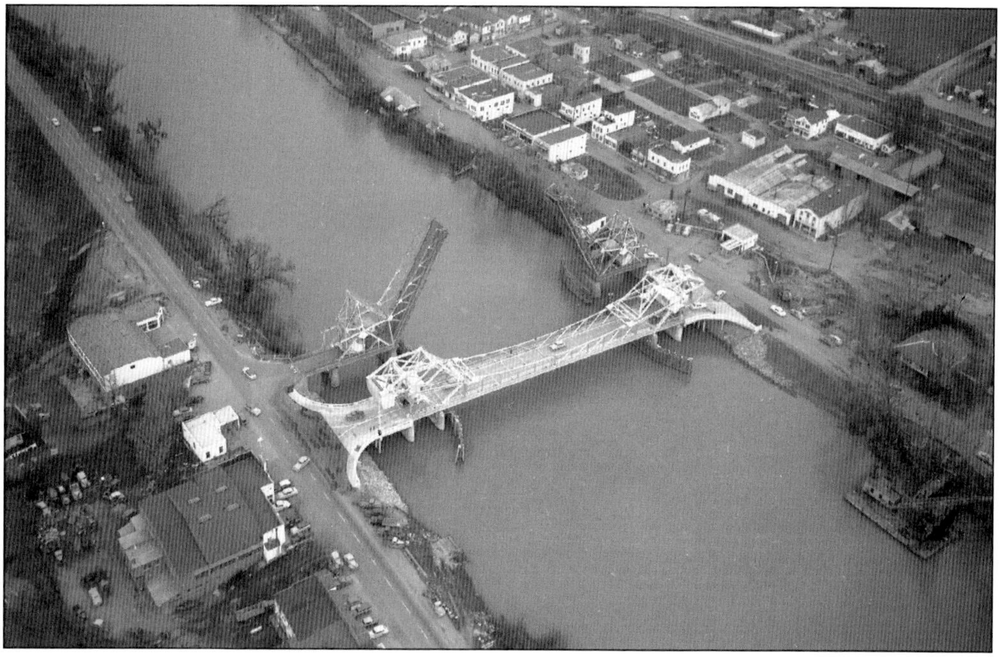

A new drawbridge across the Sacramento River was built in 1956 to replace the older one (top) constructed in 1915. The Walnut Grove Branch passes through at upper right, and the Alex Brown packing shed is at far right. (Courtesy of the Sacramento Archives and Museum Collection Center.)

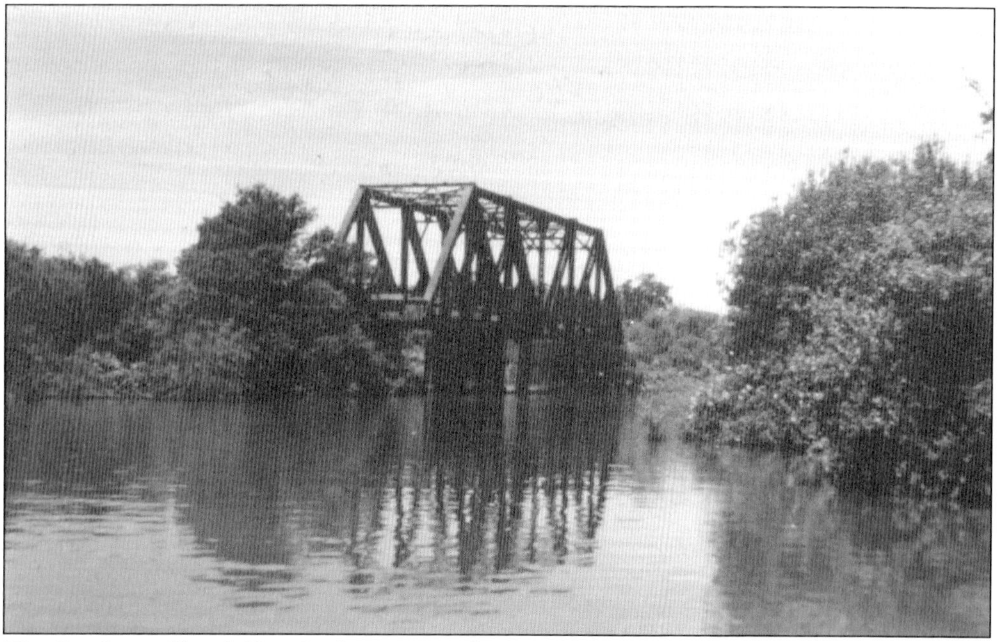

The Snodgrass Slough Drawbridge, seen under construction in chapter 2, has been left open to allow boat traffic to pass unimpeded. Little remains of this bridge today. (Courtesy of the Sacramento River Delta Historical Society.)

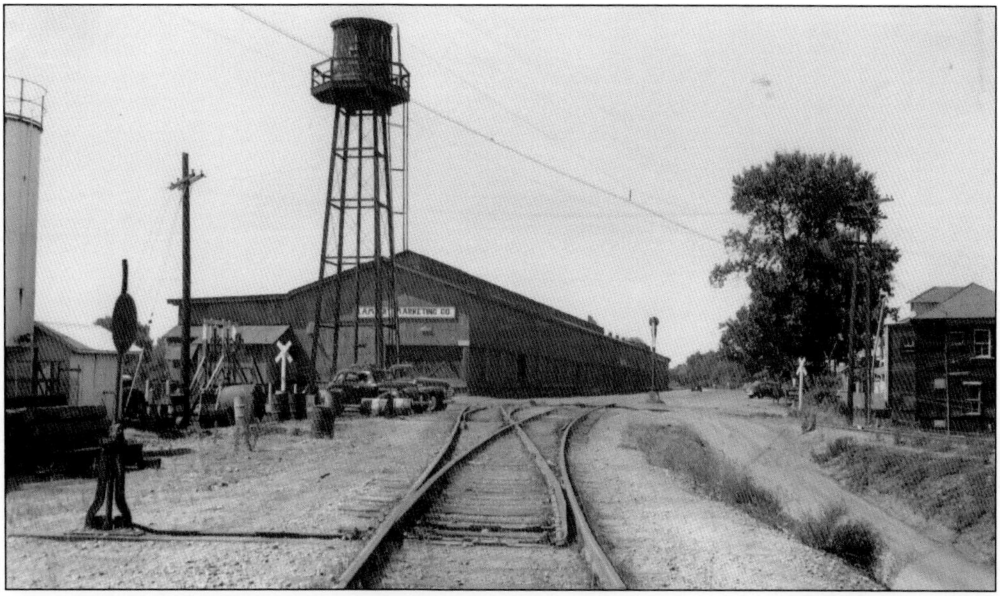

The wharf and packing shed at Locke stood less than a mile upriver from Walnut Grove. The SP reached its wharf by rail via a spur from the Walnut Grove Branch. Across River Road from the wharf stood the largely Chinese settlement begun in earnest after the 1915 fire that heavily damaged Walnut Grove's Chinese neighborhood. (Courtesy of the Roy Graves Collection, Bancroft Library, University of California, Berkeley.)

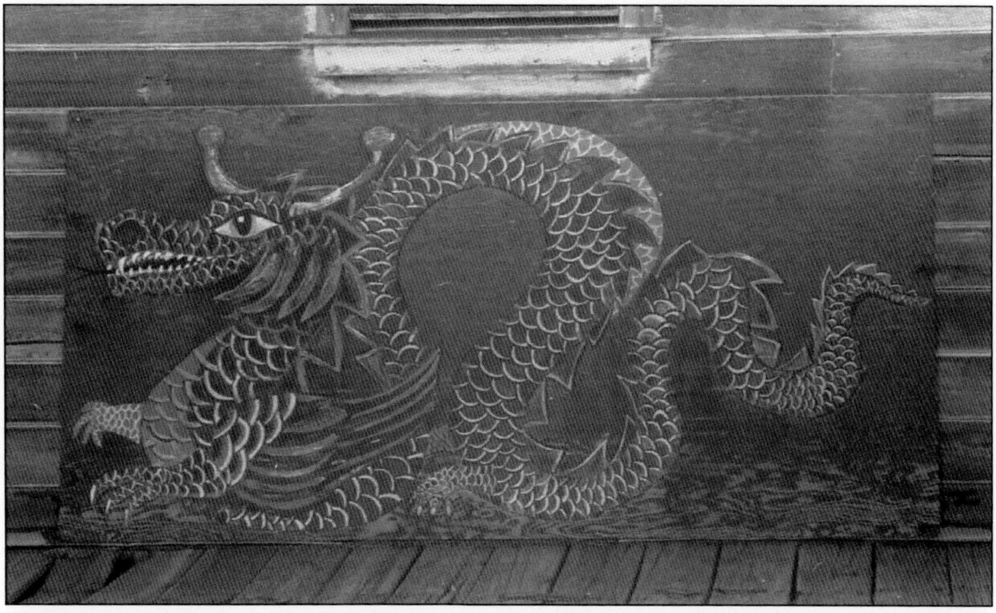

This dragon is indicative of Locke's Chinese heritage. The town was situated along the river levee across from the SP's wharf and packing shed. Most of the wood-frame buildings, erected in the 1910s, still stand; the area is now the Locke Historic District and has been declared a National Historic Landmark. (Courtesy of the Sacramento Archives and Museum Collection Center.)

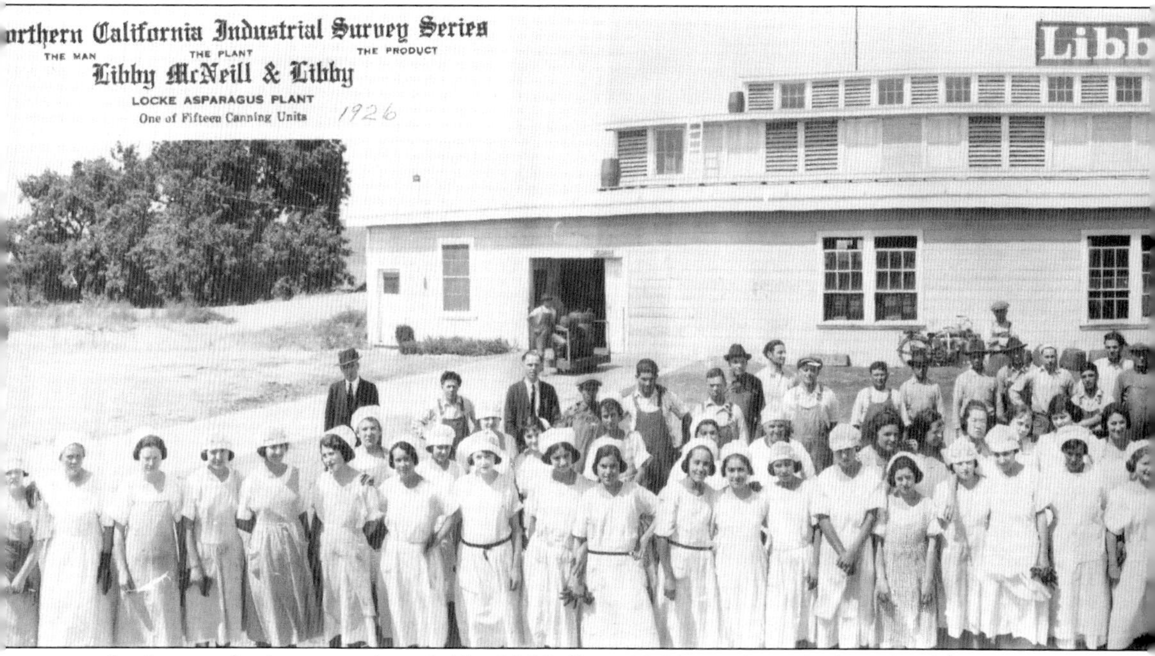

Locke was also home to a large Libby, McNeill, and Libby packing shed north of the wharf. This plant was responsible for packing asparagus from nearby delta farms. The shed had its own spur

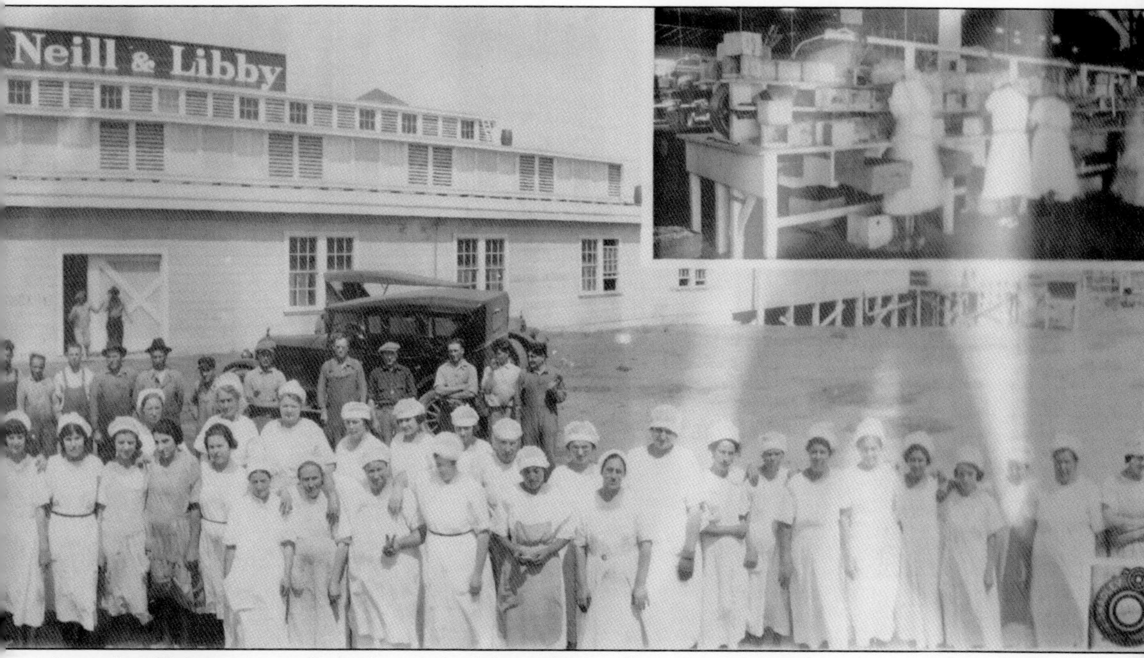

from the Walnut Grove Branch, reached from the trackage leading to the wharf. (Courtesy of the Sacramento River Delta Historical Society.)

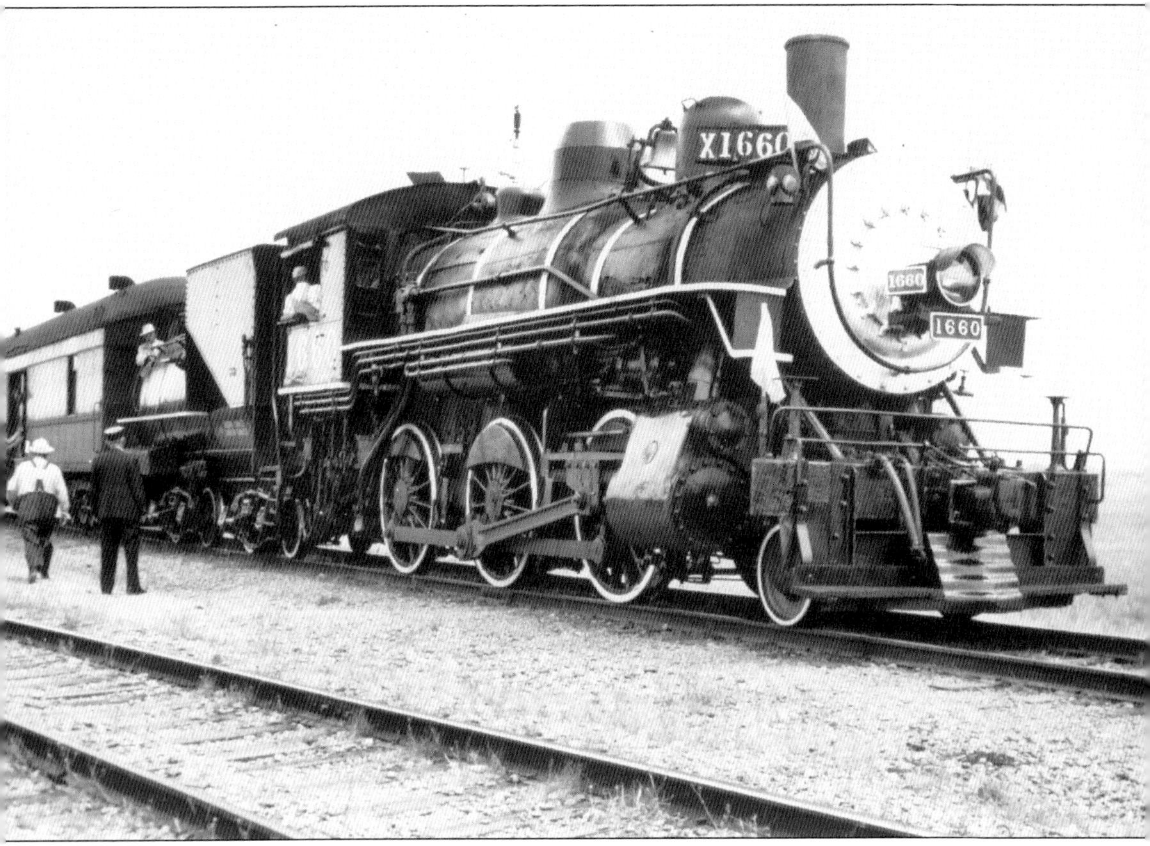

An excursion train has arrived in Locke c. 1949, long after regular passenger service on the branch had been discontinued. SP 2-6-0 No. 1660 was one of many such small-but-mighty locomotives commonly seen on SP's valley lines. They were commonly known as "Valley Mallets" on account of their ability to handle long, heavy trains. (Photograph by Alan Aske, courtesy of Marilyn Sommerdorf.)

Seven
ISLETON

The town that would become the Walnut Grove Branch's southern terminus was founded in 1874. As with Walnut Grove and Locke, agriculture was the principal business, and soon a sizable population of Chinese and Japanese immigrants sprang up. Two of Isleton's claims to fame are the yearly Crawdad Festival, held in June, and actor Pat Morita (1932–2005), of *Karate Kid* fame, who was born in Isleton to Japanese immigrants.

In its review of the SP's application to extend the branch to Isleton, the Interstate Commerce Commission—which tightly regulated railroads for much of the 20th century—took note of the presence of three canneries and a pickle plant in town, and the fact that establishment of direct rail service would spawn an increase in fruit and vegetable production. The SP estimated that the extension would carry 20,700 tons of outbound freight in its first year of operation, increasing to 23,840 tons in its fifth year.

Customers of the SP in Isleton included the National Packing Company, which was founded and operated by Chinese immigrants; Ensher, Alexander, and Barsoom, known as E&A, whose cannery and pickle plant were next door to National Packing; the H. J. Heinz Company, famous for its 57 varieties and ketchup, which maintained a pickle plant in Isleton; the Golden State asparagus cannery on the banks of the Mokelumne River, to which SP built a 3-mile spur from Isleton in 1931; and a sugar beet dump near the municipal baseball field. Spur tracks also served a granary and wharf along the Sacramento River just north of the National and E&A plants. The Union Ice Company supplied SP's refrigerator cars, or reefers, with ice to keep their perishable contents fresh.

Longtime Isleton resident John Perez, whose real estate office is situated in the former icehouse, recalls watching ball games from atop the sugar beet dump and recalls the special train the Southern Pacific sent to Isleton in 1939. This train carried Perez and his classmates to the World's Fair on Treasure Island in San Francisco Bay.

There was, alas, one other special train around 1942. The branch was used to help carry the region's Japanese American residents to internment camps.

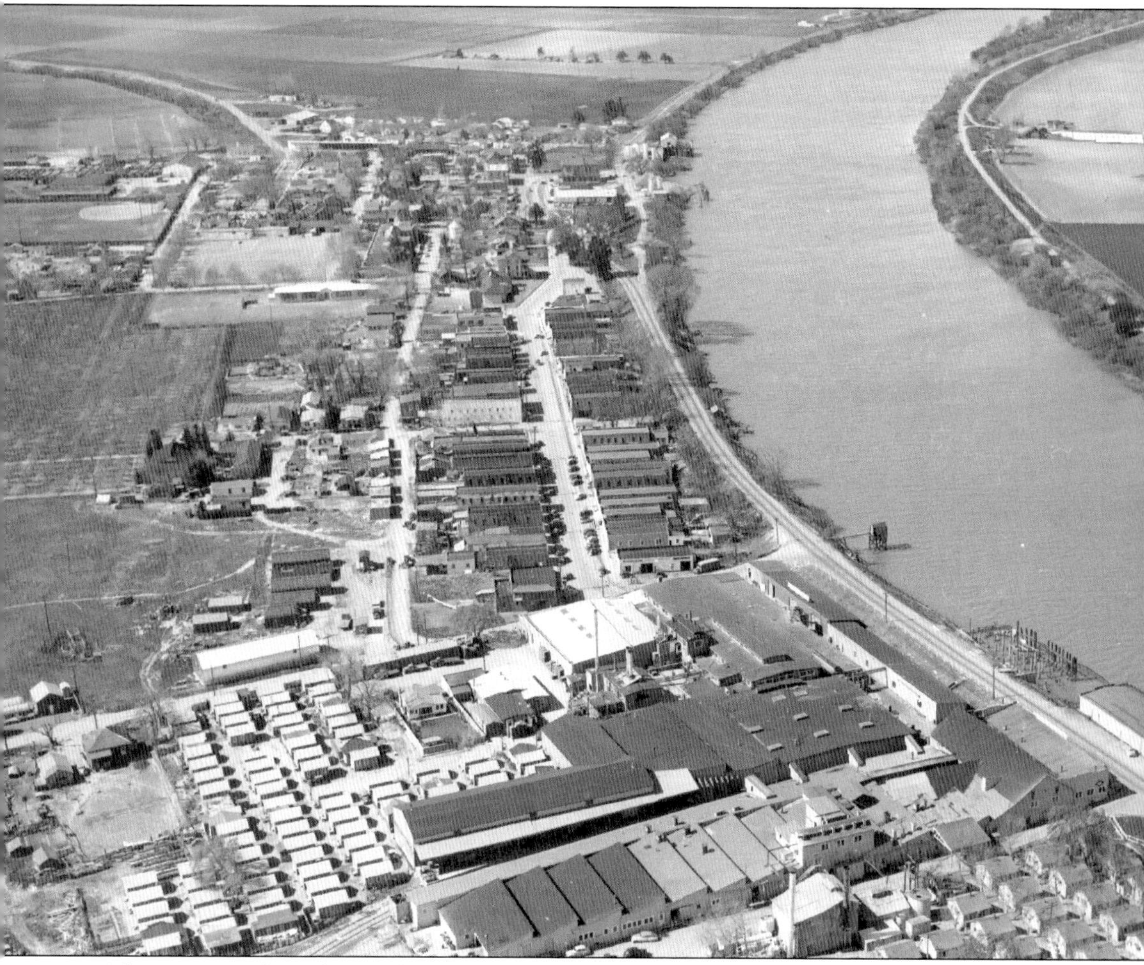

Isleton is seen from the air about 1953, looking south, with the Sacramento River at right. The packing and pickle plant nearest the bottom belonged to Ensher, Alexander, and Barsoom; John Perez worked here in his youth, doing, as he put it, a little of everything. Next door, at the foot of Main Street, is National Packing Company. The cottages near both plants housed cannery workers. The H. J. Heinz pickle plant is at upper left, next to the baseball field. The depot was near the ball field, just out of the picture. (Courtesy of the Sacramento Archives and Museum Collection Center.)

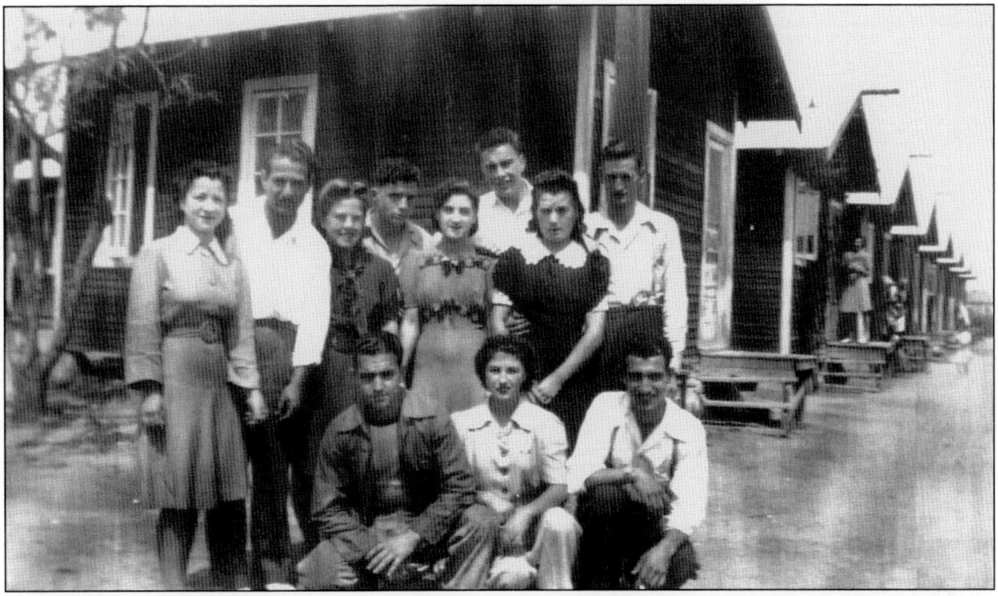

Workers from the Ensher, Alexander, and Barsoom (E&A) plant gather outside the cannery's housing. Some workers would live here year-round; others would stay only during the peak of the harvesting and canning season. Walnut Grove Branch trains served this plant and National Packing Company from the same spur track. (Courtesy of the Isleton Brannan-Andrus Historical Society.)

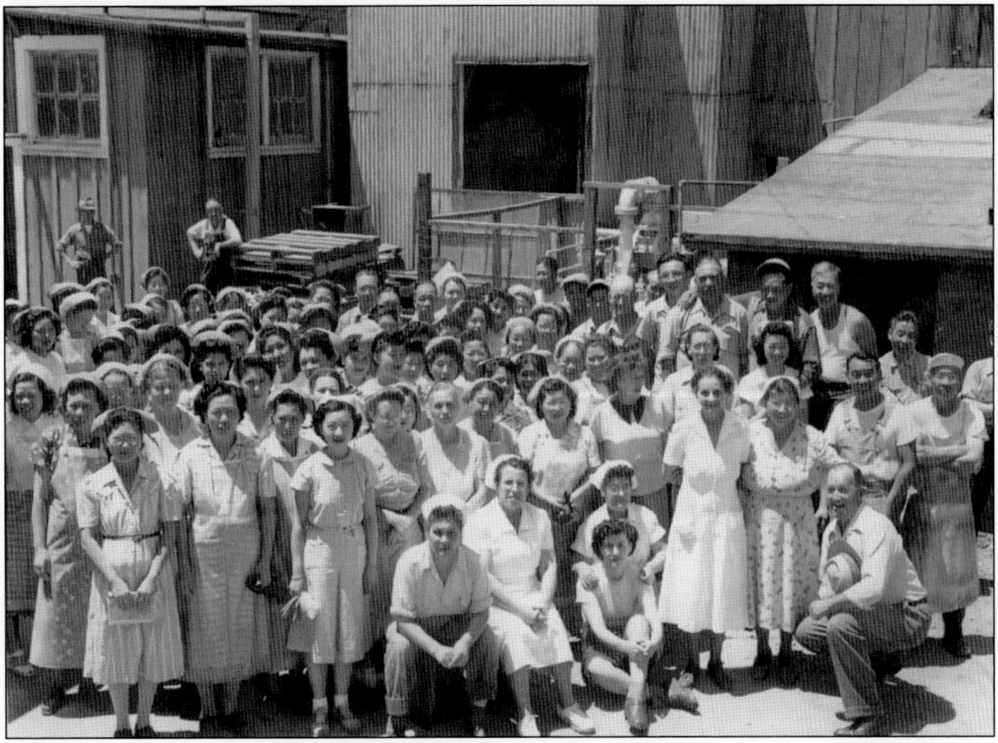

Running a cannery or packing shed was a labor-intensive process. These are just some of the people it took to keep the National Packing Company in Isleton humming. (Courtesy of the Isleton Brannan-Andrus Historical Society.)

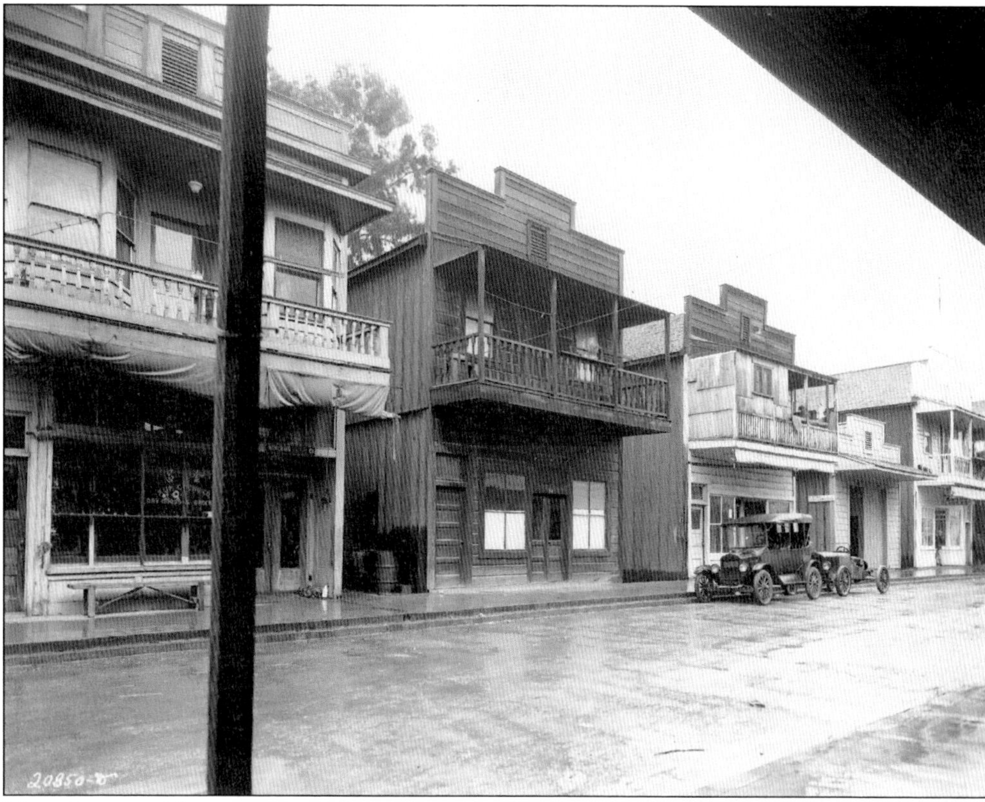

Main Street in Isleton, seen in 1926, reflects the town's once-burgeoning population of Chinese and Japanese immigrants. At left is the Kum Chong Company dry goods store. A disastrous Labor Day fire that year wiped out Main Street; everything had to be rebuilt. (Courtesy of the California History Room, California State Library.)

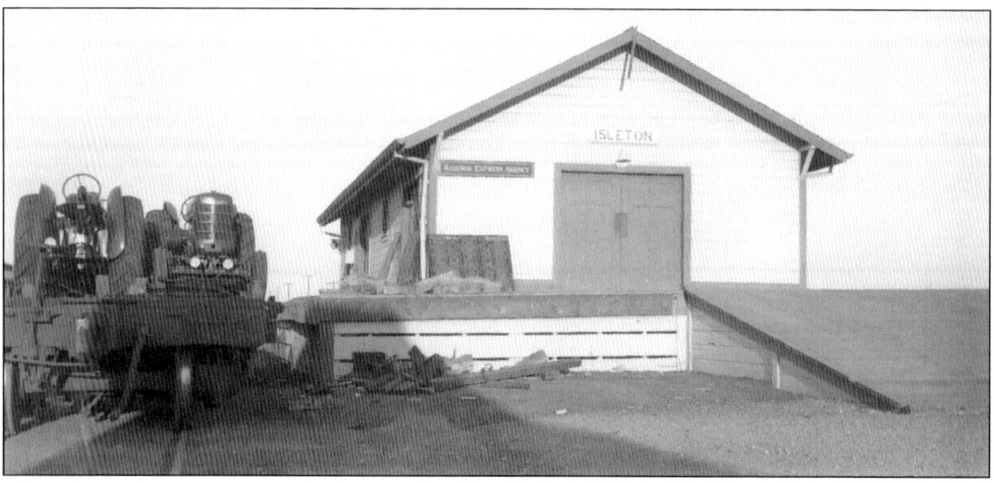

The Isleton depot stood near the southeastern edge of town, where Sixth Street is now. The depot contained a telegraph office and a Railway Express Agency office. Note the flatcar loaded with International Harvester tractors. According to John Perez, tractors were brought in by train for dealers such as Dolk and Gordon Hansen. (Courtesy of the Roy Graves Collection, Bancroft Library, University of California, Berkeley.)

The SP Sacramento Division timetable of December 1930 contained no major changes from the previous few years—with the notable exception of the line's new southern terminus. This was the extent of regular passenger service to Isleton, and it did not last long. (Courtesy of the California State Railroad Museum Library.)

EASTWARD			Time Table No. 141	WESTWARD	
FIRST CLASS			December 28, 1930		SECOND CLASS
Capacity of sidings in car lengths	532 Sacramento Isleton MIXED	Distance from San Francisco		Distance from Isleton	533 Isleton Sacramento MIXED
	Leave Daily		STATIONS		Arrive Daily
Terminal Yard WOTYPBK	8.30 AM	88.8	TO-R SACRAMENTO	32.4	s 5.55 PM
			0.5		
Yard		89.3	S. N. R. R. Crossing	31.9	
			0.3		
Yard P	8.35	89.6	JCT. SWITCH R STREET	31.6	5.50
			2.2		
Yard	f 8.42	91.8	BATHS	29.4	f 5.43
			2.4		
60	f 8.50	94.2	DEL RIO	27.0	f 5.35
			3.3		
60	f 9.00	97.5	FREEPORT	23.7	f 5.25
			7.8		
60 P	s 9.25	105.3	HOOD	17.3	s 5.00
			4.0		
55	f 9.38	107.9	LAMBERT	13.3	f 4.47
			3.3		
44	f	111.2	MOFUBA	10.0	f
			2.2		
Yard 61 PWY	s 9.55	113.4	TO-R WALNUT GROVE	7.8	s 4.30
			7.8		
Yard PWBY	s 10.30 AM	121.2	TO-R ISLETON	0.0	4.00 PM
	Arrive Daily		(32.4)		Leave Daily
	(2.00)		Time over District		(1.55)
	16.20		Average speed per hour		16.90

Additional Flag Stops to Receive or Discharge Passengers: Nos. 532 and 533 at Front and M Street, Sacramento, Charles, Pocket, Content, Cronin, Mosher, Acacia, Locke and Rosebud.

Additional Stations: Charles Mile Post 93.0, Pocket 96.4, Content 98.9, Cronin 100.1, Mosher 100.9, Acacia 102.6, Rosebud 103.3, Locke 112.6.

EASTWARD			Time Table No. 147	WESTWARD	
FIRST CLASS			April 24, 1932		SECOND CLASS
Capacity of Sidings in Car Lengths	520 Local Freight	Distance from San Francisco	Walnut Grove Branch	Distance from Isleton	529 Local Freight
	Leave Daily Ex. Sunday		STATIONS		Arrive Daily Ex. Sunday
Term. Yard WOTYPBK	3.00 PM	88.8	TO-R SACRAMENTO	32.4	9.10 PM
			0.5		
Yard		89.3	S. N. R. R. Crossing	31.9	
			0.3		
Yard P	3.05	89.6	JCT. SWITCH, R STREET	31.6	9.05
			2.2		
Yard		91.8	BATHS	29.4	8.55
			2.4		
60	3.20	94.2	DEL RIO	27.0	8.45
			3.3		
60	3.30	97.5	FREEPORT	23.7	8.35
			7.8		
60 P	3.55	105.3	HOOD	17.3	8.10
			4.0		
55	4.10	107.9	LAMBERT	13.3	7.45
			3.3		
44		111.2	MOFUBA	10.0	
			2.2		
Yard 61 PWY	4.25	113.4	TO WALNUT GROVE	7.8	7.30
			7.8		
Yard PWBY	5.00 PM	121.2	TO-R ISLETON	0.0	7.00 PM
	Arrive Daily Ex. Sunday		(32.4)		Leave Daily Ex. Sunday
	(2.00)		Time over District		(2.10)
	16.20		Average Speed per Hour		14.95

Additional Flag Stops to Receive or Discharge Passengers: Nos. 520 and 529 at Front and M Street, Sacramento, Charles, Pocket, Content, Cronin, Mosher, Acacia, Locke and Rosebud.

Additional Stations: Charles Mile Post 93.0, Pocket 96.4, Content 98.9, Cronin 100.1, Mosher 100.9, Acacia 102.6, Rosebud 103.3, Locke 112.6.

In 1932, owing to the Great Depression and the rise of the automobile, regular passenger service on the Walnut Grove Branch was discontinued. This was the only scheduled freight train on the branch, though extra trains could be called when harvest seasons were at their peak. (Courtesy of the California State Railroad Museum Library.)

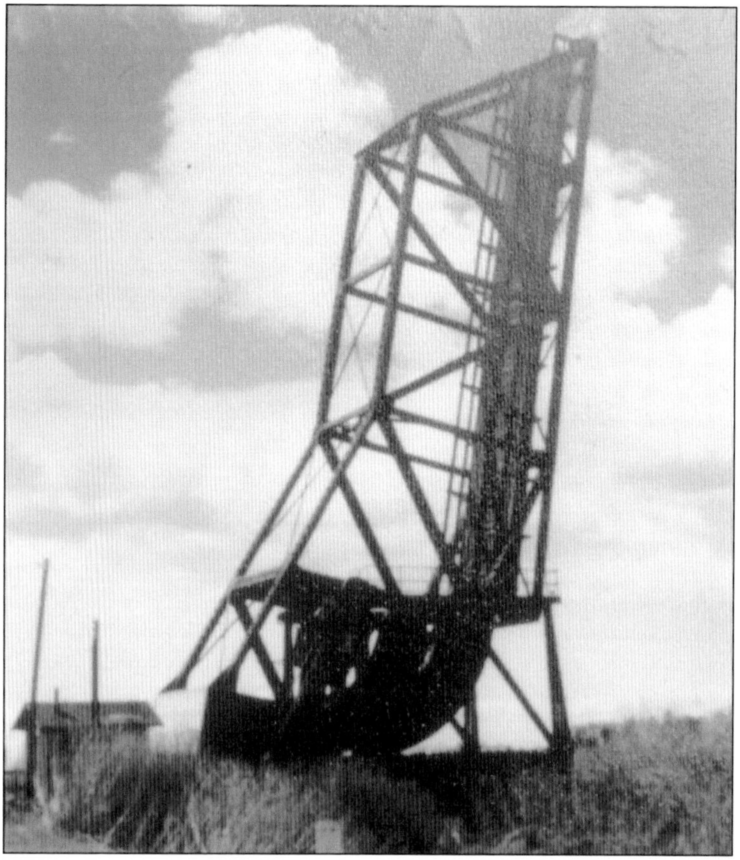

The Walnut Grove Branch reached Isleton by way of a lift bridge over the Georgiana Slough, which carried the tracks from Tyler Island to Andrus Island. Note the SP herald on the bridge's counterweight. Since rail traffic on the branch was relatively light, the bridge was normally left open to allow for unrestricted boat traffic and would be lowered as necessary. As with the Snodgrass Slough Bridge, this span was dismantled after the Walnut Grove Branch was abandoned. (Both photographs courtesy of the Sacramento River Delta Historical Society.)

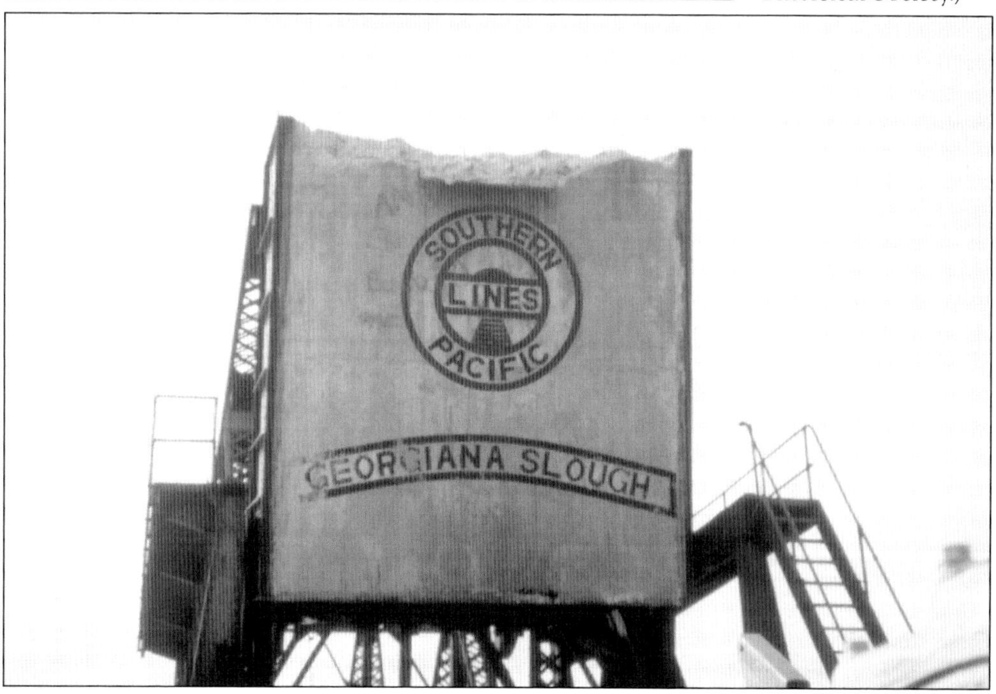

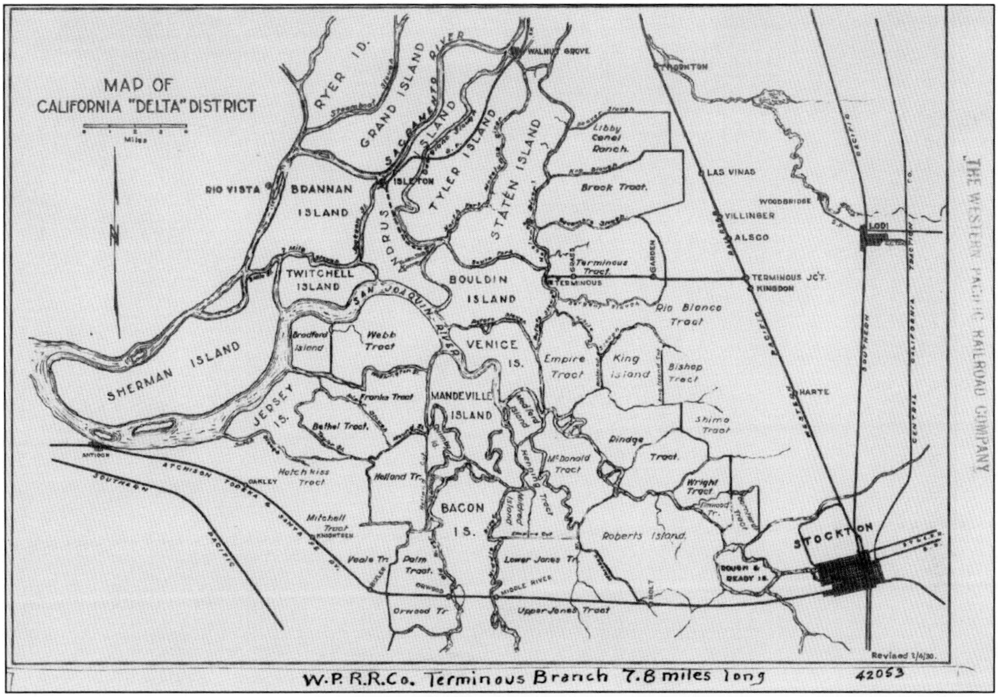

This *c.* 1930 map shows the proximity of the Southern Pacific's Walnut Grove Branch at Walnut Grove and Isleton to the Santa Fe's railhead at Antioch and the Western Pacific's Terminous wharf. All served the burgeoning delta agricultural trade. Of the three, only the Santa Fe's line through Antioch is still active, now part of the Burlington Northern Santa Fe Railway. (Courtesy of the BAERA Archives Collection/Western Railway Museum.)

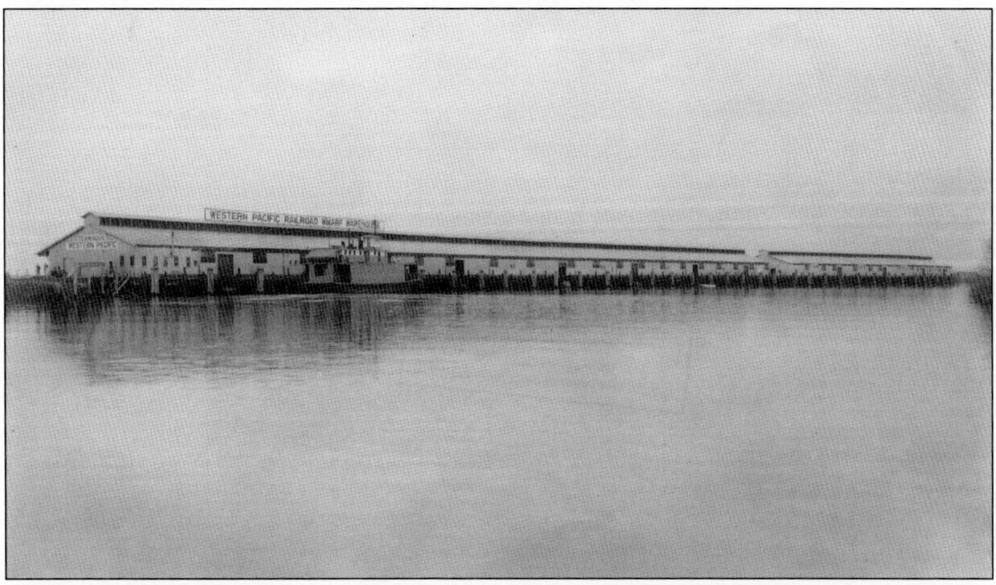

About 5 miles to the east of the Walnut Grove Branch's ultimate reach stood the Western Pacific's wharf at Terminous, on Potato Slough. This wharf was reached by a spur from the WP's own Sacramento-Stockton main line. (Courtesy of the BAERA Archives Collection/Western Railway Museum.)

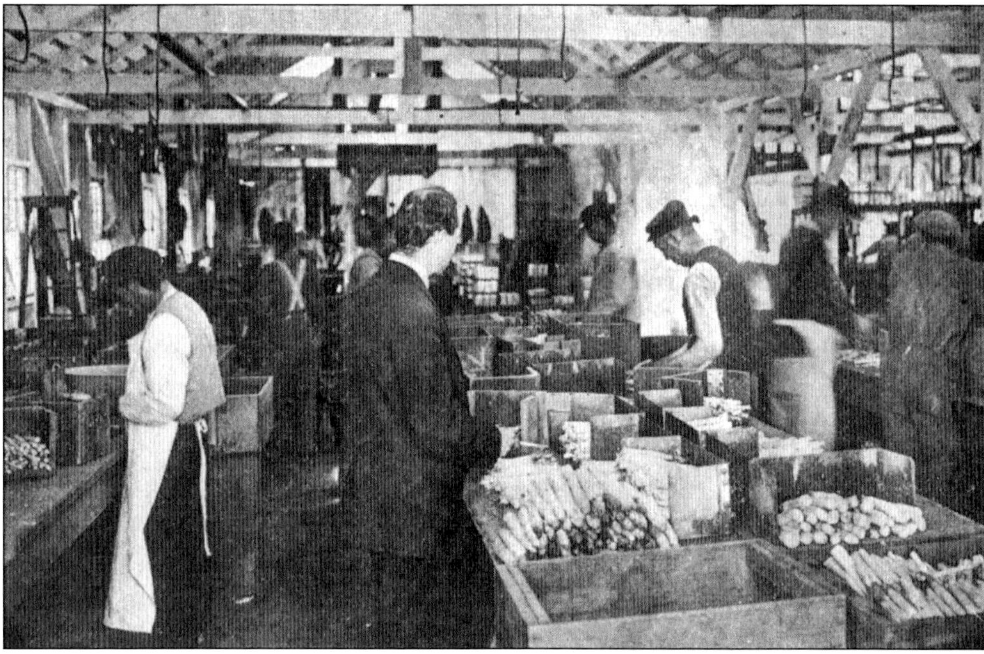

Asparagus was, and still is, a prime delta crop. (Stockton, for example, celebrates the vegetable with an annual Asparagus Festival.) Packing sheds, such as these, would either box up fresh asparagus for shipment or can the spears for longer shelf life. Ice-cooled refrigerator cars made it possible for railroads to move these goods to markets around the country while keeping them fresh. (Above, courtesy of the Isleton Brannan-Andrus Historical Society; below, the California History Room, California State Library.)

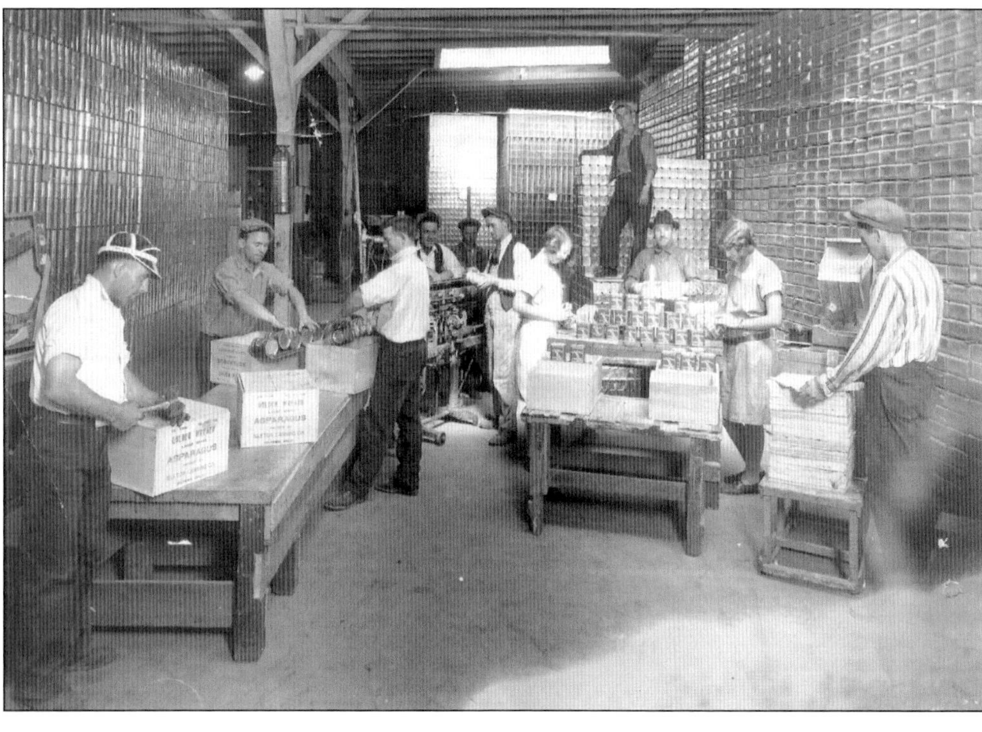

Eight

Decline and Abandonment

From the 1950s onward, it was all downhill for the Walnut Grove Branch. The first segment abandoned was the spur from Isleton to the Golden State cannery in 1951, only 20 years after it was built. As in much of the country, trucks began taking more and more of the traffic off the rails. By the early 1970s, train operations were down to several trips per week. Then Mother Nature got involved. Early on the morning of June 21, 1972, a levee break led to a disastrous flood that nearly wiped out Isleton. Among other things, the SP's facilities on Andrus Island were heavily damaged. Never again did a Southern Pacific train operate to Isleton, although the city remained in SP's timetable until 1977.

In June 1975, with the flood having caused business to dry up, the SP filed to abandon the branch from Hood Junction to Isleton. Despite a protest from the city of Isleton, the Interstate Commerce Commission approved the application. This abandonment took effect in 1977. In July 1976, SP filed to abandon the Miller Park–Hood Junction segment of the line. A protest was received from fruit canner Del Monte Corporation, but it came to naught, as the ICC approved this abandonment, too. The SP, however, was told to keep the right-of-way intact in case the California Department of Parks and Recreation was interested in acquiring it. The last SP train to Hood Junction operated on October 10, 1978. Only the Old Sacramento–Miller Park portion of the line remained active, and that was mainly to store freight cars in need of minor repairs. Otherwise, the onetime would-be main line to San Francisco was left to rust in the weeds.

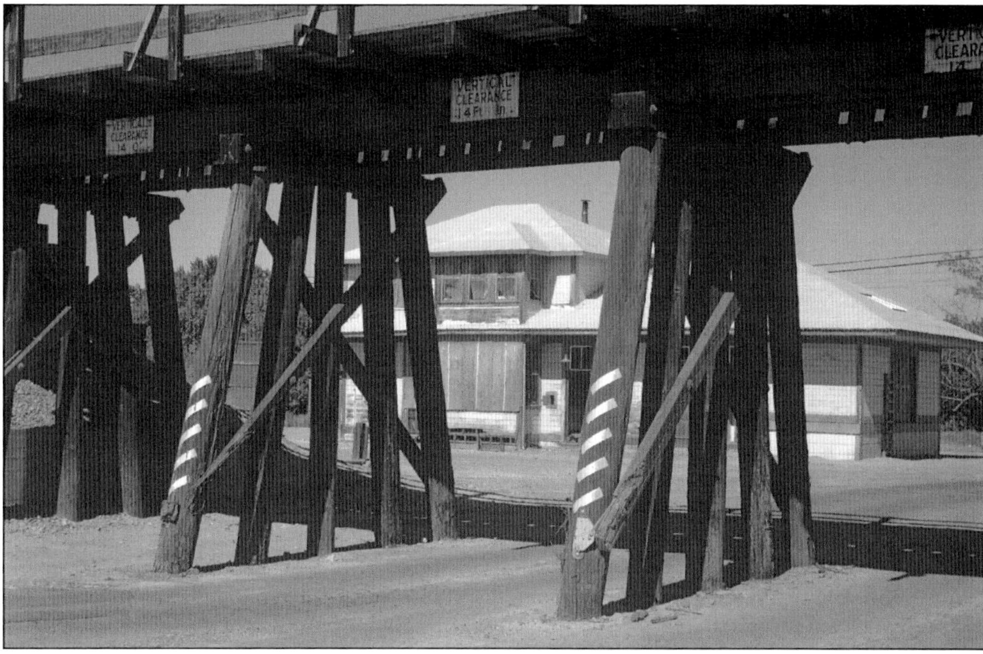

The Walnut Grove depot had been taken out of service and boarded up by the fall of 1973. Photographer Marilyn Sommerdorf reports that, dissatisfied with the lighting, she went back a few days later to reshoot this photograph. Too late—Walnut Grove's depot had been demolished. (Photograph by Marilyn Sommerdorf.)

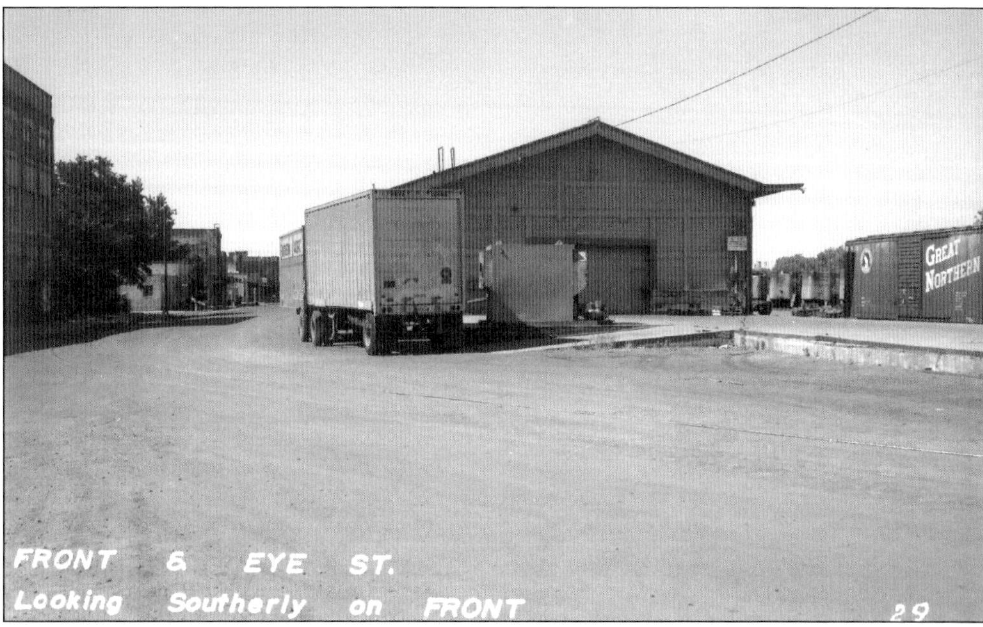

By 1969, Sacramento's waterfront had devolved into a skid row of wide renown. This photograph is one of many made for the city's redevelopment department. The Southern Pacific freight shed, seen from the intersection of Front and I Streets, is still in business—but not for long. Note that the truck trailers outnumber the railcars. (Courtesy of the Sacramento Archives and Museum Collection Center.)

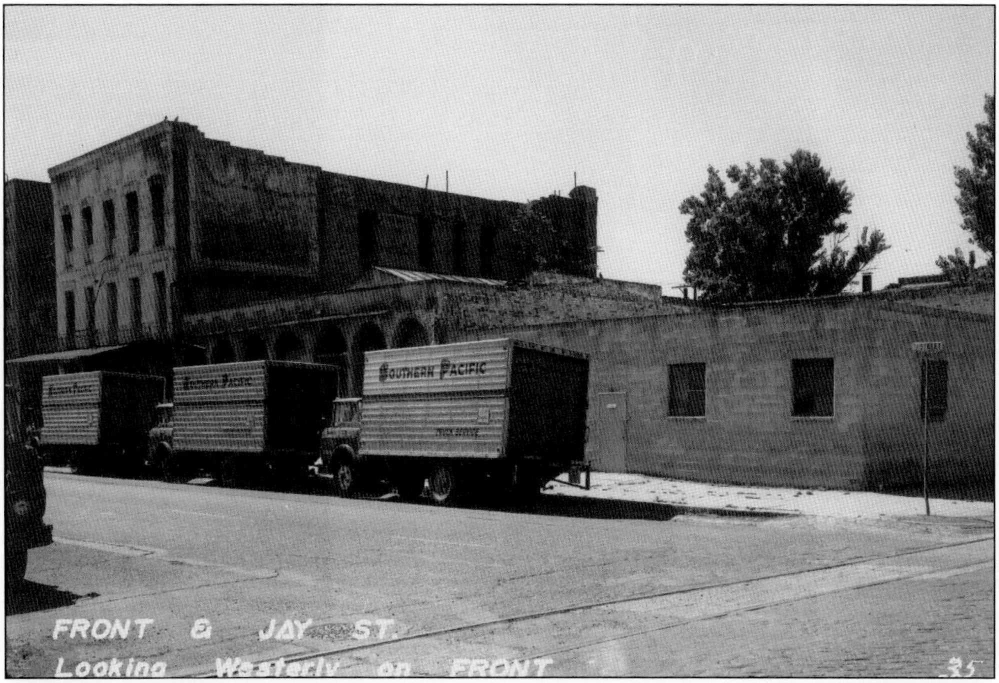

The scene at Front and J Streets was not much better. At least the Southern Pacific is still in business, even if all of the vehicles seen here are of the rubber-tire variety. (Courtesy of the Sacramento Archives and Museum Collection Center.)

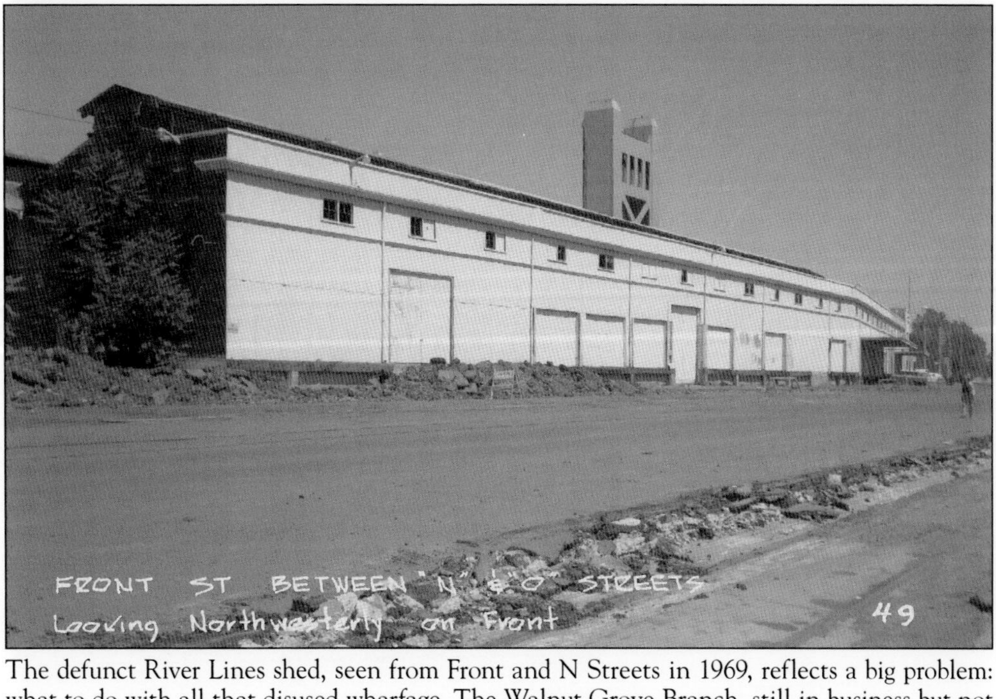

The defunct River Lines shed, seen from Front and N Streets in 1969, reflects a big problem: what to do with all that disused wharfage. The Walnut Grove Branch, still in business but not very busy, can be seen in the pavement. A public promenade now occupies this spot. (Courtesy of the Sacramento Archives and Museum Collection Center.)

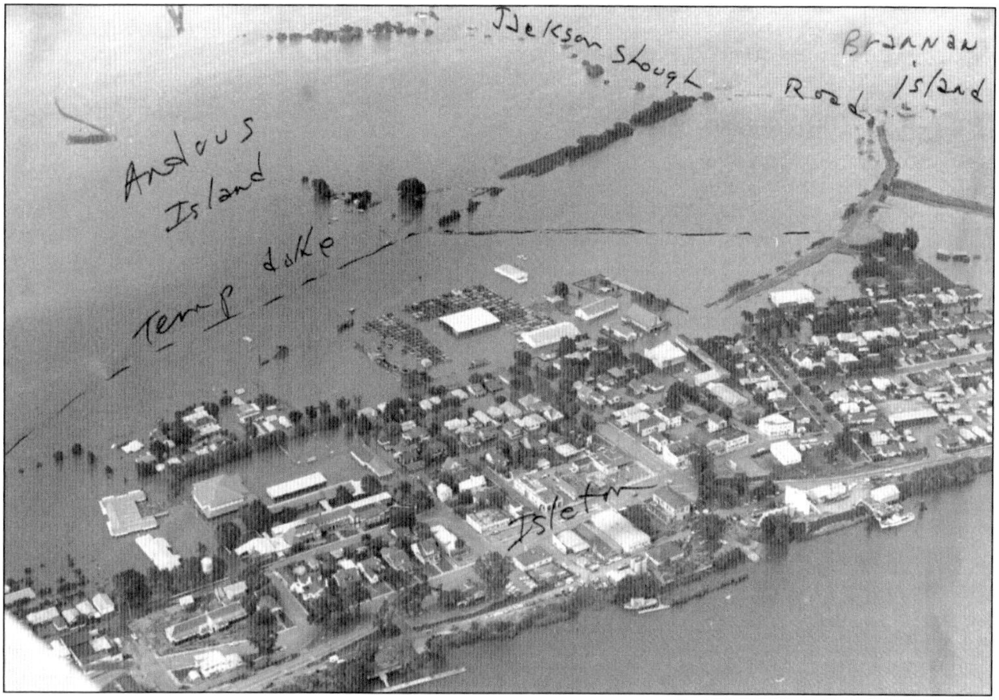

Just after 1:00 a.m. on June 21, 1972, a levee under repair broke, inundating most of Isleton. The flooded Heinz pickle plant is at center; all of the Southern Pacific's trackage is underwater. The Sacramento River is at bottom. (*Sacramento Bee* photograph, courtesy of the Sacramento Archives and Museum Collection Center.)

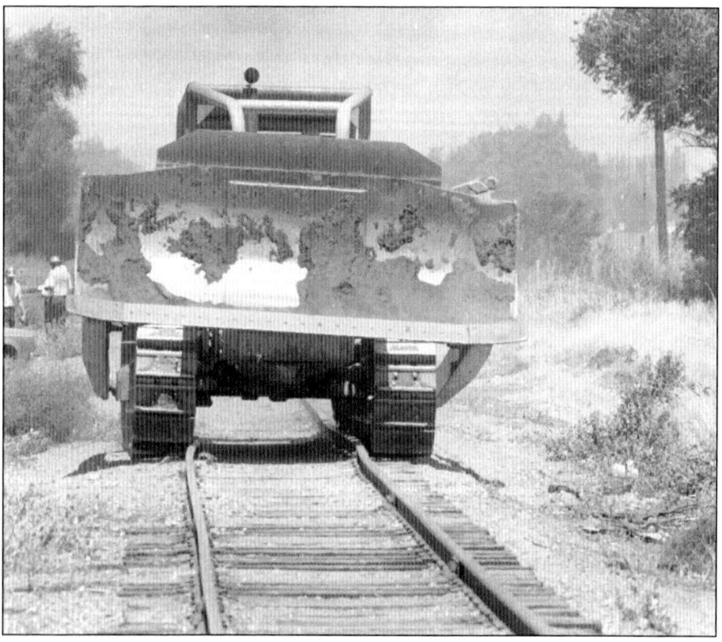

A bulldozer travels along the Southern Pacific's tracks on Andrus Island en route to flood cleanup operations. The floods brought SP operations in Isleton to a permanent halt. (*Sacramento Bee* photograph, courtesy of the Sacramento Archives and Museum Collection Center.)

	Walnut Grove Branch		
89.0 88.7	Yd. Lmts. BKIYPQ TO-R **SACRAMENTO**	23050	33.2
97.5	8.8 **FREEPORT**	23214	24.4
104.6	7.1 **HOOD JCT.**	23221	17.3
113.4	Yd. Lmts. 8.8 **WALNUT GROVE**	23243	8.5
121.9	8.5 **ISLETON**	23250	0.0
	(33.2)		

This Sacramento Division timetable entry from 1977 represents the last time Isleton and Walnut Grove would appear as stations on Southern Pacific's Walnut Grove Branch. That year, the Hood Junction–Isleton portion of the line was abandoned. Much of the right-of-way has since been sold. (Courtesy of the California State Railroad Museum Library.)

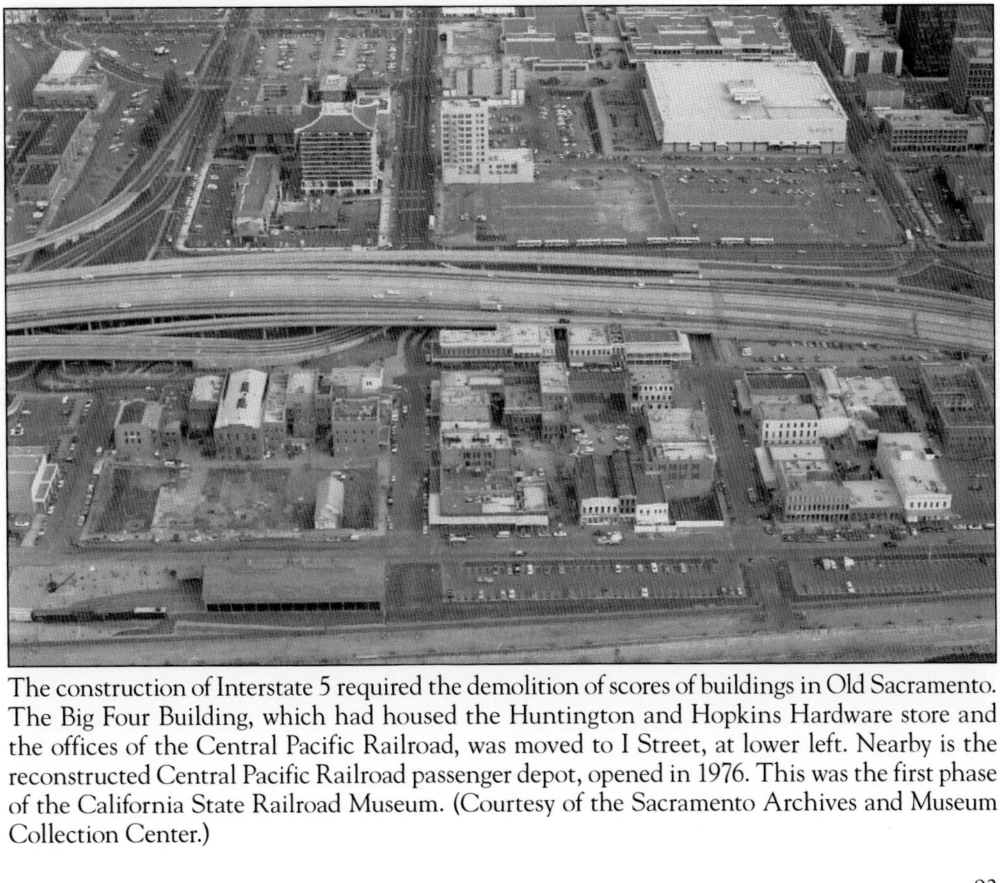

The construction of Interstate 5 required the demolition of scores of buildings in Old Sacramento. The Big Four Building, which had housed the Huntington and Hopkins Hardware store and the offices of the Central Pacific Railroad, was moved to I Street, at lower left. Nearby is the reconstructed Central Pacific Railroad passenger depot, opened in 1976. This was the first phase of the California State Railroad Museum. (Courtesy of the Sacramento Archives and Museum Collection Center.)

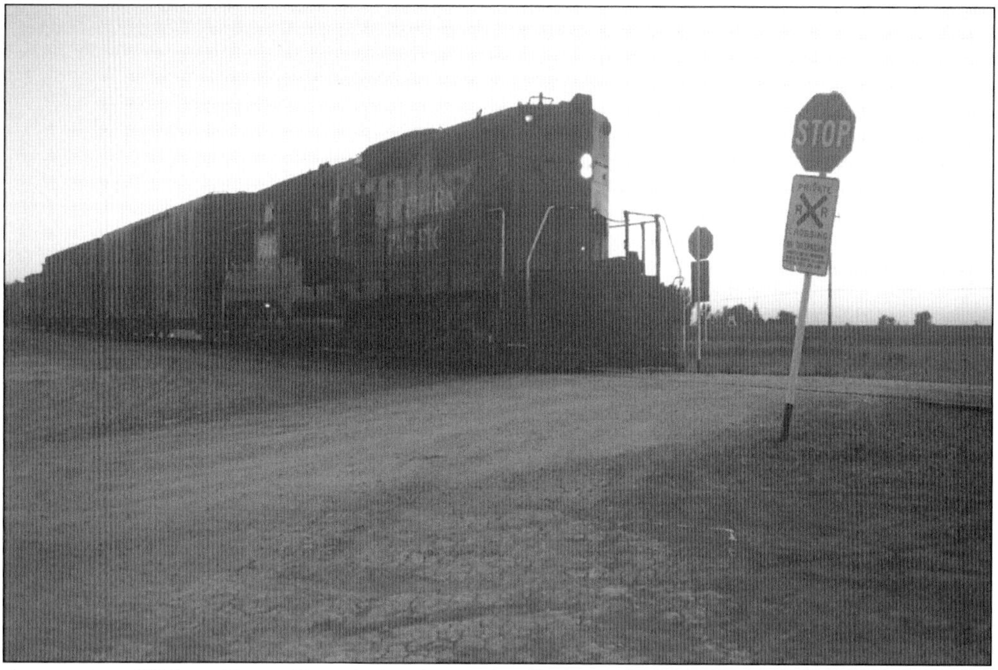

A very short Walnut Grove Branch freight train rolls toward Sacramento just north of Freeport about 1976. Between the GP9 locomotive and the caboose are two boxcars. The private crossing leads to the Klotz family's property near the river. (Photograph by Marilyn Sommerdorf.)

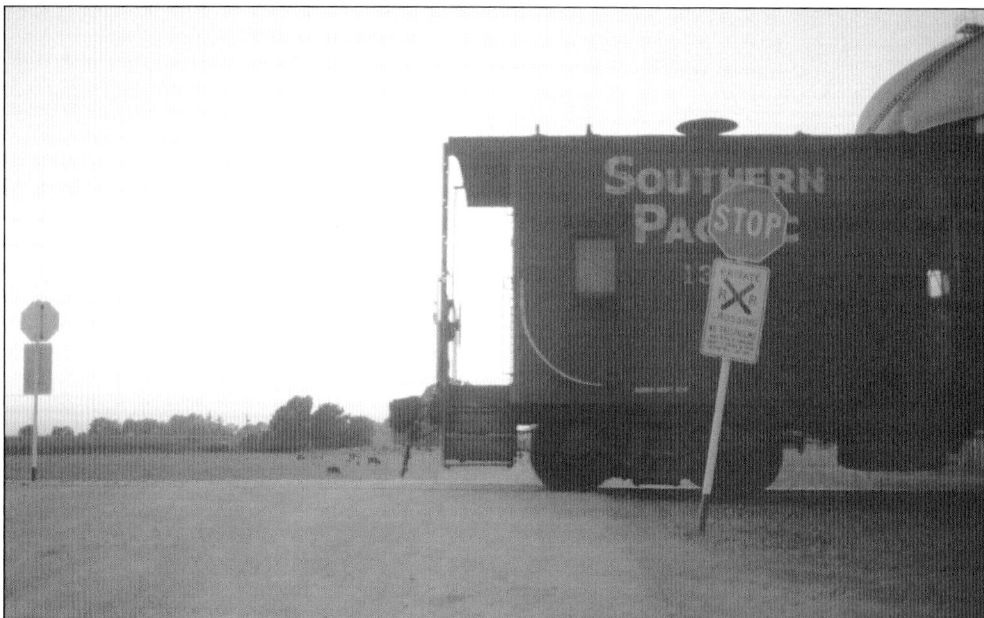

The short freight's caboose rolls through the Klotz crossing. Southern Pacific made heavy use of bay window cabooses, where trainmen watched over their train from bay windows extending from the side rather than a cupola up top. The increasing height of freight cars obscured trainmen's view from above. (Photograph by Marilyn Sommerdorf.)

The Sacramento Division timetable of January 9, 1978, marked the final appearance of the Walnut Grove Branch in a Southern Pacific timetable. Hood Junction is now the end of the line. Most of the remaining portion will be abandoned before the year is over. (Courtesy of the California State Railroad Museum Library.)

EAST-WARD ↓ Mile Post Location	STATIONS SIDING CAPACITIES AND FACILITIES	Station Number	WEST-WARD Distance
	Walnut Grove Branch		
89.0 88.7	Yd. Lmts. BKIYPQ R **SACRAMENTO**	23050	16.8
	8.8		
97.5	**FREEPORT**	23214	8.0
	8.0		
104.6	**HOOD JCT.**	23226	0.0
	(**33.2**)		

ADDITIONAL STATIONS

Capacity and Direction of entry into spurs		Mile Post	NAME	Station Number
			Walnut Grove Branch	
..	..	91.8	Baths....................	23204
..	..	94.2	Del Rio................	23208

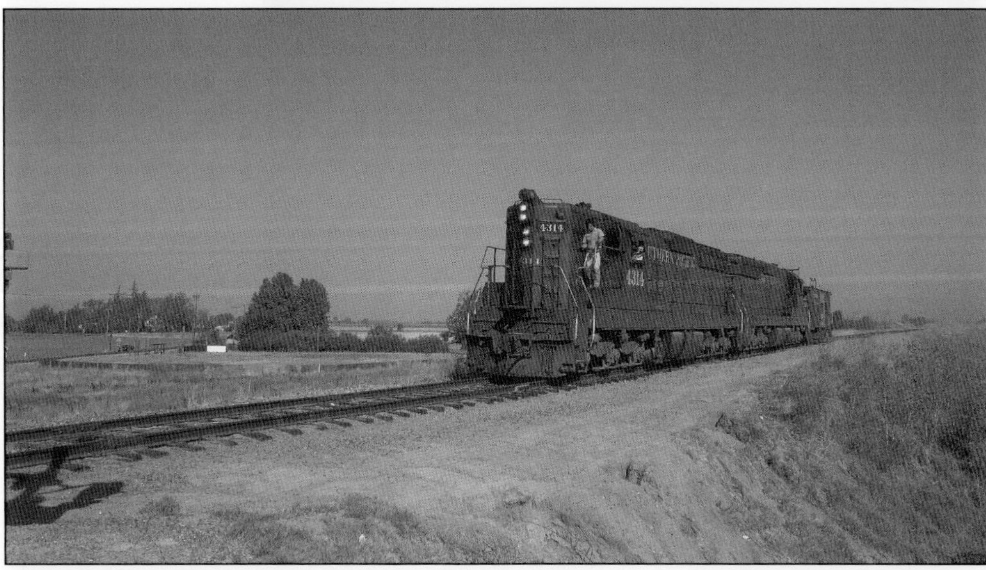

This is the beginning of the end. It is October 10, 1978, and two Southern Pacific locomotives have traveled from Sacramento to Hood Junction to gather up the derelict freight cars and take them home, bringing down the curtain on the Walnut Grove Branch. These locomotives are SD9's (Special Duty), built by General Motors' Electro-Motive Division. Their smooth ride earned them the nickname "Cadillacs." (Photograph by Marilyn Sommerdorf.)

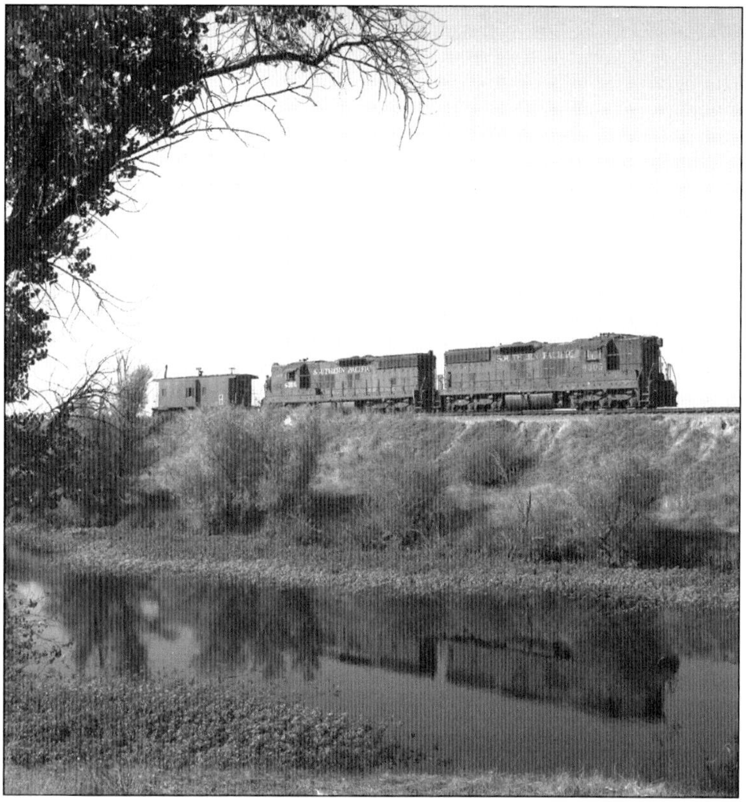

The SP locomotives have run around their caboose at Hood Junction in preparation for coupling onto the string of derelicts, out of the picture to the left. The waterway in the foreground is a slough created long ago by a dredger operating in the area. (Photograph by Marilyn Sommerdorf, courtesy of the California State Railroad Museum Library.)

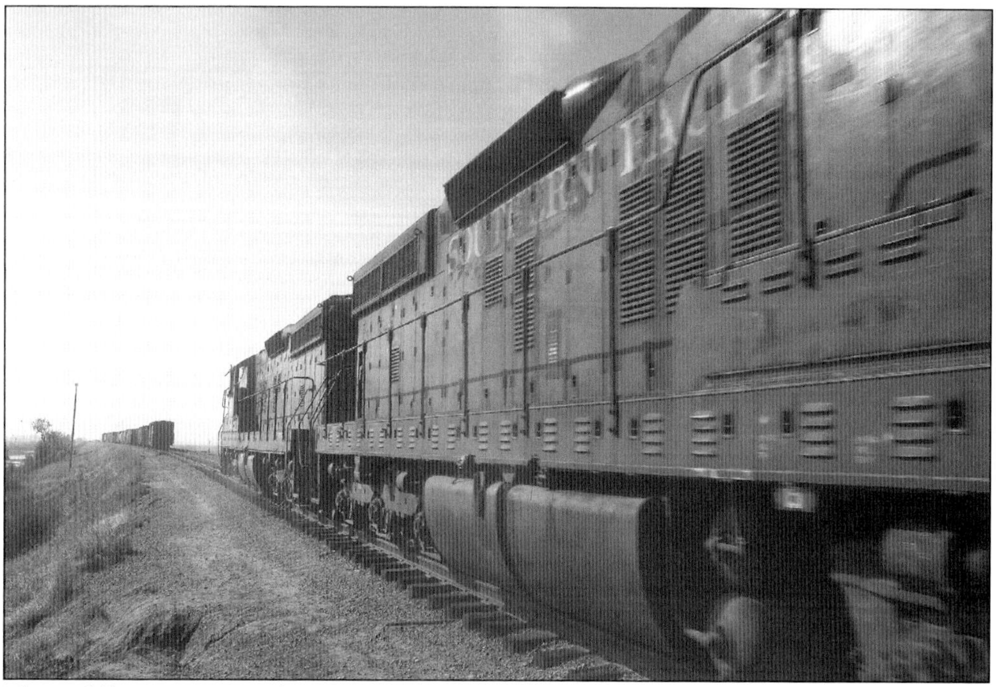

The Cadillacs move toward a cut of cars at Hood Junction to couple up. (Photograph by Marilyn Sommerdorf, courtesy of the California State Railroad Museum Library.)

With all of the derelicts coupled into one train, the Southern Pacific's last Walnut Grove Branch train prepares to head for home. The mostly hidden caboose is in an unusual spot: sandwiched between the locomotives and the rest of the train. (Photograph by Marilyn Sommerdorf, courtesy of the California State Railroad Museum Library.)

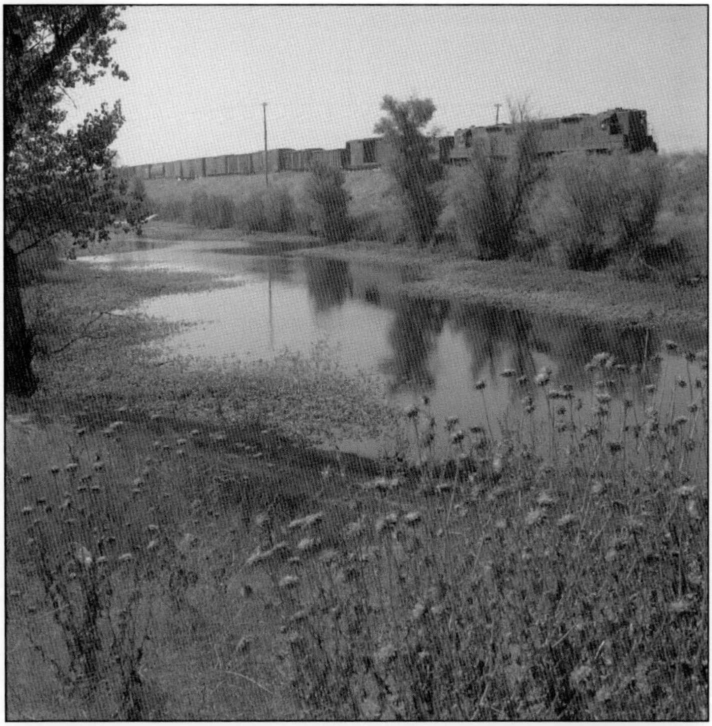

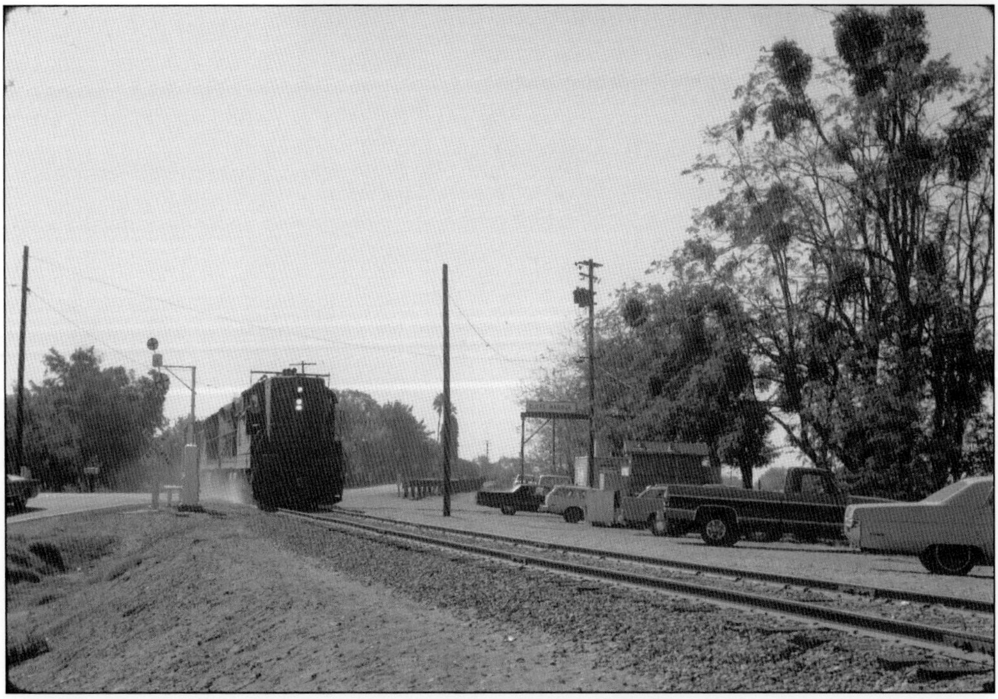

The last train on the old Sacramento Southern Railroad/Walnut Grove Branch crosses River Road near Cliff's Marina, south of Freeport. The grade crossing signal is known as a wigwag, or a "mechanical flagman." The wigwag's red light comes on and the signal "wags" to warn motorists of the train's approach. (Photograph by Marilyn Sommerdorf.)

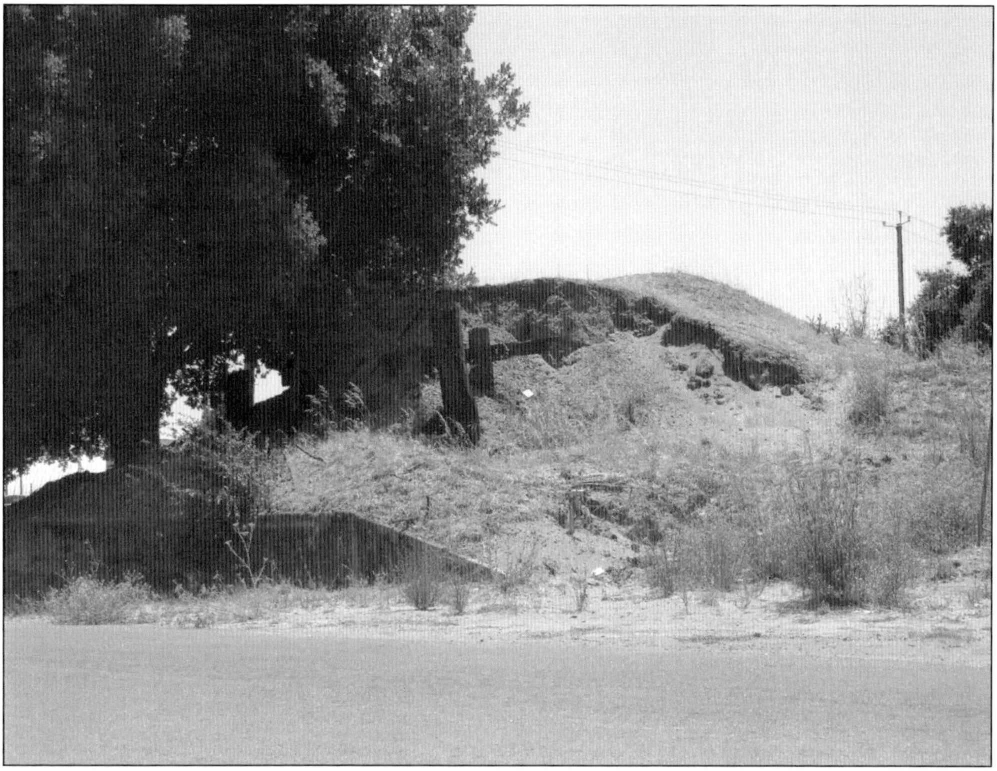

Thirty-one years after the last train left Walnut Grove, this is about all that remains of the old embankment at Depot Road. A parking lot, a street extension, and a park now occupy much of the old right-of-way. (Photograph by author.)

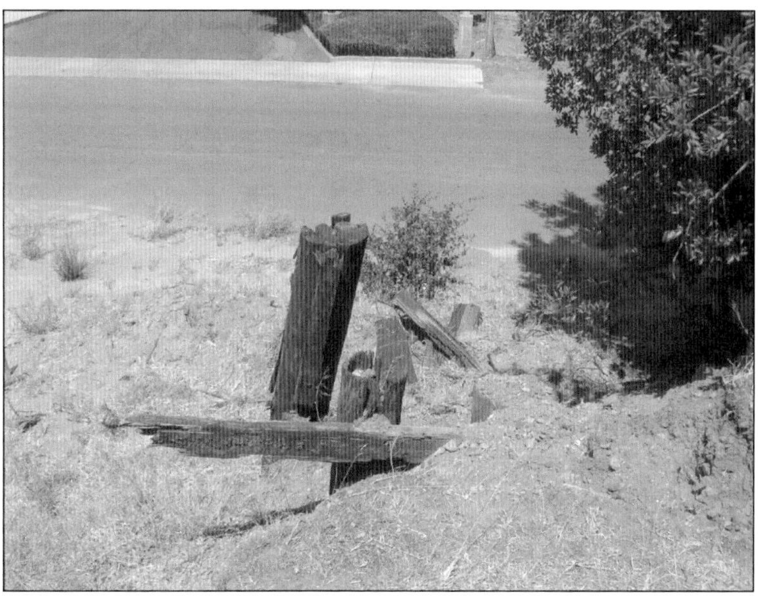

Pieces of the trestle that used to carry Sacramento Southern Railroad/Walnut Grove Branch trains over Depot Road are still visible, testifying to the town's railroading past. (Photograph by author.)

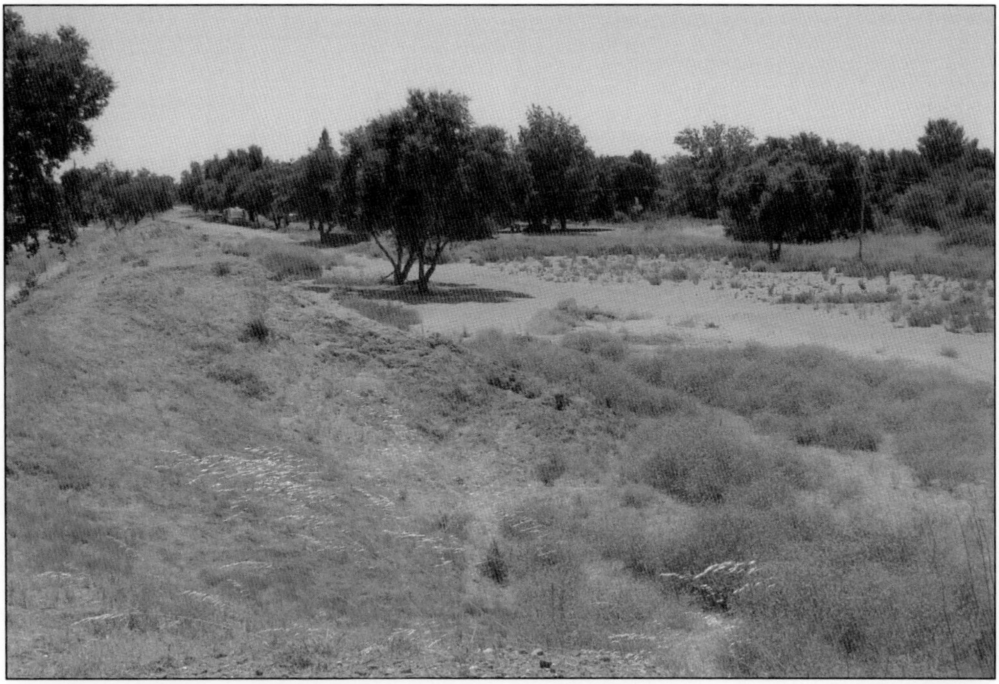

Atop the embankment in July 2008, one sees only empty land and weeds where once the Walnut Grove depot stood, at right. Tracks continued south on the land at left. Compare this with the view of the depot at the bottom of page 72. (Photograph by author.)

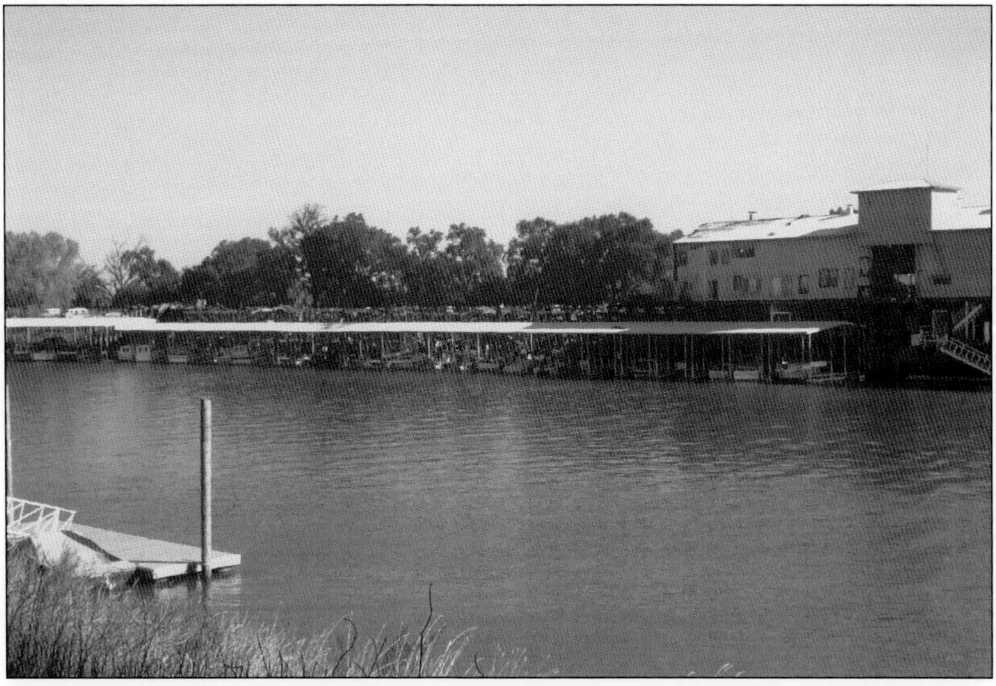

The wharf and packing shed at Locke remained standing long after the Southern Pacific left town. About half of the shed burned down in 1988; this was the scene after the fire was extinguished. (Photograph by Marilyn Sommerdorf.)

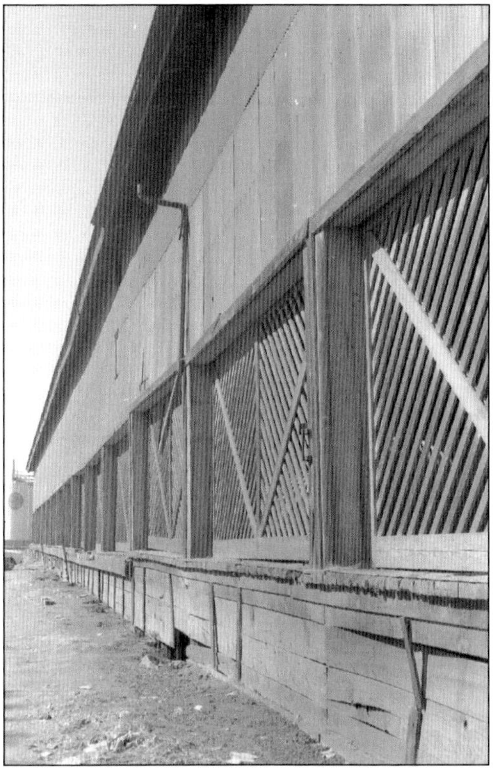

The remaining half of the Locke shed still stands today; it is now a privately owned boathouse. A visitor to the area today can still see rails in the ground across River Road from the shed. (Left, courtesy of the Sacramento Archives and Museum Collection Center; below, photograph by author.)

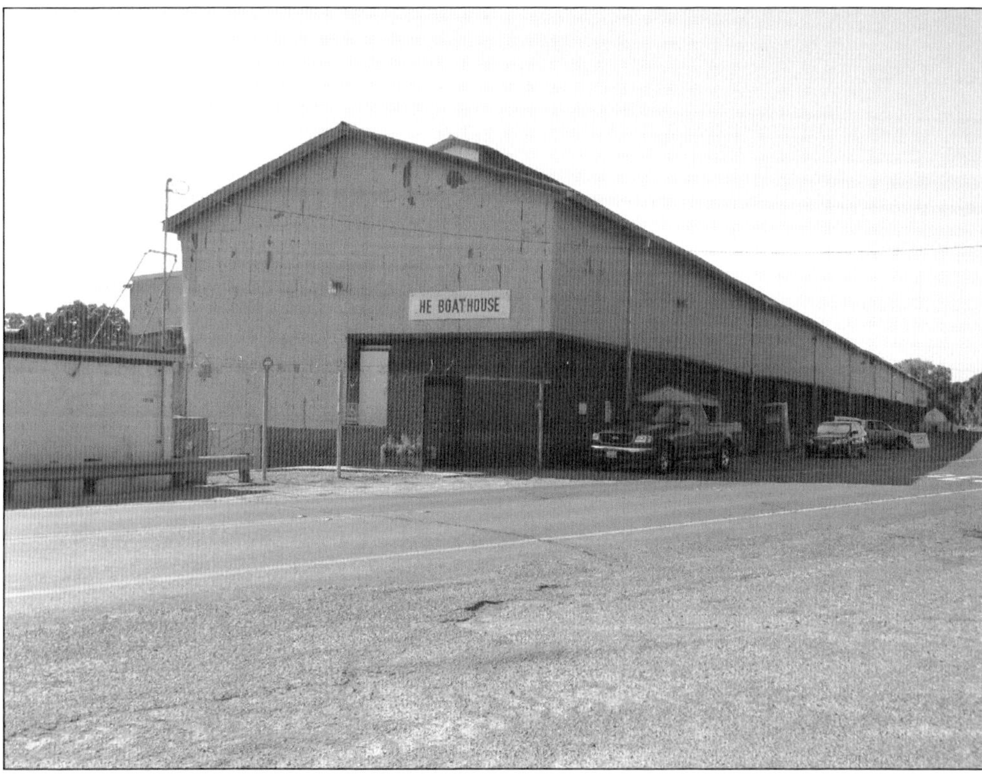

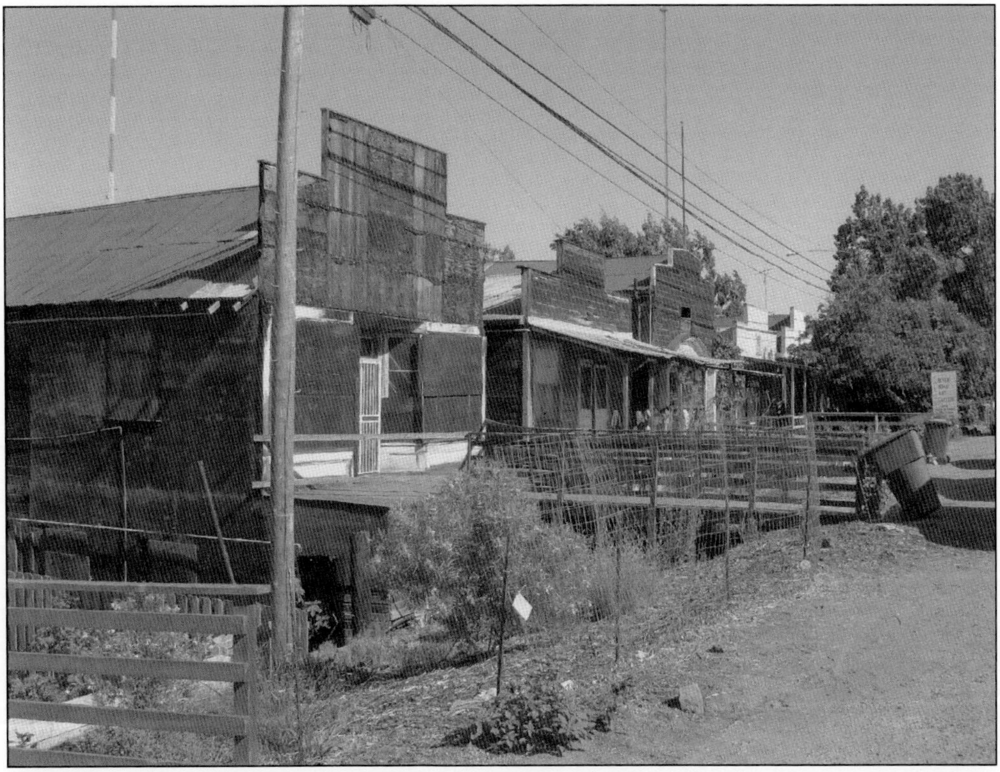

Many of Locke's buildings still stand in various states of repair. The town is now very sleepy, a contrast to its heyday as a bustling Chinatown. (Photograph by author.)

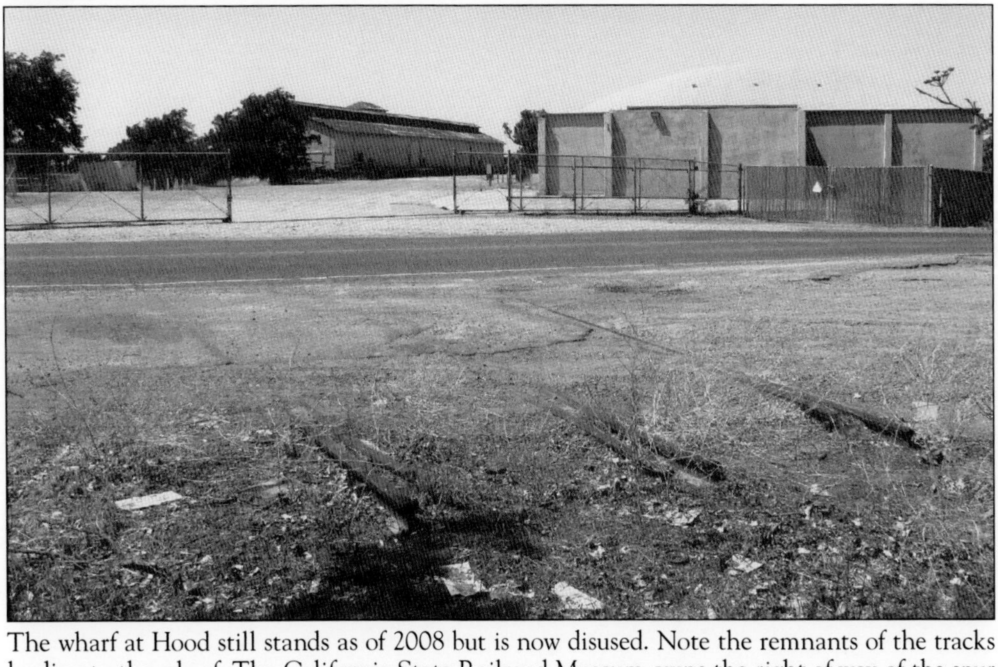

The wharf at Hood still stands as of 2008 but is now disused. Note the remnants of the tracks leading to the wharf. The California State Railroad Museum owns the right-of-way of the spur from Hood Junction, although most of the tracks have been pulled up. (Photograph by author.)

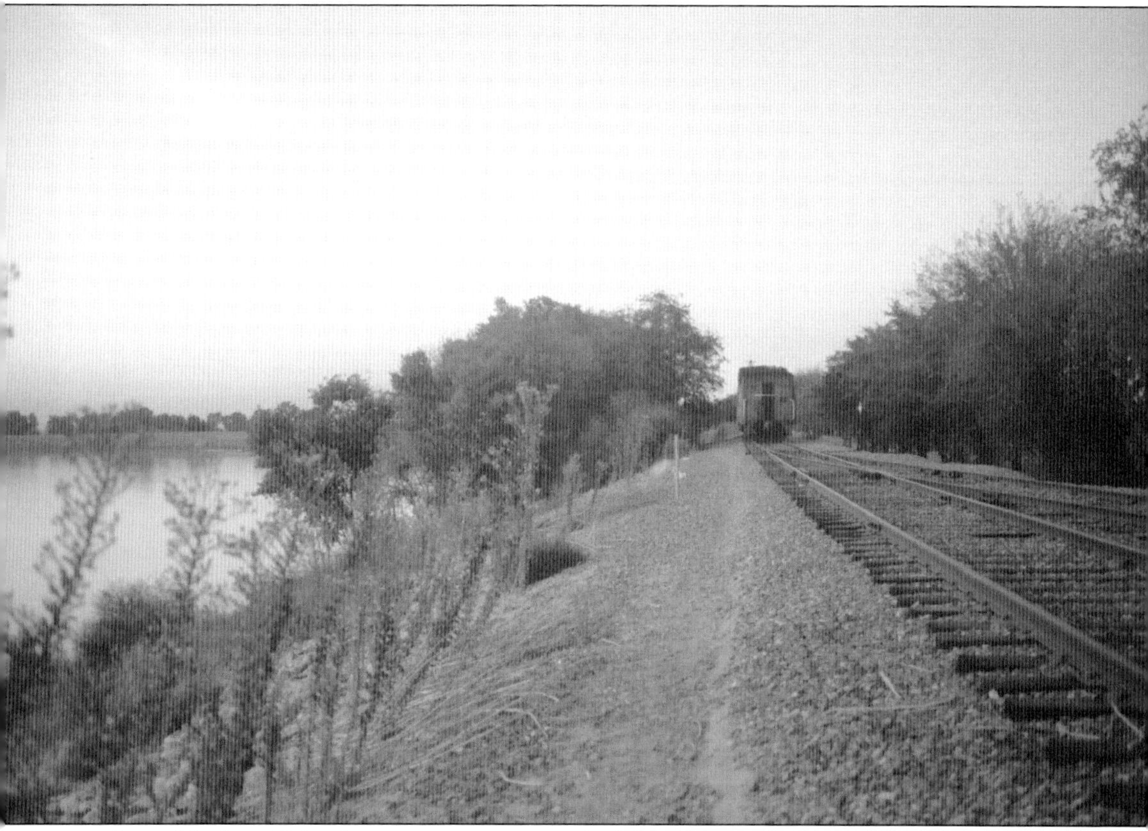

One of the last SP freight trains to operate on the Walnut Grove Branch rolls north past Freeport with the Sacramento River at left. Times may have looked bleak for the Walnut Grove Branch, but as seen in the next two chapters, the story is not over. (Photograph by Marilyn Sommerdorf.)

Nine

Revival

Even as the SP was leaving the scene, the Walnut Grove Branch was being eyed as a potential heritage railway. Two studies were commissioned to investigate the possibility of such an operation. One, produced in April 1979 by Sacramento State University professor Cary J. Goulard, solicited the public's opinion about the idea of a steam-train ride out of Old Sacramento and found the reception positive. Another, put together by International Engineering Company of San Francisco and released in June 1979, investigated the possibility of reviving the abandoned portion of the branch all the way to Isleton under the working title "Old Sacramento Railway." The opening of the California State Railroad Museum's main building in 1981 was celebrated with a huge Railfair in Old Sacramento. Visiting locomotives would often venture to the remnant of the Walnut Grove Branch south of Old Sacramento for layover and servicing. After Railfair, plans for excursion trains began to come together. The program assembled by Walter Gray, Terry Stefani, Mark Spellman, Cathy Taylor, and Dick Noonan called for all volunteer crew members to serve as car attendants. In addition, volunteers could also train for brakeman and fireman positions. Initially engineers came from the ranks of active and retired locomotive "hoggers;" now all of the Sacramento Southern's engineers are volunteers who must meet the same federal training and licensing requirements as their Union Pacific and Amtrak counterparts. About 1985, the Sacramento Southern Railroad name—disused since the corporation's dissolution in 1916—was resurrected. Though trains presently operate only between Old Sacramento and Baths, extension of service to Hood Junction (or even Hood itself) has long been contemplated. As of August 2008, the California State Railroad Museum is investigating several possibilities for service to Hood.

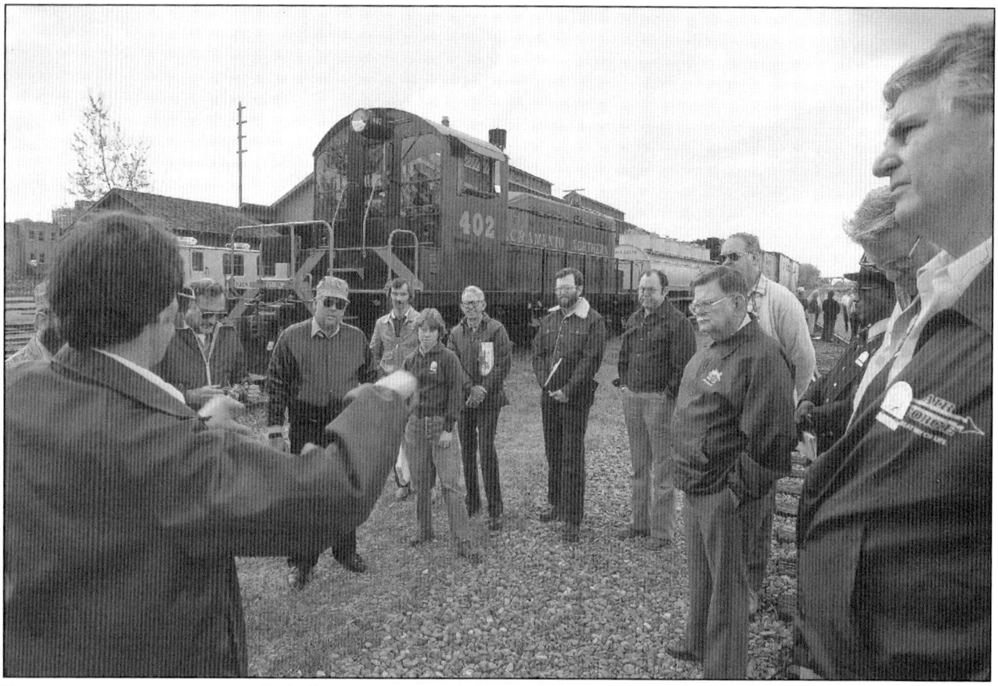

Extensive training preceded the opening of the California State Railroad Museum's excursion service. Potential brakemen spent many hours learning the basics of the trade, such as hand signals and how to operate switches, some of 19th-century design. Today, as in the past, brakeman is the beginning level of the operating crew; from brakeman, crew members are eligible to move into train service (conductor) or engine service (engine helper, fireman, engineer) positions. (Both Richard H. Denison photographs, courtesy of the California State Railroad Museum Library.)

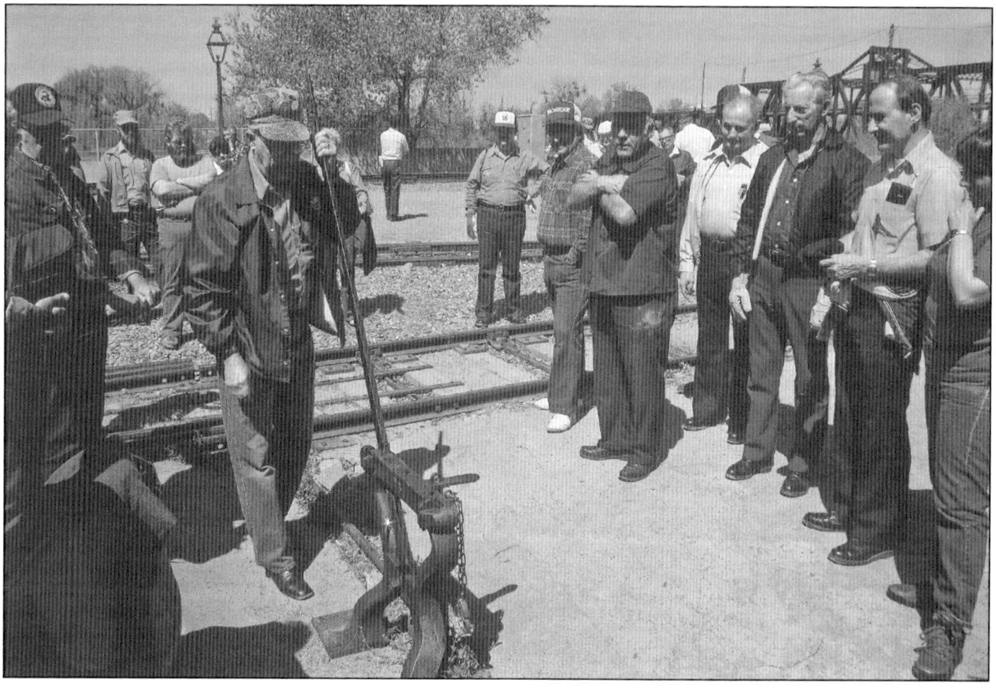

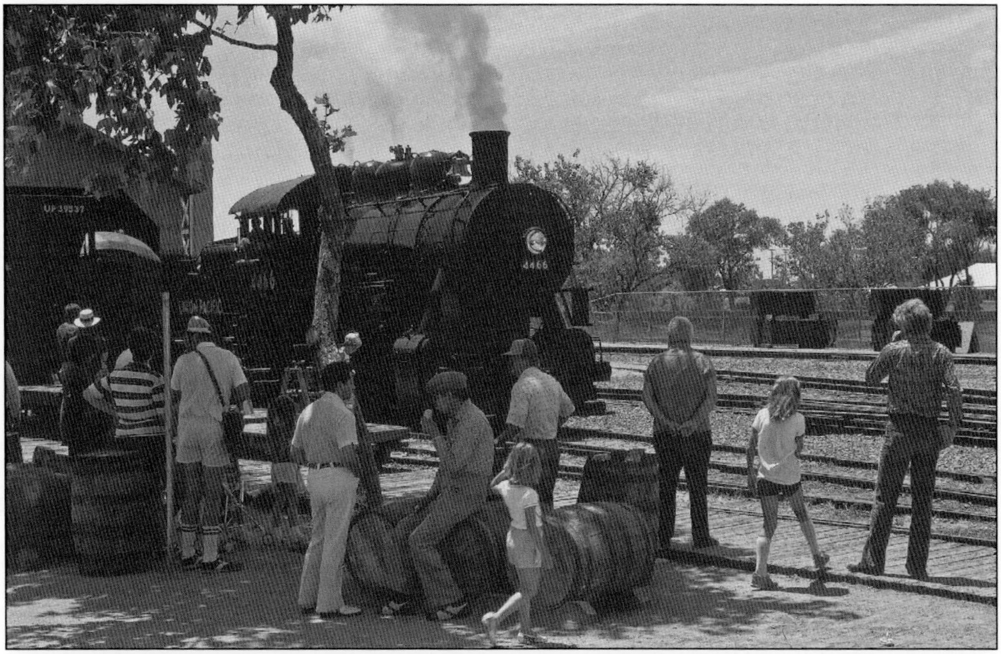

This is it! The hard work and training paid off on June 2, 1984, with the operation of the California State Railroad Museum's first volunteer-operated excursion trains. Power was provided by the Union Pacific No. 4466, a coal-fired steam switcher built in 1920 by Lima Locomotive Works of Lima, Ohio. The cars—two ex-SP coaches and two former boxcars converted to open-air excursion cars—remain in service today. (Courtesy of the California State Railroad Museum Library.)

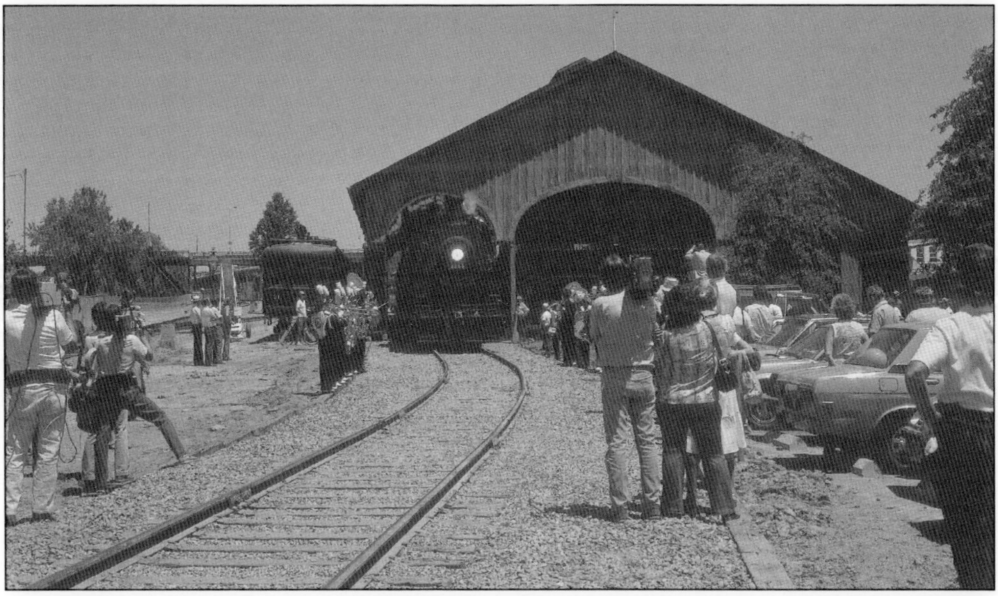

The 4466 and train roll south out of the Central Pacific passenger station amid much fanfare, including an appearance by the University of California band. The excursion trains initially used the rebuilt 1876 passenger depot; today's Sacramento Southern trains use the Central Pacific freight depot, which was reconstructed in the late 1980s where the parking lot stands, at right. The 4466 is rolling past the foot of J Street. (Courtesy of the California State Railroad Museum Library.)

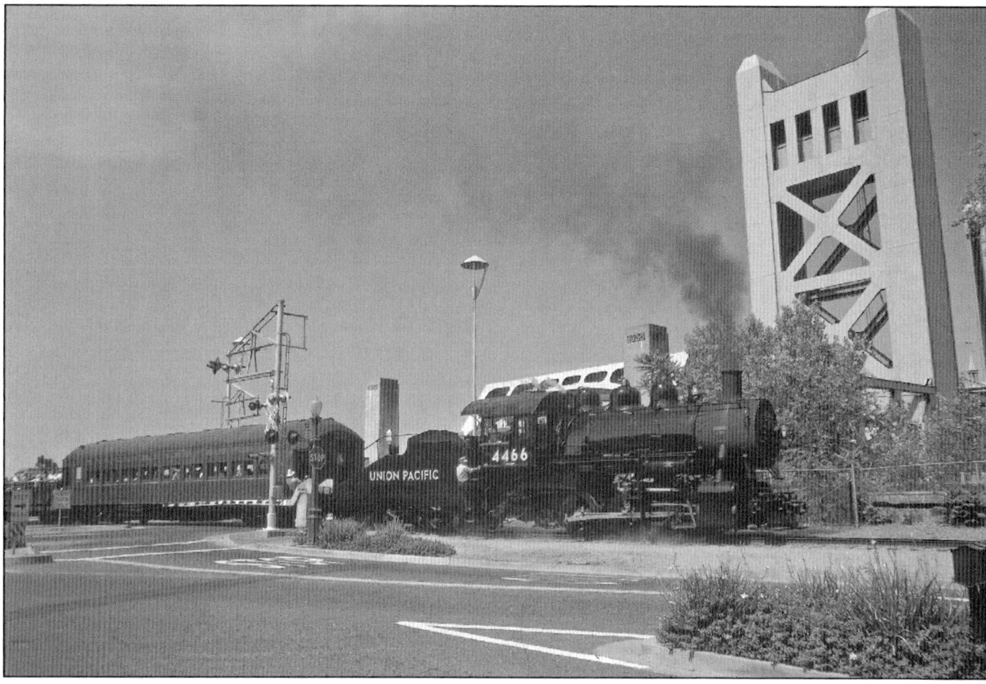

The 4466 rumbles north across Capitol Mall past Tower Bridge. The coach is a former Southern Pacific "Harriman" coach, so called because the design was conceived while Edward H. Harriman was president of the Union Pacific and Southern Pacific Railroads during the first decade of the 20th century. This car is a veteran of, among other things, the SP's San Francisco–San Jose commute service. (Courtesy of the California State Railroad Museum Library.)

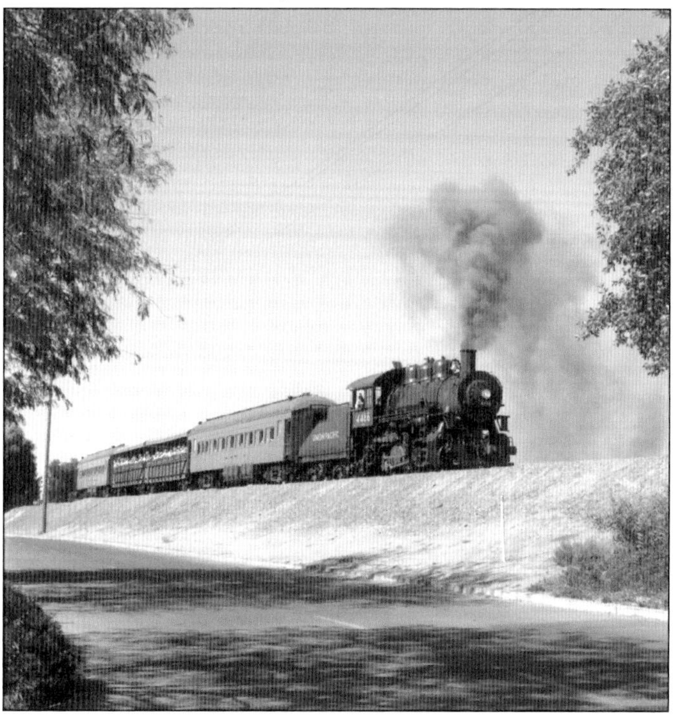

The 4466 nears the initial southernmost point of excursion operations at Miller Park, about a mile and a half south of Sacramento. Service was extended to Baths, about 3 miles south of Old Sacramento, by the end of the decade. (Courtesy of the California State Railroad Museum Library.)

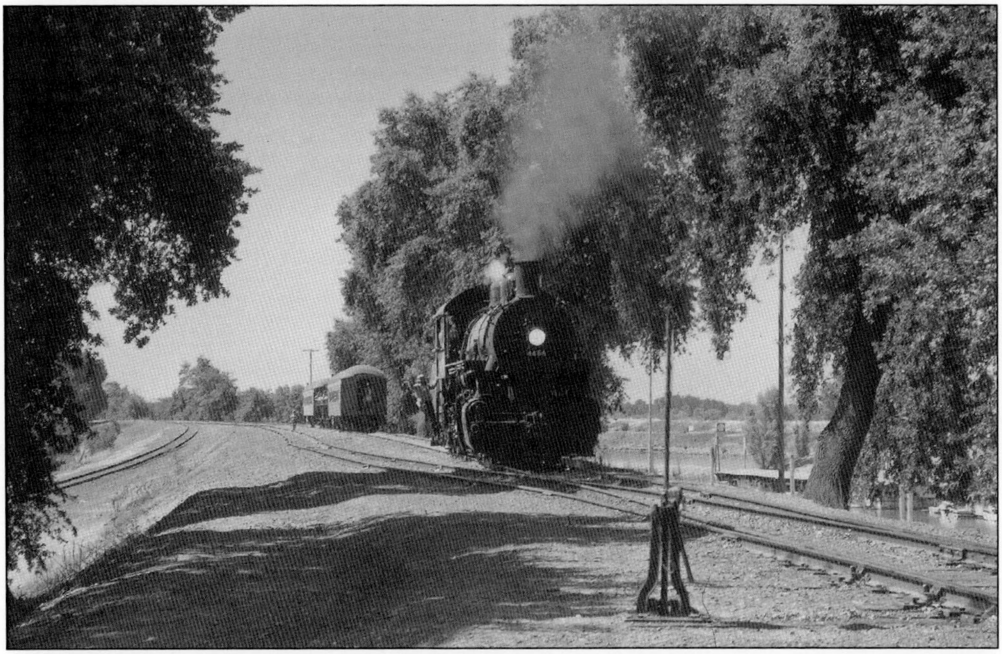

The 4466 has run around her train at the Miller Park siding and is about to back down to the train standing on the main line. The downhill track at left leads to Setzer Forest Products, the Sacramento Southern's major freight customer. (Courtesy of the California State Railroad Museum Library.)

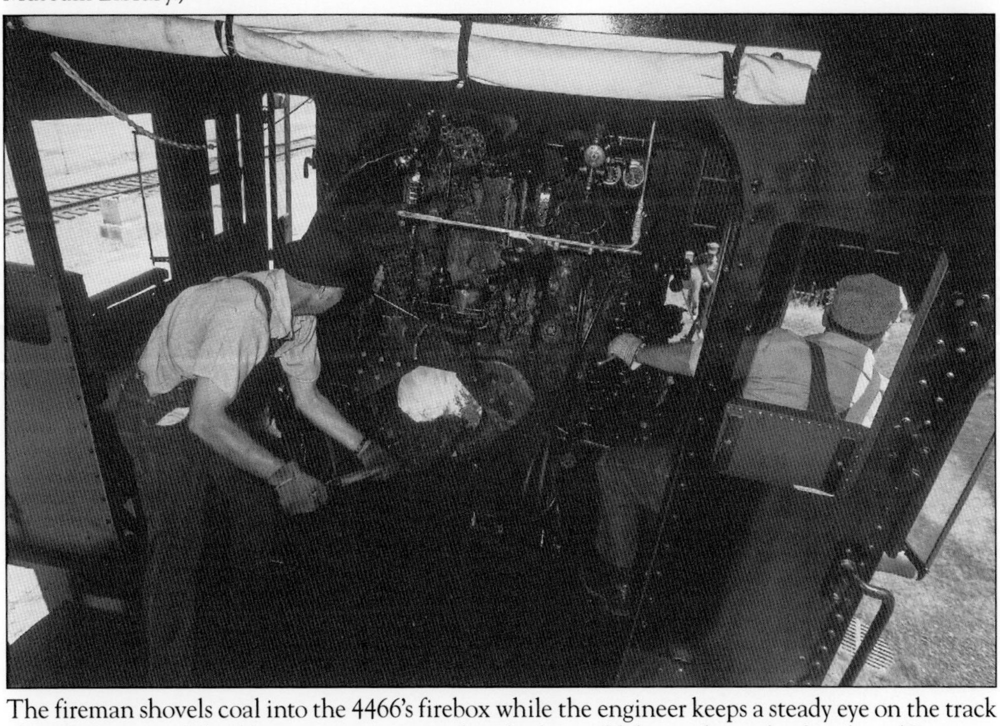

The fireman shovels coal into the 4466's firebox while the engineer keeps a steady eye on the track ahead. Many coal-fired locomotives required such physical labor to keep the fires hot. (Courtesy of the California State Railroad Museum Library.)

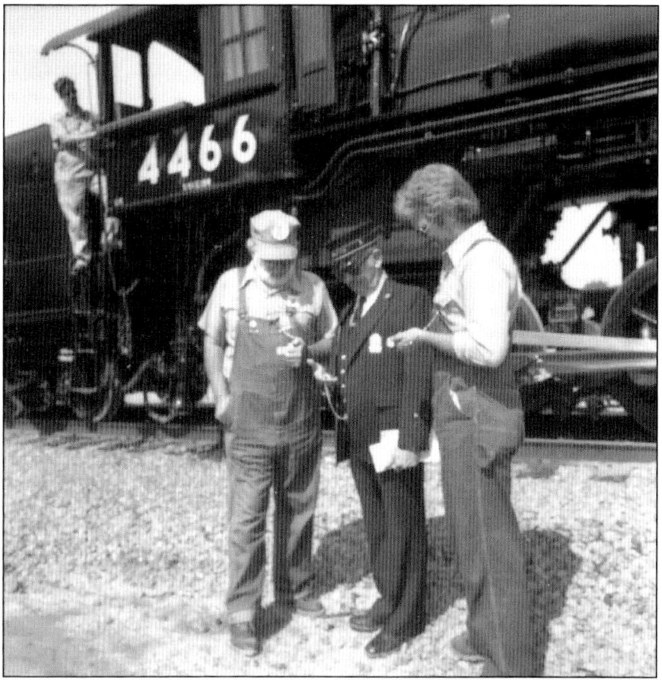

A timeless railroad scene comes back to life in Old Sacramento: the conductor comparing watches with his engine crew. (Courtesy of the California State Railroad Museum Library.)

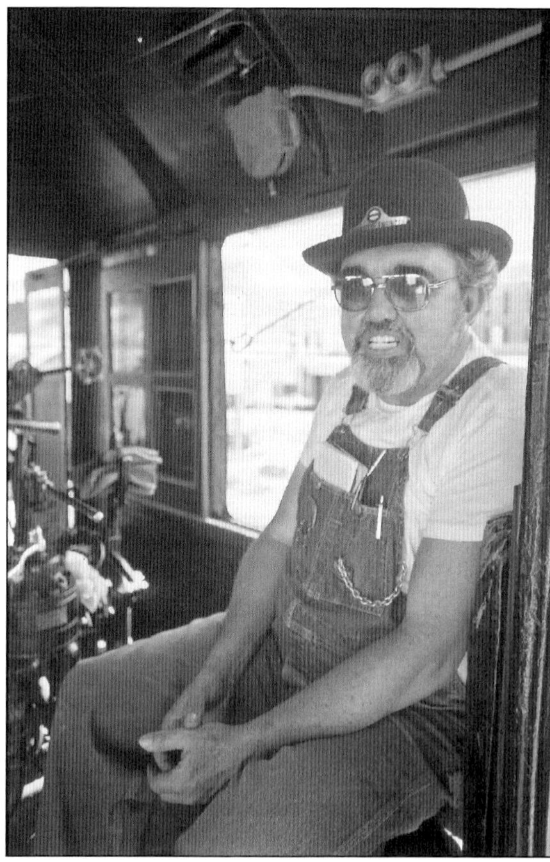

Al Shelley worked for the Southern Pacific from 1946 to 1984, working on the Walnut Grove Branch among other places. When the California State Railroad Museum launched its excursion service, Shelley became one of the line's first engineers. Shelley served the railroad as engineer and as road foreman of engines until 1999. His wife, Mary, served as a crew dispatcher. Al Shelley "took the last train" in 2005. (Courtesy of the California State Railroad Museum Library.)

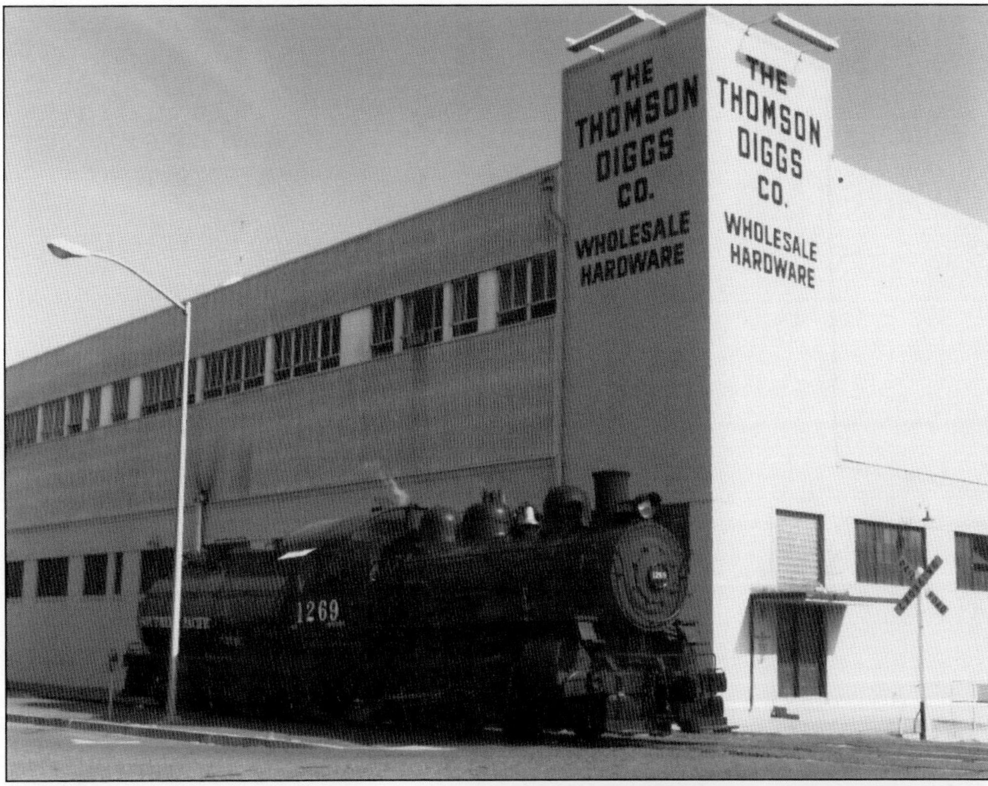

The industrial trackage leading from the Sacramento Southern to R Street saw its last movement in May 1987. Former Southern Pacific switcher No. 1269, built at SP's Sacramento shops in 1921 and on loan from the Pacific Locomotive Association, had the honor of trundling over the R Street Bridge (made necessary by the construction of Interstate 5). The locomotive paused next to Thomson-Diggs, between Second and Third Streets. (Photograph by Marilyn Sommerdorf, courtesy of the California State Railroad Museum Library.)

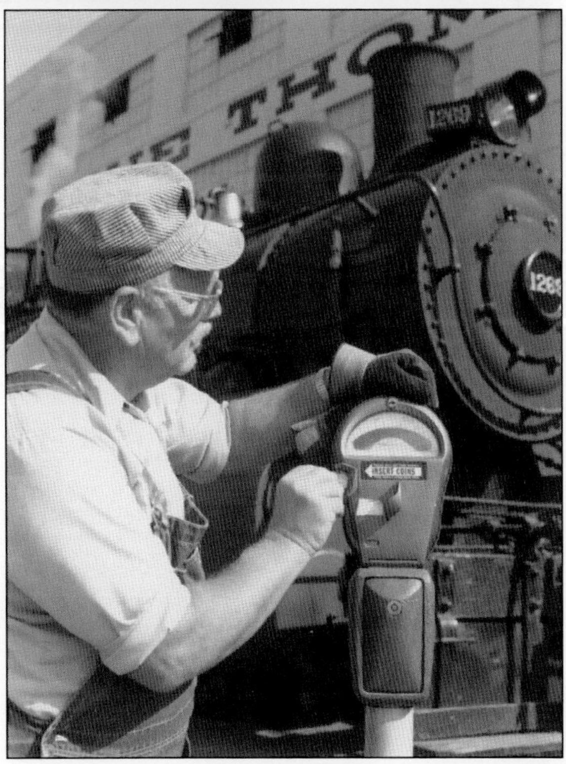

Just to make sure the locomotive does not get towed, crew member John Herman feeds the meter next to the 1269's R Street parking spot. (Photograph by Marilyn Sommerdorf, courtesy of the California State Railroad Museum Library.)

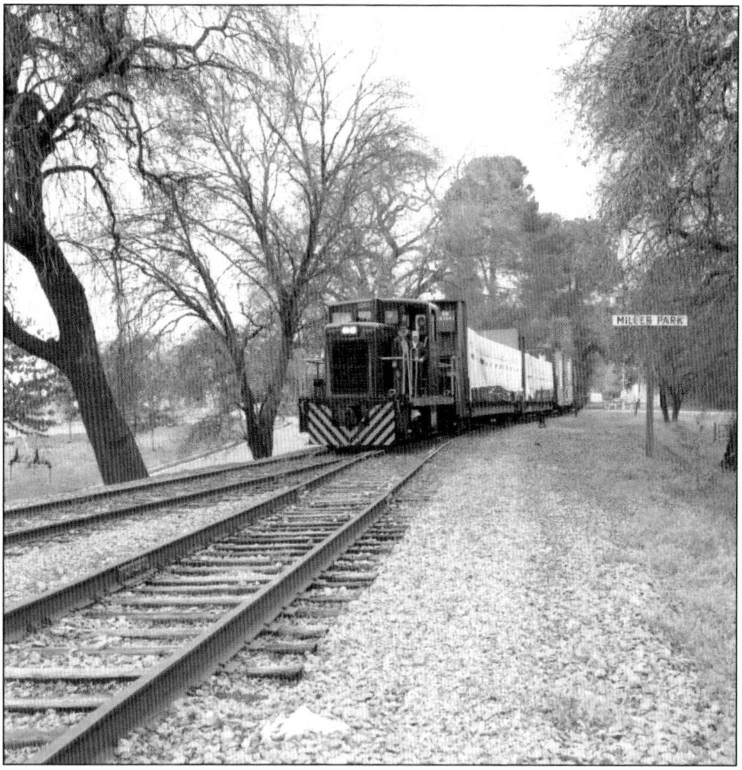

Museum visitors were not the only beneficiaries of the Sacramento Southern's revival. Setzer Forest Products has freight service once again. SSRR crews pick up loads dropped off by the Union Pacific in Sacramento and forward them to Setzer's plant, then return the empties to the UP interchange. As with the excursion trains, freights are operated by fully qualified volunteer crews. (Courtesy of the California State Railroad Museum Library.)

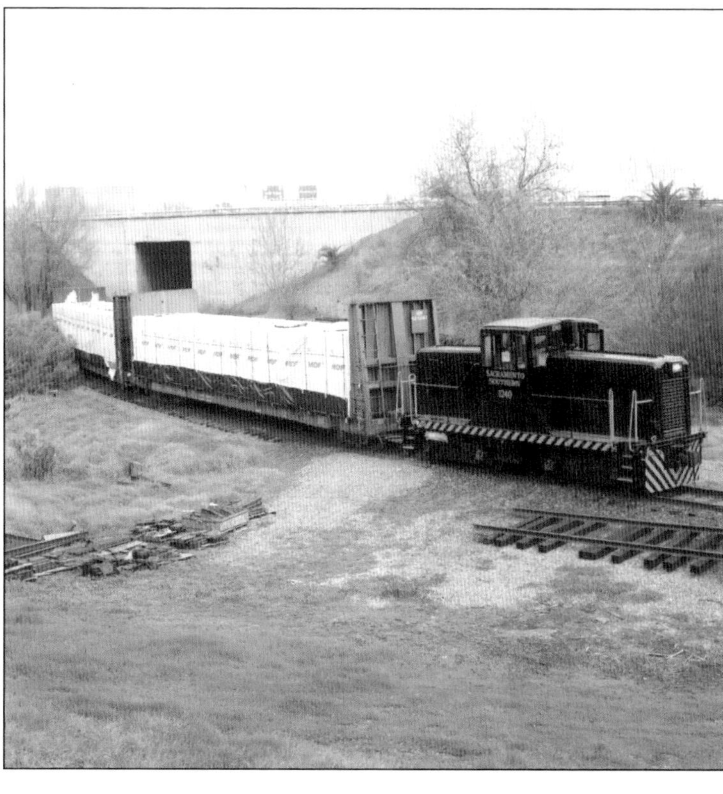

Sacramento Southern diesel No. 1240 pushes two carloads of wood products toward the tunnel leading under Interstate 5 to the Setzer plant c. 2000. No. 1240 is a General Electric 44-ton industrial switcher. This locomotive is an armed services veteran, used by the U.S. Army and U.S. Air Force before coming to the Sacramento Southern in 1993. Before the train can proceed, two brakemen have to walk the tunnel to check for "hobos." (Courtesy of the California State Railroad Museum Library.)

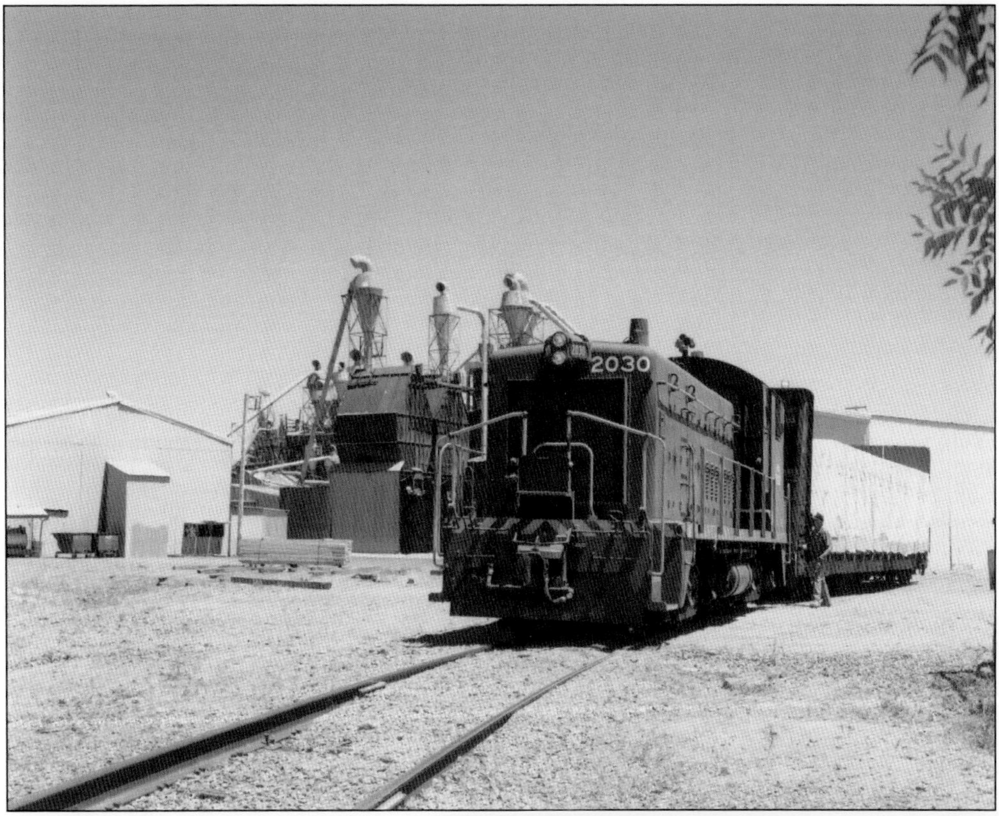

On another day, Sacramento Southern No. 2030 spots a load of woodstuffs at the Setzer plant. The 2030 came to the museum in 1995 from the U.S. Army, for whom General Motors' Electro-Motive Division built this SW8 switcher in 1951. (Courtesy of the California State Railroad Museum Library.)

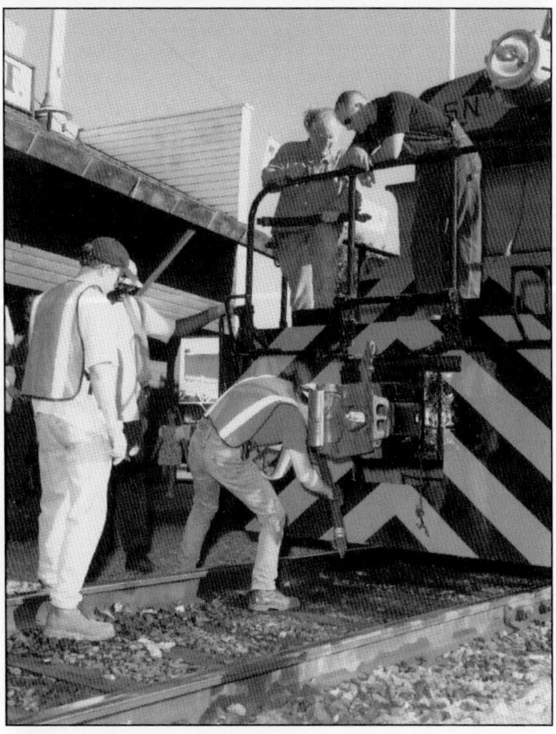

Sacramento City College conducts a training program for those interested in going into railroading for a living. The school rents the Sacramento Southern Railroad so that potential future train crews can gain practical hands-on experience, as seen here around 1999. (Courtesy of the California State Railroad Museum Library.)

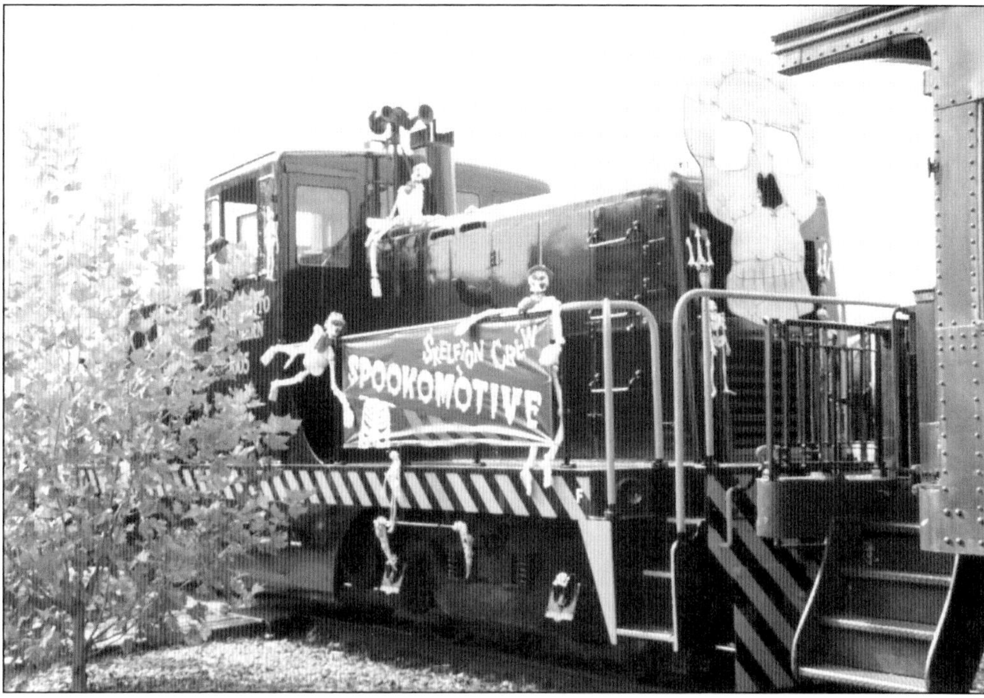

October brings a frightening development: Halloween trains. A diesel painted black and orange is transformed into a "Spookomotive," and the passenger cars are festooned with skeletons, jack-o'-lanterns, crows, cobwebs, and other Halloween items. These trains are operated, naturally, with "skeleton crews." (Both courtesy of the California State Railroad Museum Library.)

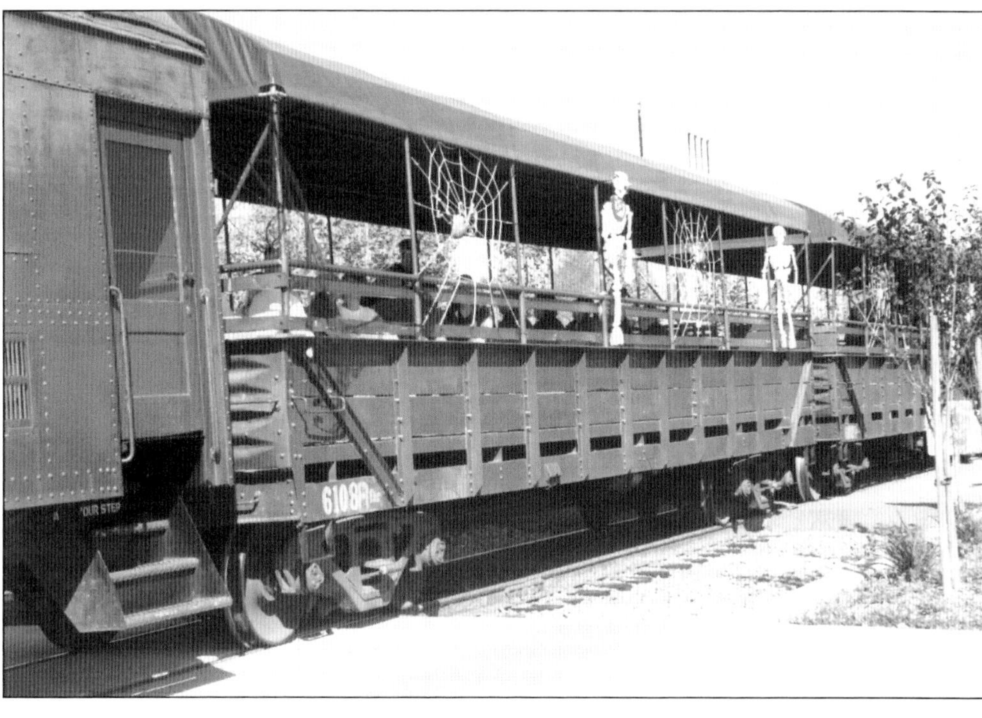

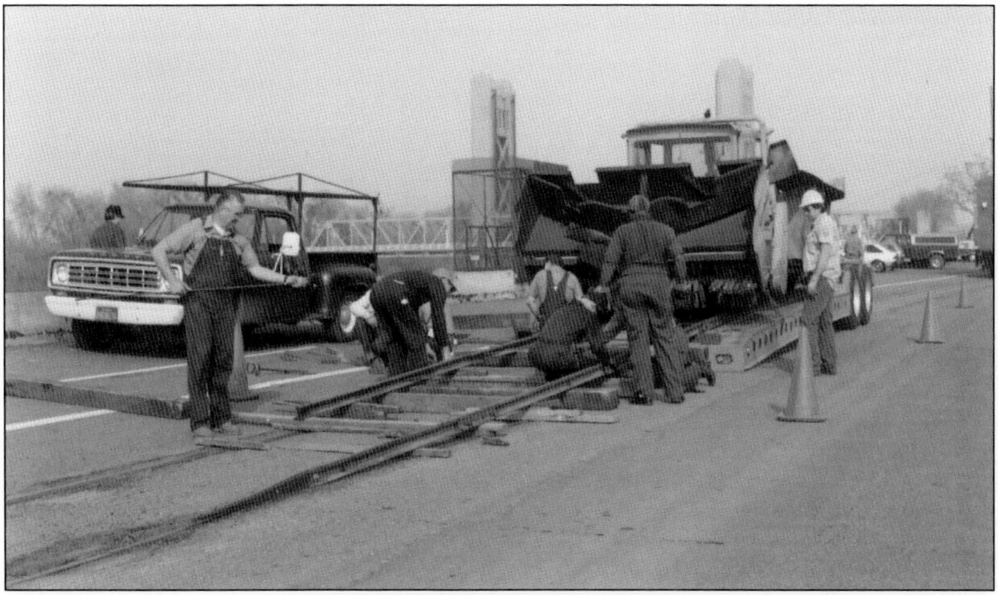

If it were not for the railroad's all-volunteer Maintenance of Way department, trains would never roll. The MOW personnel are chiefly responsible for keeping the tracks in a state of good repair. A crew takes care of some trackage along Front Street south of Capitol Mall in the late 1980s. (Courtesy of the California State Railroad Museum Library.)

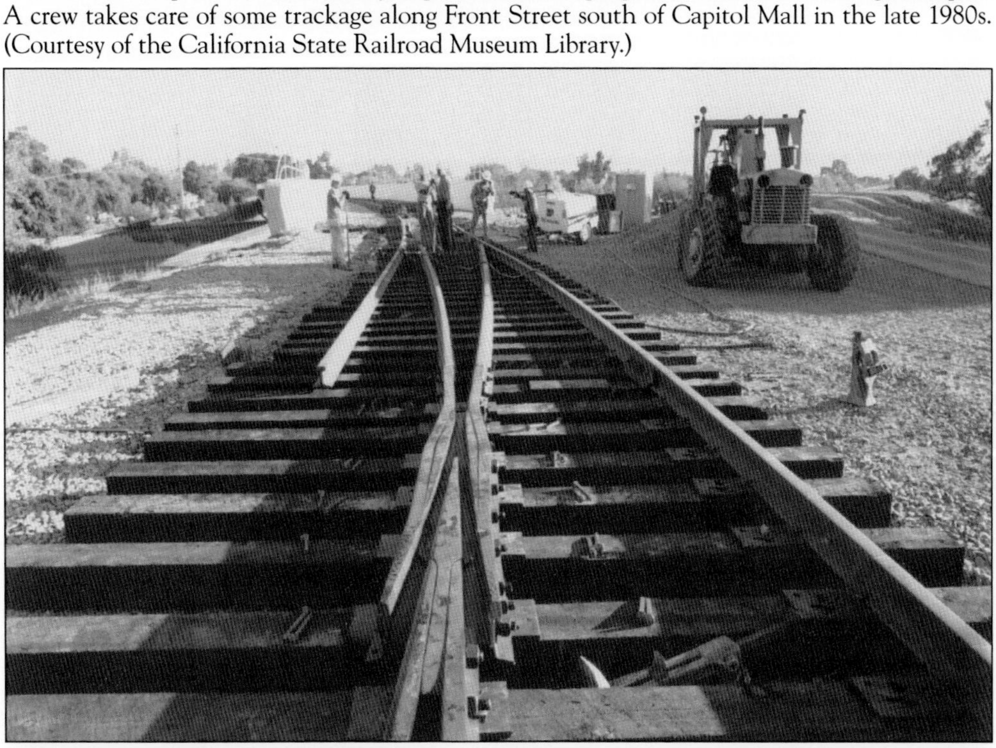

A new siding at Baths was constructed around 1990 so that locomotives could perform the end-of-line runaround here instead of Miller Park. The Walnut Grove Branch here had been realigned from a straight shot into an S curve when Interstate 5 was constructed in 1973. The concrete bridge in the background leads over I-5 to the dormant portion of the Sacramento Southern; it replaced the bridge seen on page 54. (Courtesy of the California State Railroad Museum Library.)

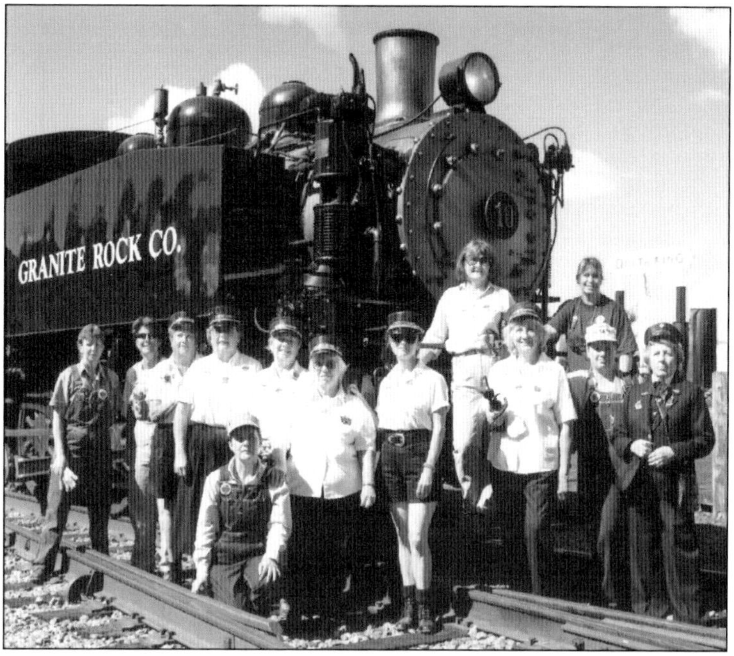

On several occasions, the Sacramento Southern has operated its steam-powered excursion train with an all-female crew. One such occasion was on August 29, 1997, as part of an event marking the ratification of the 19th Amendment to the Constitution, which gave women the right to vote. (Photograph by Richard H. Denison, courtesy of the California State Railroad Museum Library.)

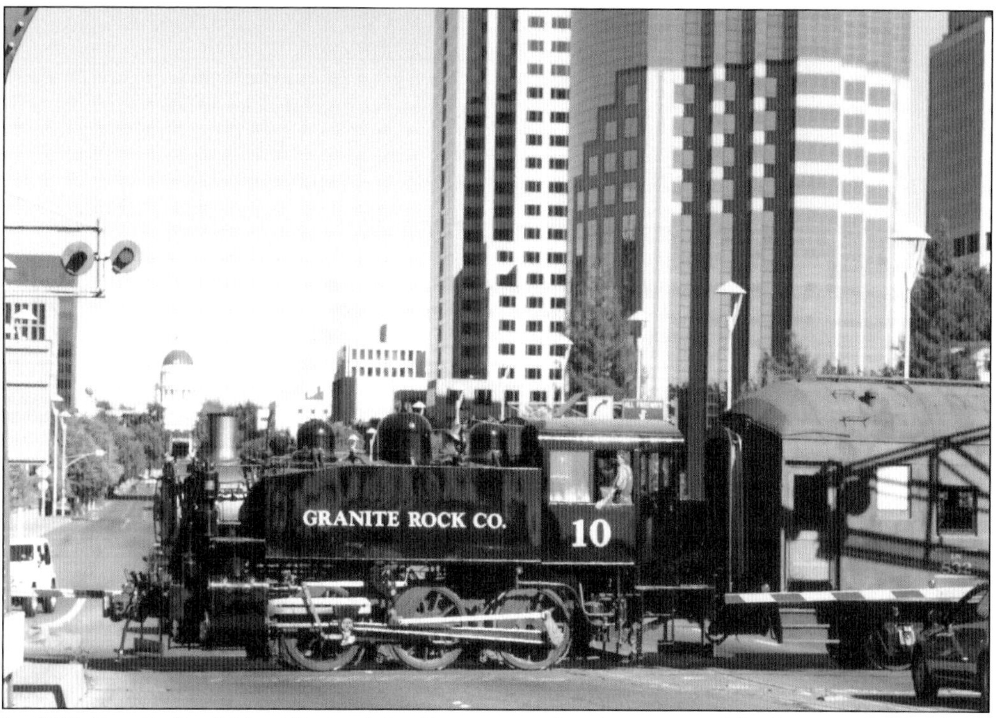

In 1997, Granite Rock No. 10 joined the Sacramento Southern roster. This locomotive was built in 1942 for the U.S. Army Transportation Corps and used at the army depot in Tracy. After the war, it was sold to Granite Rock Company, which used the locomotive at its quarry near Logan until about 1960. The locomotive was donated to the museum in 1995 by Granite Rock, which also underwrote its restoration. (Photograph by Marilyn Sommerdorf, courtesy of the California State Railroad Museum Library.)

Ten

STILL WORKIN' ON THE RAILROAD

Though run by volunteers, today's Sacramento Southern Railroad thinks and acts as a professional operation that goes beyond steam trains on summer weekends.

Freight trains still operate on the branch; a volunteer crew of railroaders moves cars for Setzer Forest Products as traffic warrants. The Car Department inspects and cleans the passenger cars before operating weekends and makes minor repairs as necessary. The Signal Department maintains the gates and lights at the line's grade crossings. Maintenance of Way inspects and repairs tracks and switches and also keeps trees and brush from intruding upon the right-of-way. Volunteers in the shops keep the locomotives and cars in running order.

The photographs in this chapter give a glimpse at the railroad's operations in the summer of 2008, the railroad's 25th operating season.

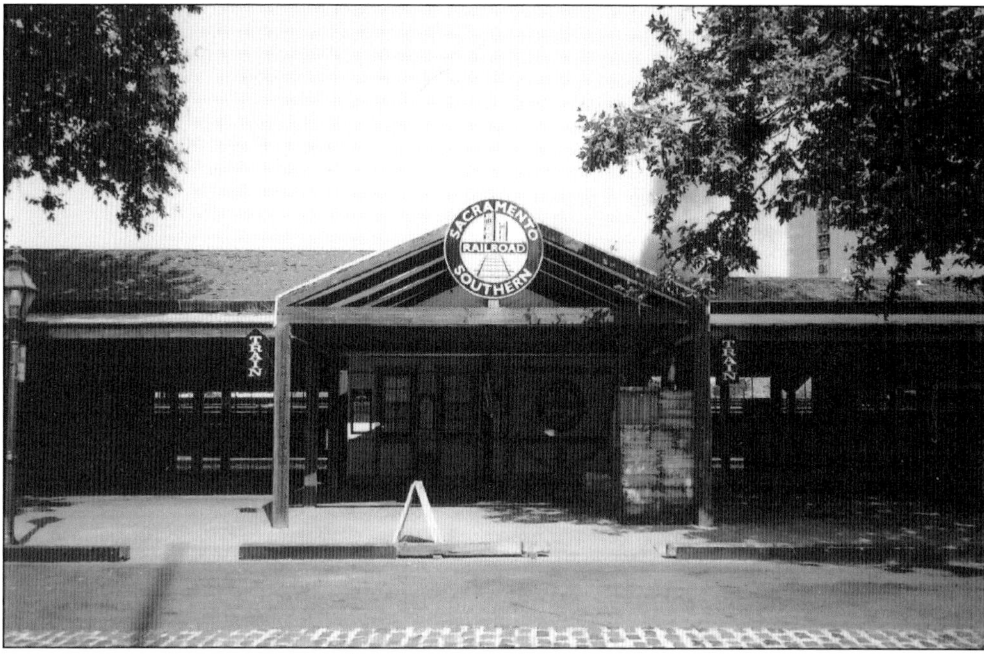

The reconstructed Central Pacific freight depot on Front Street, between J and K Streets, is the boarding point for the Sacramento Southern's excursion trains. (Photograph by author.)

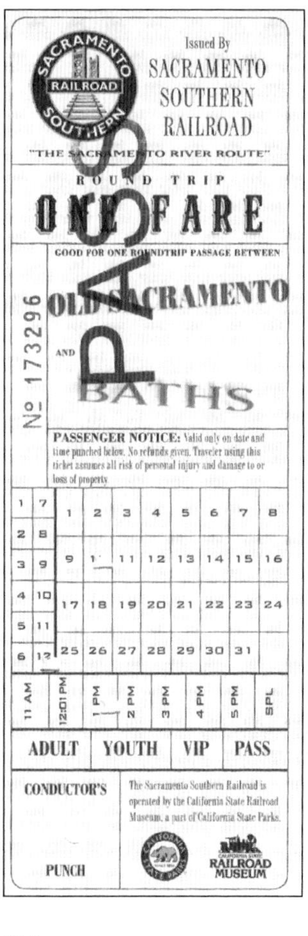

The Sacramento Southern's tickets hark back to an earlier time in train travel. (Author's collection.)

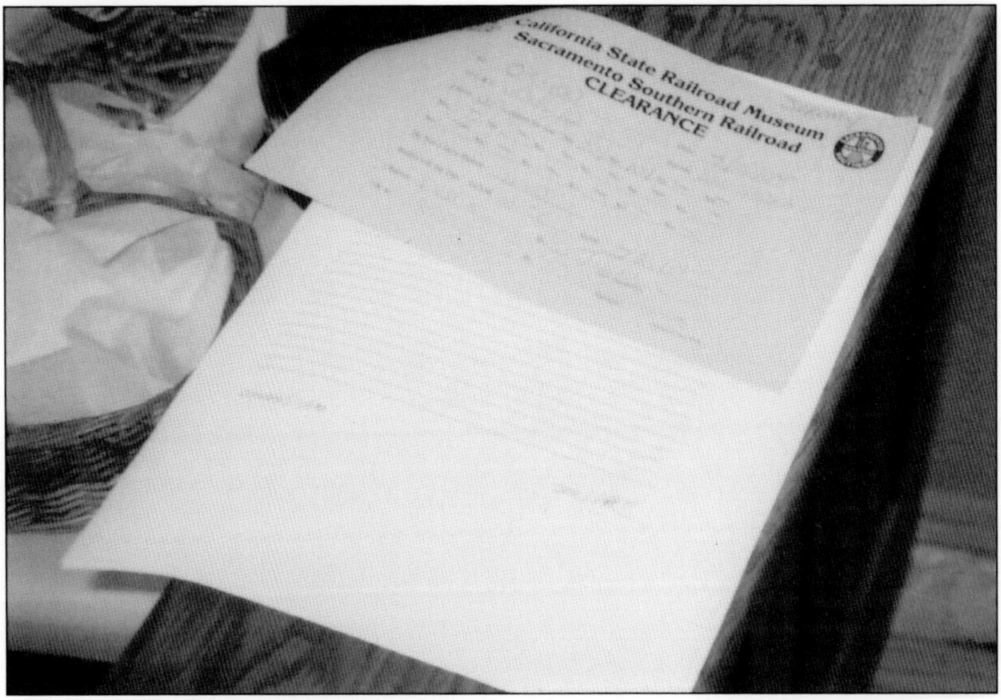

Trains are still dispatched the old-fashioned way—with clearance cards and train orders. Clearance cards authorize a train to occupy a certain segment of track at a certain time; train orders advise conductors and engineers of any special instructions. (Photograph by author.)

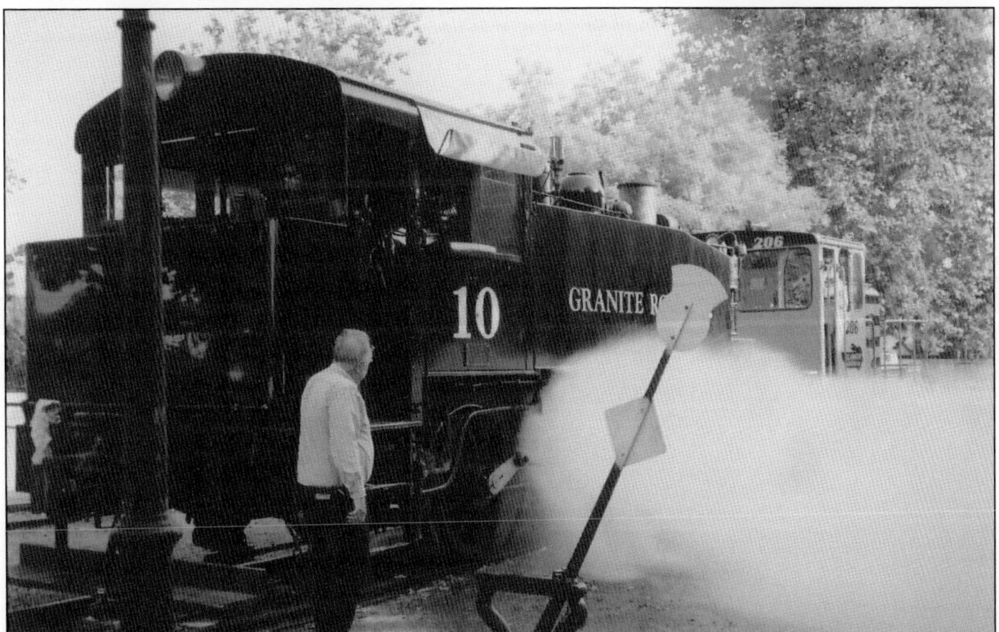

The engine crew's day begins several hours before the first train rolls. At about 8:00 a.m. on a Sunday morning in July, road foreman Red Hadler oversees the dumping of cold water from the boiler. (Photograph by author.)

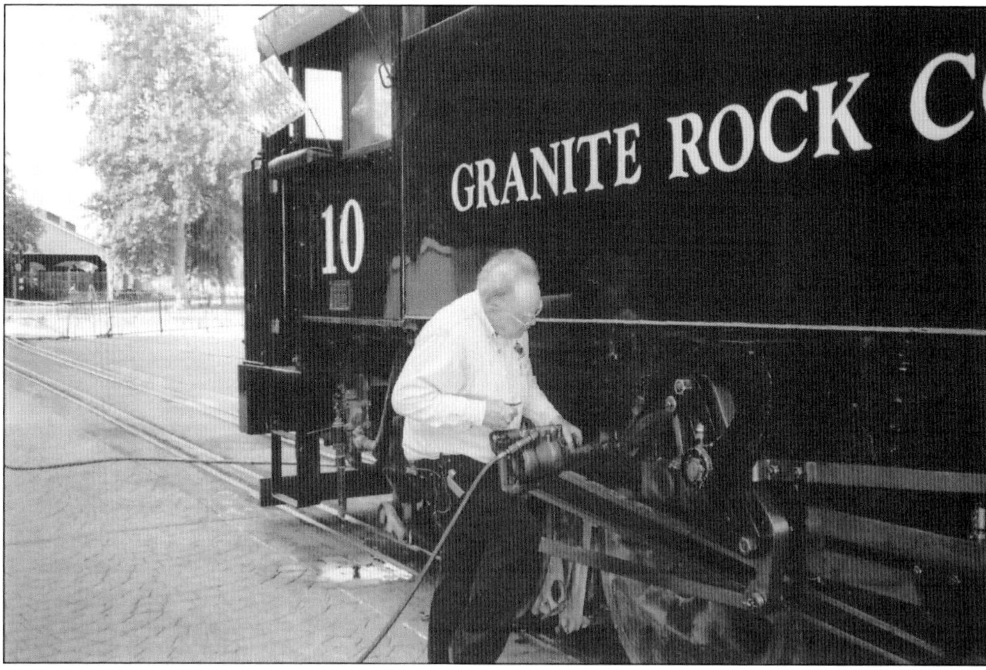

Red Hadler uses an air-powered grease gun to lubricate Granite Rock 10's running gear. Granite Rock 10 is presently the Sacramento Southern's lone operational steam locomotive, the 4466 having been retired to display in the museum roundhouse in 1999. (Photograph by author.)

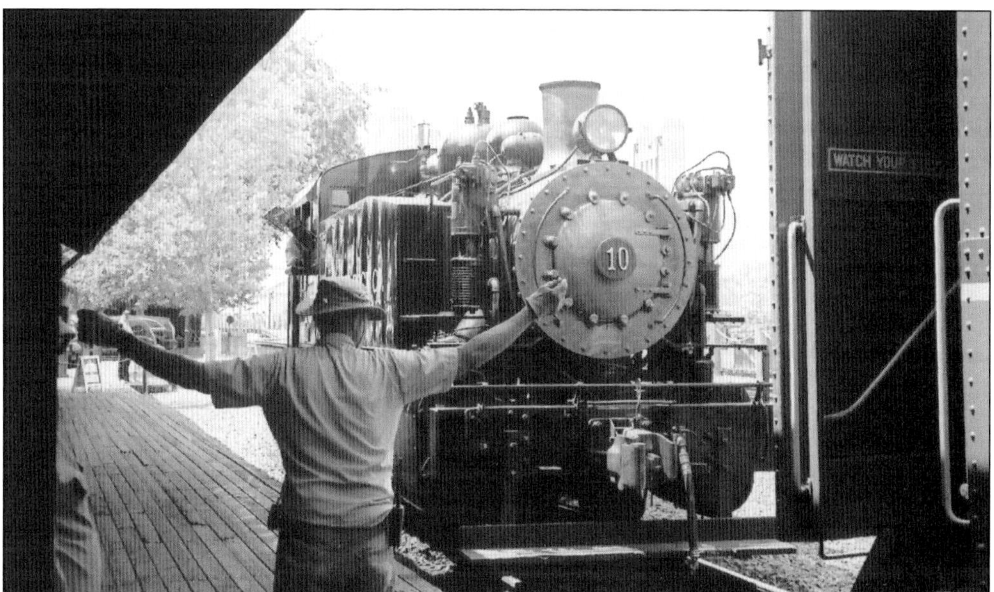

With steam up, Granite Rock 10 moves to the depot to couple to the train. Brakeman Chuck Zailer guides engineer Jeremy Levish to a smooth coupling. The engineer cannot see the couplers from the cab and relies on the brakeman's hand signals. (Photograph by author.)

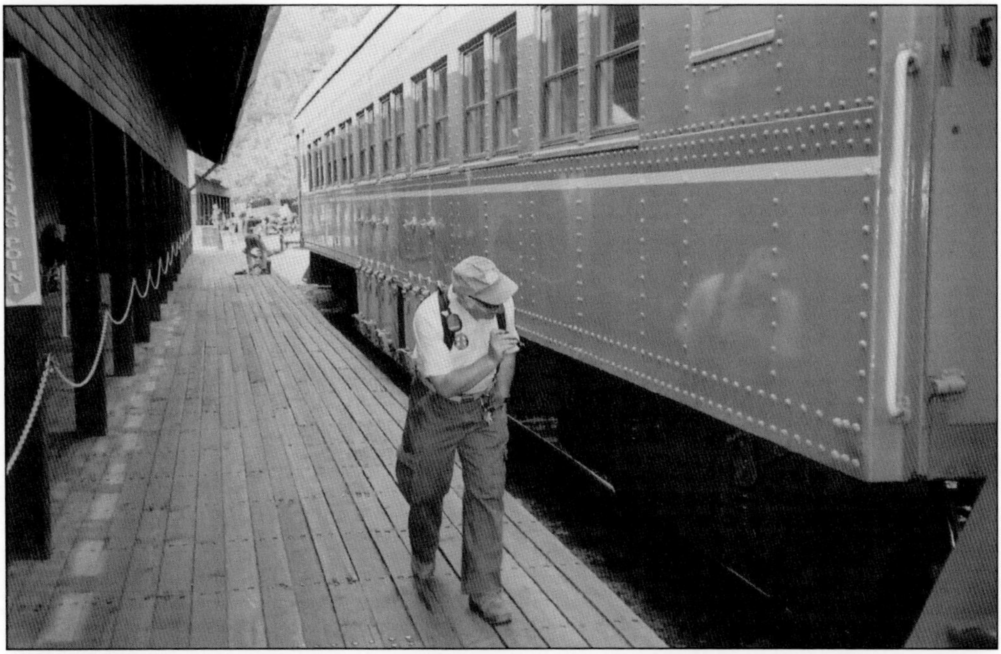

After coupling, the air hoses are connected and the brakes tested. Brakeman Eric Peak is inspecting the brake shoes on each car to ensure the train's air brakes are operating properly. (Photograph by author.)

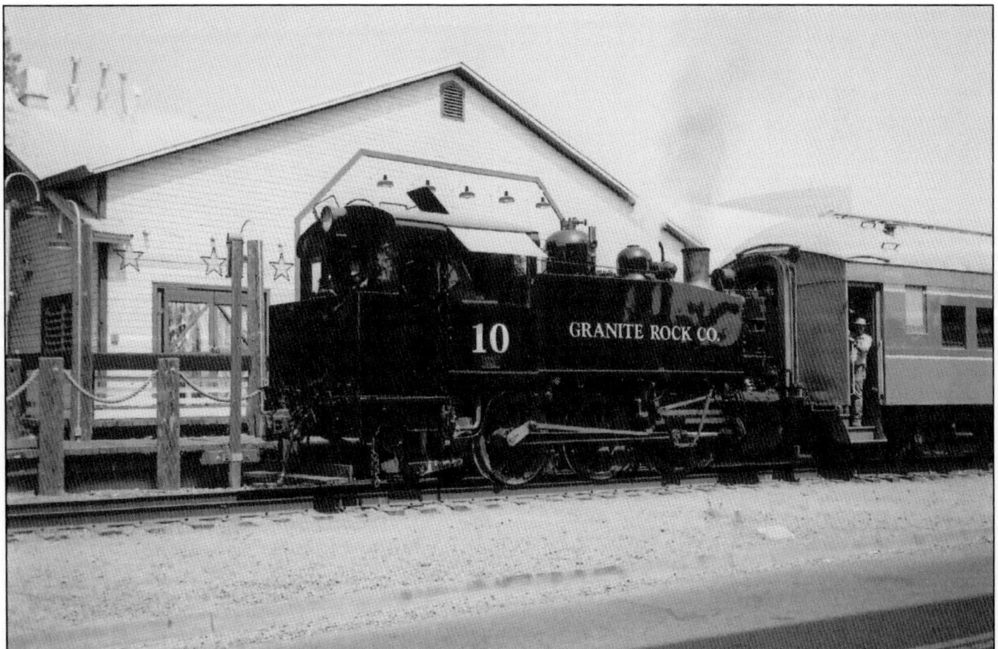

The first train of the day leaves Old Sacramento, passing Joe's Crab Shack on the way out of town. Joe's sits on the riverfront where the Southern Pacific Steamer Terminal once did. Compare this shot with the one on page 41. (Photograph by author.)

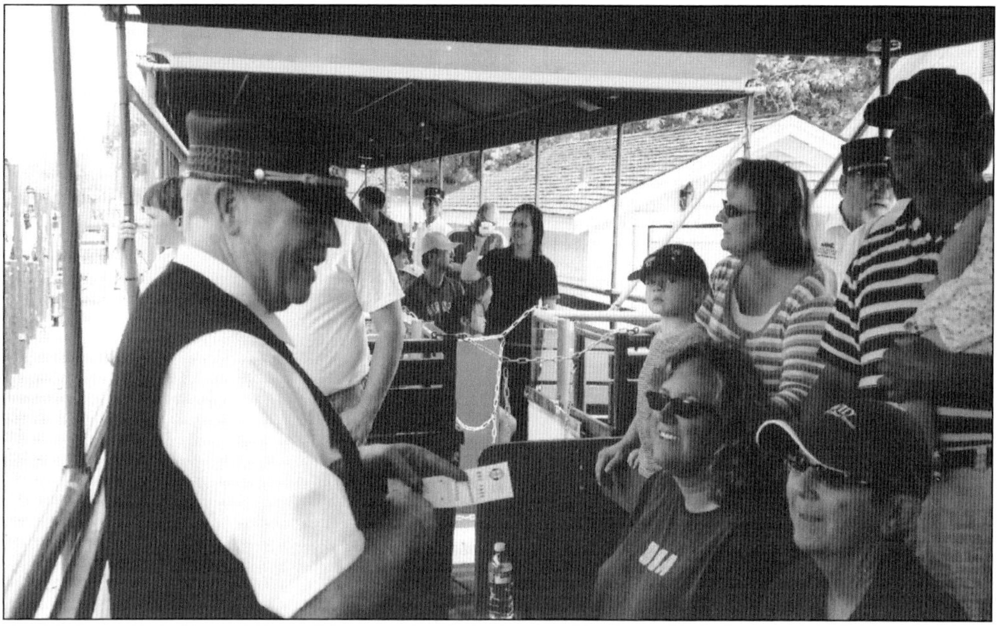

As the train rambles out of Old Sacramento, conductor Rusty Murchison punches tickets and chats with the passengers. (Photograph by author.)

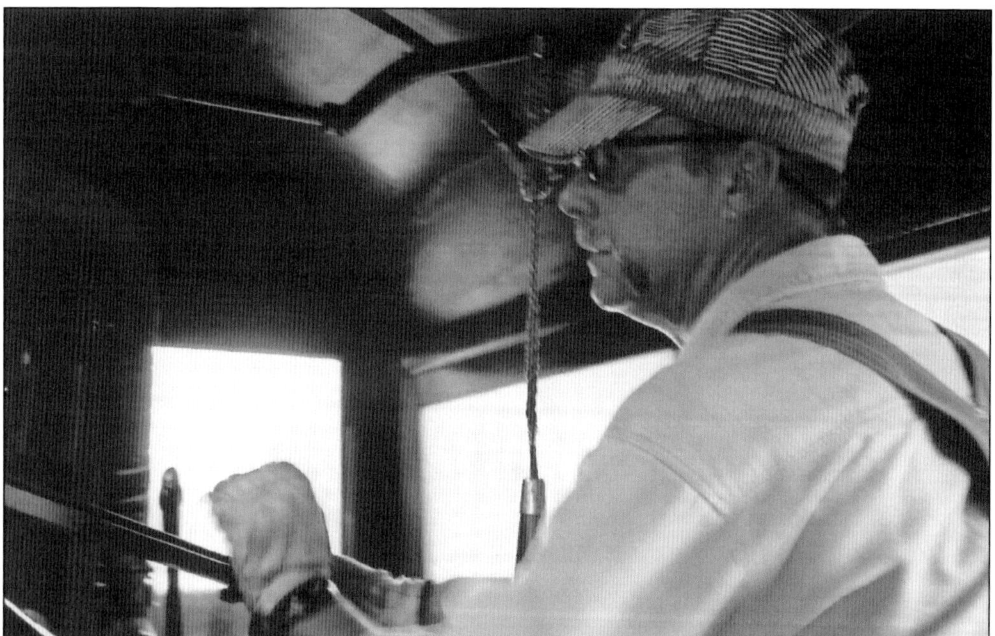

Engineer Jeremy Levish keeps an eye on his locomotive's steam pressure and water level and a steady hand on the throttle. Across the cab, the fireman is responsible for ensuring the boiler is producing sufficient steam to keep the locomotive moving. (Photograph by author.)

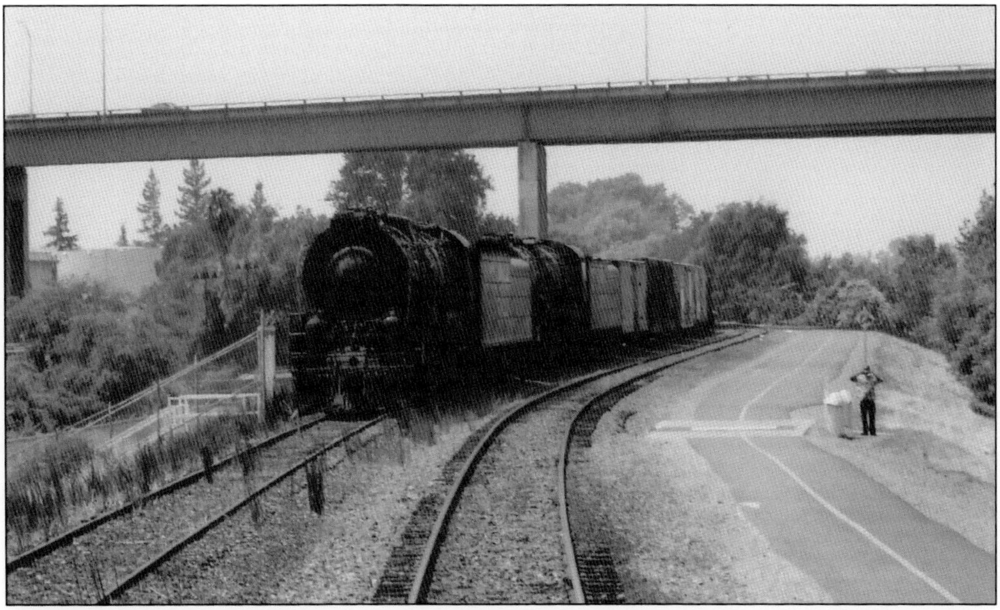

At Clunie siding, two former Santa Fe steam locomotives and a string of vintage freight cars have been parked for temporary storage while the Sacramento shops area is cleaned up for development. The lead locomotive, No. 5021, is a rare 2-10-4 "Texas" type; the trailing locomotive, No. 2925, is a more common 4-8-4 "Northern." (Photograph by author.)

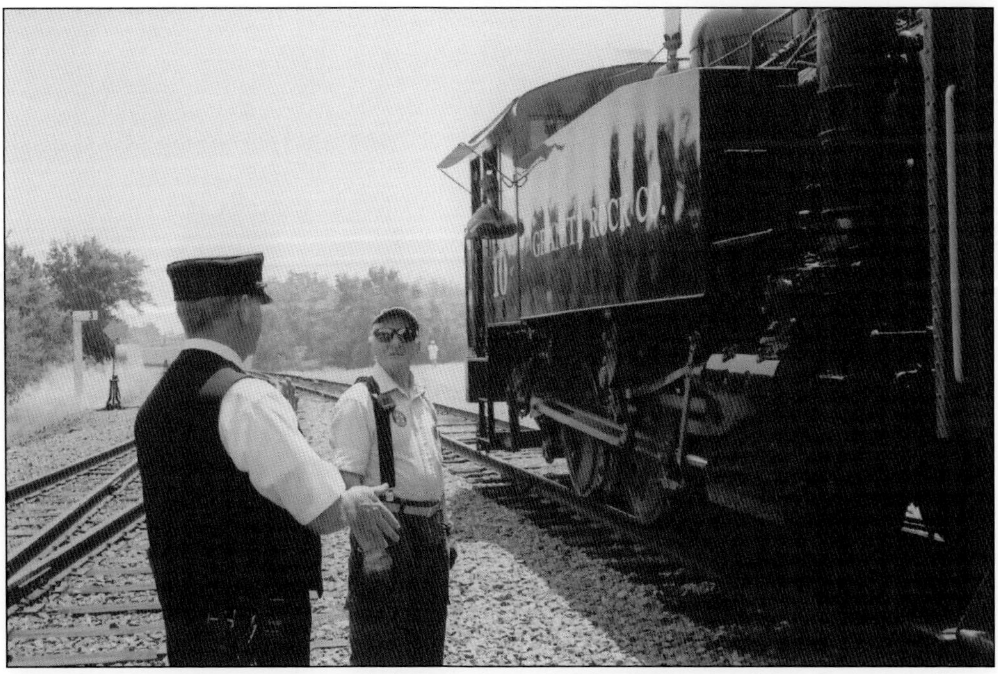

After about 15 minutes on the road, the train has arrived at Baths. Conductor Rusty Murchison is giving brakeman Eric Peak the signal to cut the locomotive away. (Photograph by author.)

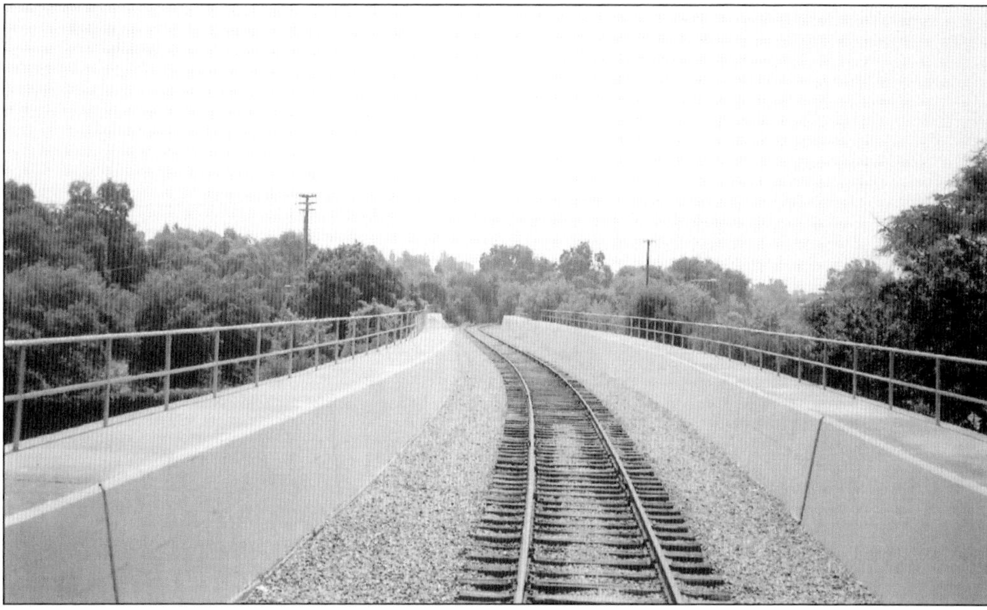

This is the I-5 bridge near Sutterville Road as seen from Granite Rock 10's cab looking south. This bridge replaced the steel truss bridge seen on page 52. This is as far south as Sacramento Southern trains go—at least for now. (Photograph by author.)

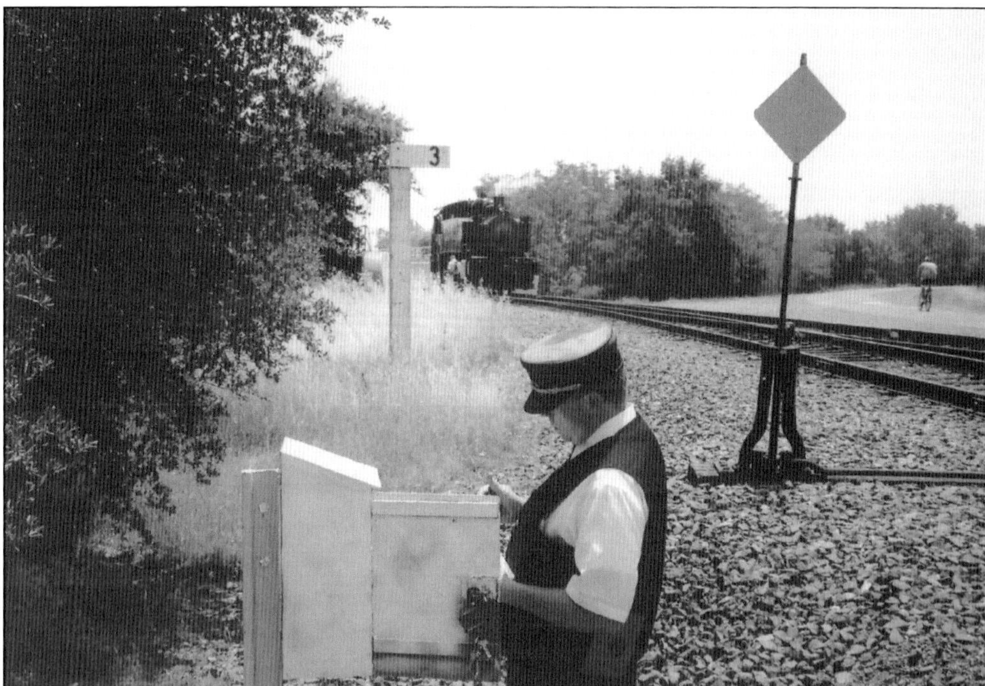

As Granite Rock 10 prepares to run around its train, conductor Rusty Murchison performs a ritual familiar to conductors of yore—signing the register kept at the Baths station to log the times of train movements. There is no depot here; a sign and a timetable designation were all it took to establish Baths as a station. (Photograph by author.)

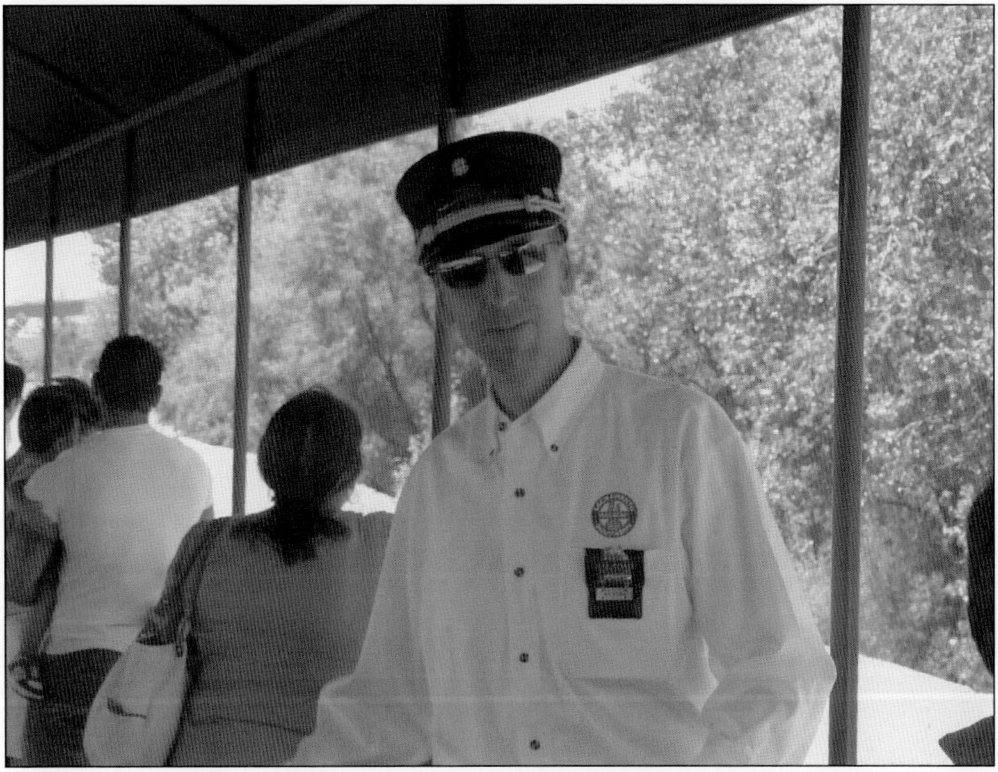

Friendly car attendants, such as Richard Paul, keep an eye out for passenger safety, answer questions, and tell stories relating to the history of California, Sacramento, and railroading in general. (Photograph by author.)

Maintenance of Way forces spend several days a week keeping museum and railroad trackage in good running condition. Here Chris Carlson (left) and Steve Mathias help rebuild a section of track in the Central Pacific passenger depot on a warm summer day in 2008. (Photograph by author.)

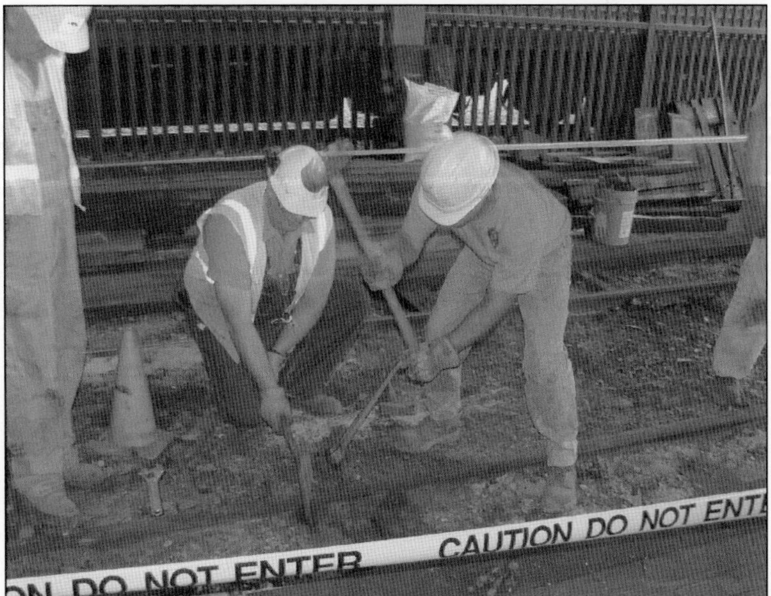

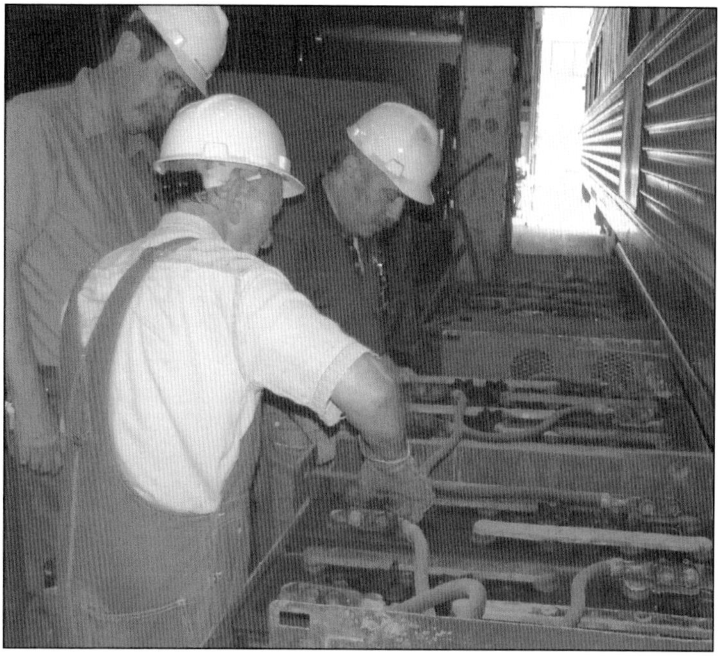

The Car Department cleans the excursion consist prior to each operating weekend and performs minor repairs. Jon Wiltshire, Eric Peak, and Jeff Allen inspect and repair batteries on one of the museum's vintage lounge cars. (Photograph by author.)

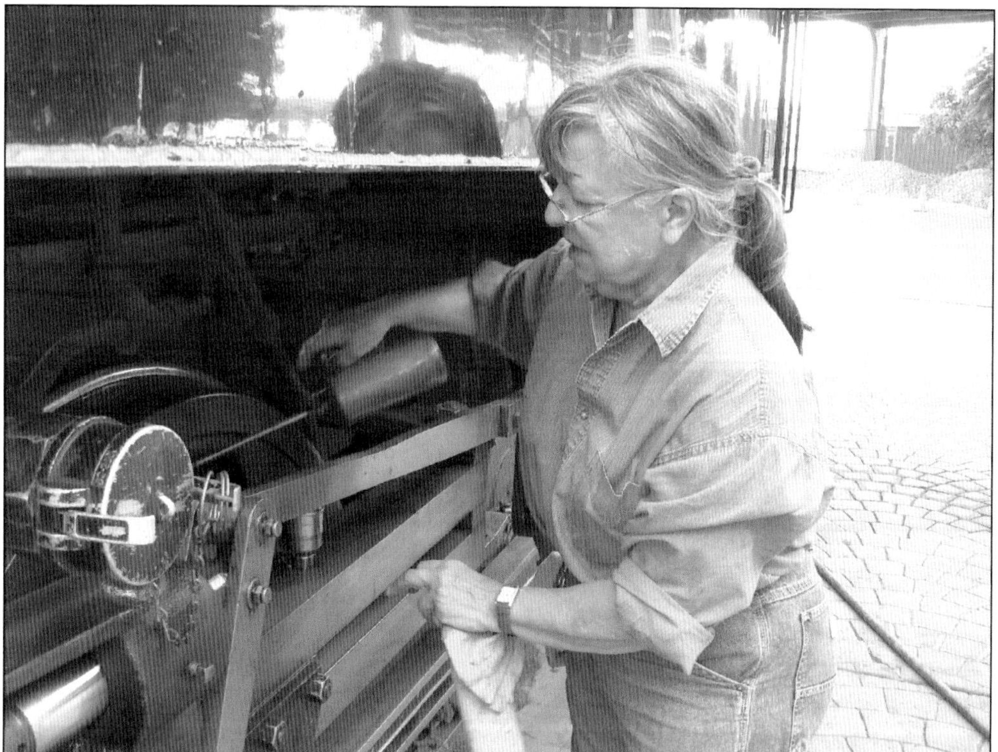

The Sacramento Southern is by no means a man's world. Virginia Baron is one of many women who serve on the railroad in all roles. Baron was acting as an engine helper on this day. Engine helpers assist with cleaning and lubrication of the locomotive in the morning as well as fueling and watering during the course of the day. (Photograph by author.)

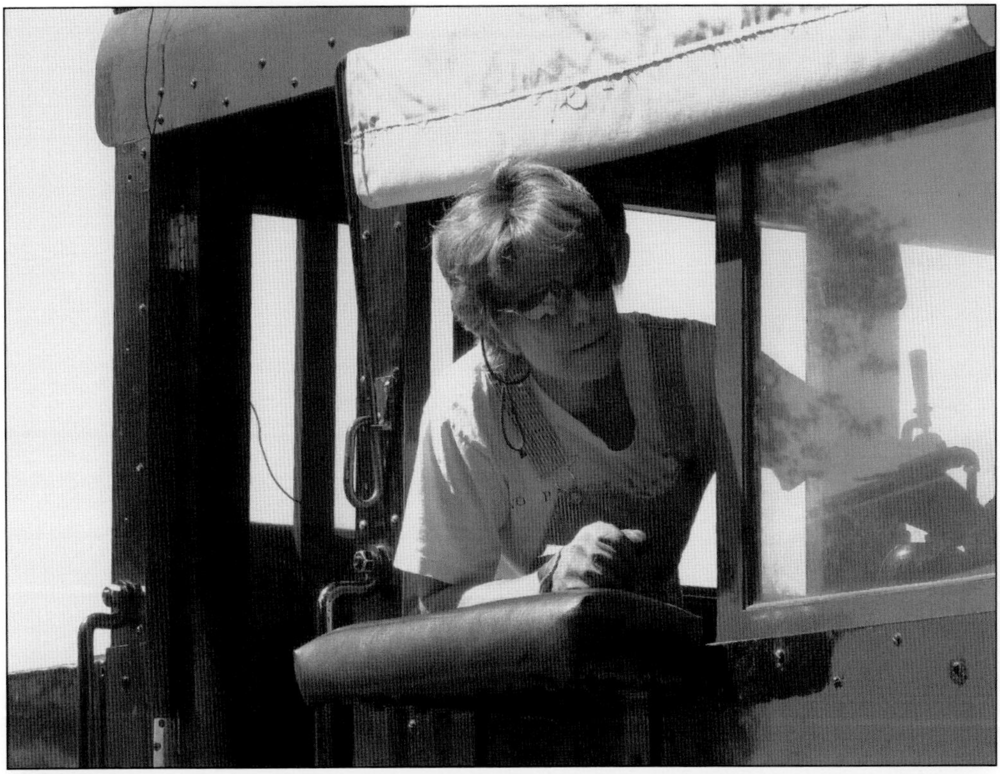

Cheryl Meyer is at present the only qualified female engineer on the Sacramento Southern. She started volunteering on the railroad in 1986 and became engineer in 1997. (Photograph by author.)

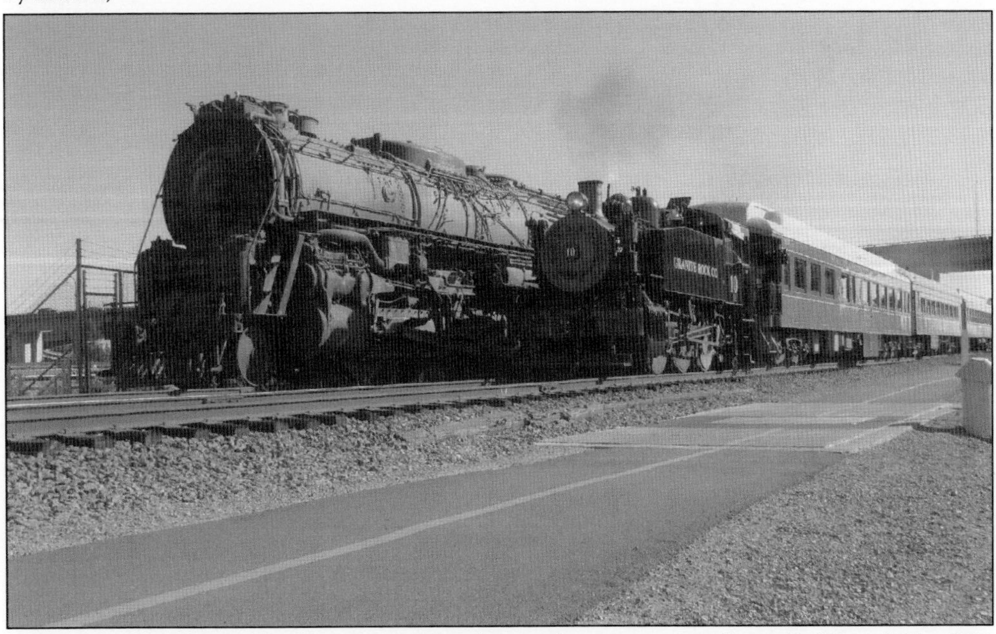

Granite Rock 10 brings the last train of the day north past inactive Santa Fe "Texas" No. 5021 at Clunie siding on August 10, 2008. (Photograph by author.)

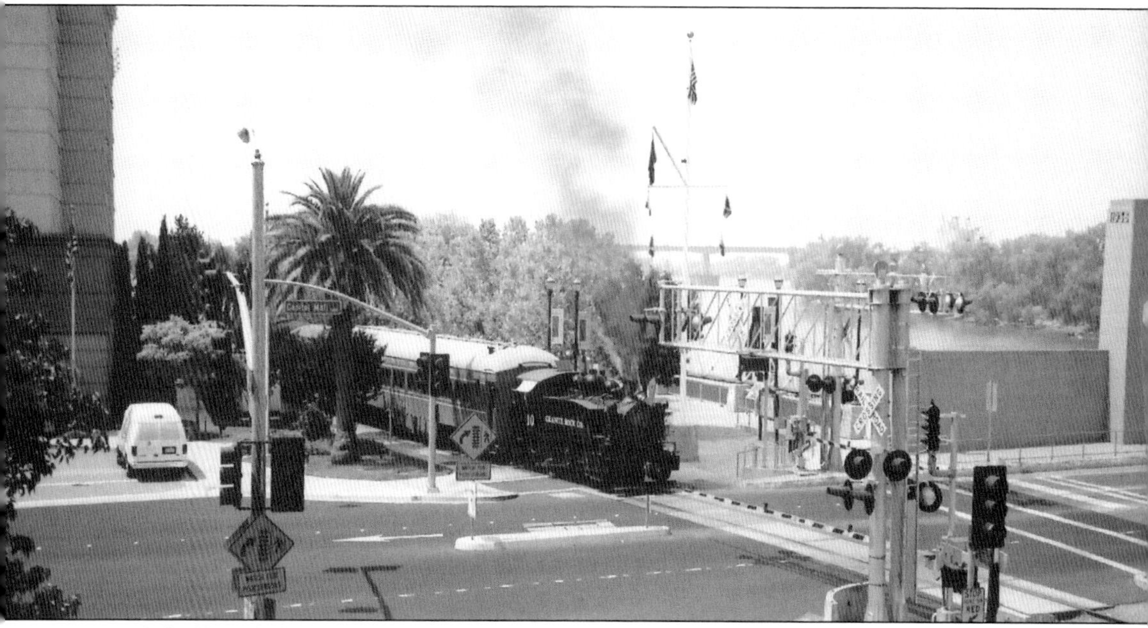

Only half a mile from home, Granite Rock 10 crosses Capitol Mall, formerly M Street, and steams past the eastern end of Tower Bridge. Compare this shot with the ones on page 40. (Photograph by author.)

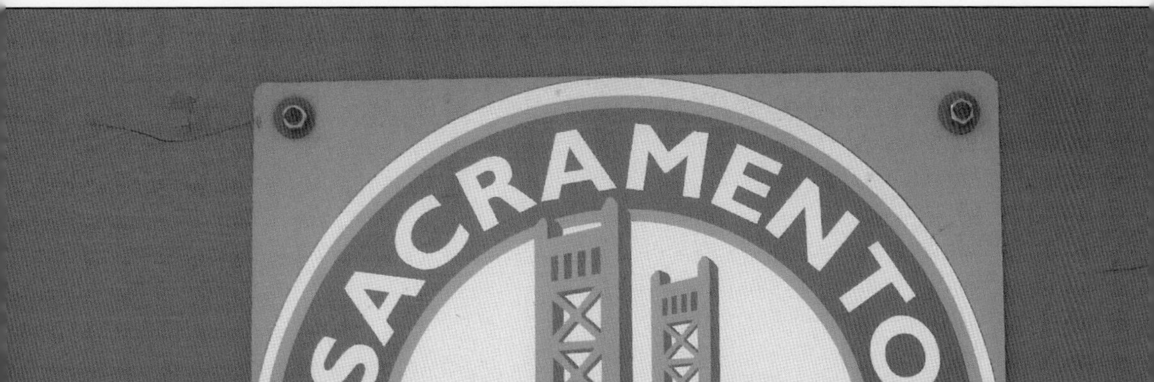

The Sacramento Southern Railroad's herald is based on that of Southern Pacific Lines, with Tower Bridge replacing the rays of the setting sun. (Photograph by author.)

About the Organization

The Sacramento Southern Railroad of today is operated by volunteers from the California State Railroad Museum, part of the California State Parks system. Steam-powered excursion trains operate from the Central Pacific freight depot on Front Street in Old Sacramento from April through September. Halloween trains operate in October and Christmas-themed trains in November and December. For more information, write the California State Railroad Museum, 111 I Street, Sacramento, CA, 95814; call (916) 445-6645; or visit www.californiastaterailroadmuseum.org.

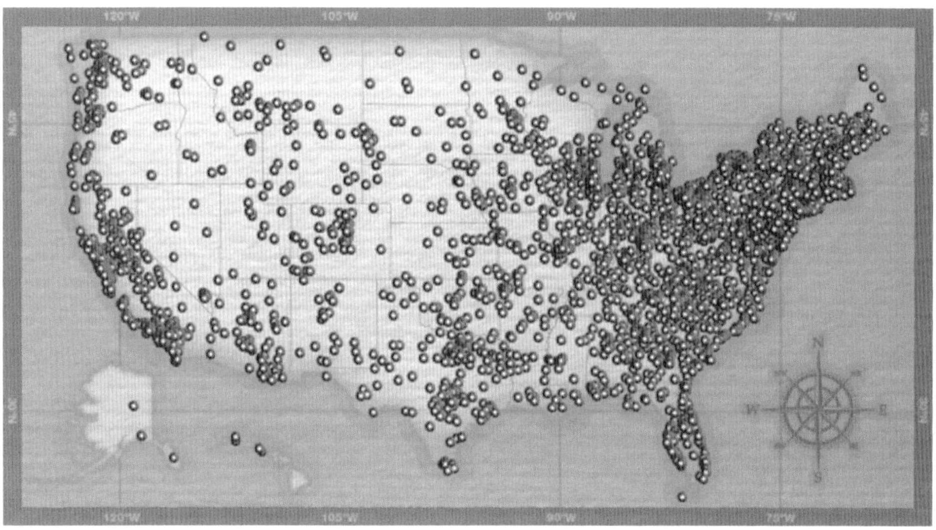